Shane Meadows

Critical Essays

Edited by Martin Fradley, Sarah Godfrey
and Melanie Williams

EDINBURGH
University Press

© the chapters their several authors, 2013

Edinburgh University Press Ltd
22 George Square, Edinburgh EH8 9LF
www.euppublishing.com

Typeset in Monotype Ehrhardt by
3btype.com, and
printed and bound in the United States of America

A CIP record for this book is available from the British Library

ISBN 978 0 7486 7639 2 (hardback)
ISBN 978 0 7486 7640 8 (webready PDF)
ISBN 978 0 7486 7642 2 (epub)

The right of the contributors
to be identified as authors of this work
has been asserted in accordance with
the Copyright, Designs and Patents Act 1988.

Contents

Acknowledgements

The editors would like to thank all the contributors for their commitment to this project. We would also like to thank colleagues in the School of Film, Television and Media Studies at the University of East Anglia for supporting the 2010 conference 'Straight Outta Uttoxeter' from which this project has emerged, particularly Yvonne Tasker and Mark Jancovich for their help in getting the ball rolling. Many thanks to the delegates who attended the conference and gave us two great days of debate and discussion. Our thanks also to Gillian Leslie and Michelle Houston at Edinburgh University Press for their enthusiasm and support throughout the planning and production of this book, and thanks also to Seb Manley for his essential editorial assistance. A special mention must go to Dave Clark at shanemeadows.co.uk, Libby Durdy and Ally Gipps at Warp Films, and Jared Wilson for the interviews which, in the end, couldn't make it into the book but will be available via leftlion.co.uk. Connected to this, we would like to acknowledge the enthusiasm and assistance of Shane Meadows, Mark Herbert and Andrew Shim, and thank them for their involvement and for giving up their valuable time.

Martin thanks: collectively, my many students at the universities of Aberdeen, Central England, Derby, Edge Hill, Keele, Manchester, Staffordshire and East Anglia. Individually: Mary Ainslie, Caiomhe Austin, Jessica Booth, Jenna Boult, Emily Chant, Francisca Fuentes, Chris Gadd, Anna Grove (*née* Savage), Natalie Hester, Ben Lockwood, John Riley, Claire Roarty, Sarah Robinson and Catherine Wagstaff. Special thanks to Pamela Craig.

Sarah would like to thank her colleagues in the School of Film, Television and Media Studies for their support throughout this project. Special thanks of course must go to my family, Darren, Ori and Zak, for their love and understanding, as ever.

Melanie would also like to thank colleagues, students, family and friends for their interest, support and encouragement.

This book is dedicated to Mark Brownrigg.

Notes on the Contributors

Paul Elliott is the author of *Hitchcock and the Cinema of Sensations*, a study that deals with embodiment and philosophy in the work of Alfred Hitchcock, and *Guattari Reframed*, an introductory volume on the French psychoanalyst and activist Felix Guattari. He has a PhD in film studies and has written widely in the area of cinema and British film. He is currently researching a book on the British crime film.

Louise FitzGerald is a lecturer in film and screen studies at the University of Brighton. Her primary research interests are the politics of representation, race, gender and cultural theory, feminism, postfeminism and maternalism. She has written articles on these topics for the *European Journal of Cultural Studies* and in her co-edited book *Mamma Mia the Movie: Exploring a Cultural Phenomenon* (2013). Her PhD, 'Negotiating Lone Motherhood: Gender, Politics and Family Values in Contemporary Popular Cinema', is presently being prepared for publication.

David Forrest is lecturer in film studies at the University of Sheffield. His research is concerned primarily with British social realism in film and television, with particular interests in representations of space and place. He has had articles and book chapters published on contemporary British cinema, British television drama, and cinema and landscape.

Martin Fradley is a former lecturer at the University of Aberdeen and Manchester University. He is a regular contributor to *Film Quarterly* and his recently published work has also appeared in the anthologies *Falling in Love Again: Romantic Comedy in Contemporary Cinema* (2009), *American Horror Film: The Genre at the Turn of the Millennium* (2010), *Fifty Contemporary Film Directors* (2010), *Handbook of Gender, Sex and Media* (2012), *Directory of World Cinema: Britain* (2012), *Postfeminism and Contemporary Hollywood Cinema* (2013) and *Tainted Love: Screening Sexual Perversities* (2013).

Sarah Godfrey is a lecturer in film and television studies at the University of East Anglia. Her research is primarily concerned with questions of gender in British film and television; in addition to writing on Shane Meadows she has recently completed work on Mike Leigh and Nick Love.

Séan Kingston obtained an MA in film studies from University College Dublin in 2010. His thesis focused broadly on the work of Shane Meadows, with an effort to contextualise the director's work in the canon of contemporary British cinema. He is currently working in film and television post-production in Dublin.

Brett Mills is head of the School of Film, Television and Media Studies, and a senior lecturer in television studies, at the University of East Anglia. He is the author of *Television Sitcom* (2005) and *The Sitcom* (Edinburgh University Press, 2009) and co-author of *Reading Media Theory: Thinkers, Approaches, Contexts* (2009, 2012). He is the principal investigator on the three-year (2012–14) AHRC-funded project 'Make Me Laugh: Creativity in the British Television Comedy Industry' (www.makemelaugh.org.uk).

Robert Murphy is Emeritus Professor in Film Studies at De Montfort University. His books include *Realism and Tinsel* (1989), *Sixties British Cinema* (1992), *British Cinema and the Second World War* (2000) and (as editor) *The British Cinema Book* (3rd edition, 2009) and *Directors in British and Irish Cinema* (2006). He is currently writing a book about British Film Noir and researching early British sound feature films.

Jack Newsinger is lecturer in media and communication at the University of Leicester. His research interests are in the political economy of the media and cultural industries, particularly focusing on institutions, policy and creative practice. He has published on the history and theory of the creative industries, UK film policy, and low-budget, documentary and short filmmaking.

Sarah N. Petrovic is an assistant professor of English at Oklahoma Wesleyan University, where she teaches world and British literature and film. Her research and teaching interests additionally include film adaptation, visual culture and pedagogy.

David Rolinson is lecturer in film and television at the University of Stirling. He is the author of *Alan Clarke* (2005) and articles for various books and journals, including *No Known Cure: The Comedy of Chris Morris* (2013) and *British Social Realism in the Arts since 1940* (2011). He has written several DVD booklets, including *Tales Out of School* (2011), and he contributes regularly to the BFI's *Screenonline*. He is writing a book on

Stephen Frears, partly facilitated by AHRC research leave, and edits the website www.britishtelevisiondrama.org.uk.

Clair Schwarz has recently submitted her PhD thesis on Meadows (entitled 'Shane Meadows: Representations of Liminality, Masculinity and Class') at the University of the West of England, where she also teaches various courses on film and visual culture and supervises third-year dissertations. Her particular interests are the representations of gender in film, feminist theory and approaches, and British cinema. She has been published in *The Journal of British Cinema and Television* and has contributed a chapter to an edited collection of Dublin-based films: 'Craicing the safe: the gangster figure in Dublin cinema', in Conolly and Whelan (2011) (eds), *World Film Locations: Dublin*, Bristol: Intellect, pp. 104–21.

Tim Snelson is lecturer in media history at the University of East Anglia. His research addresses the relationship between media and social history and has been published in journals including *Media History*, *Cultural Studies* and *New Review of Film and Television Studies*.

Jill Steans is a senior lecturer in international relations at the University of Birmingham and a Shane Meadows fan.

Emma Sutton is a graduate of the film studies BA at Hull and the MA in cult cinema at Brunel University. She has also taught on the undergraduate film programme at the University of York. Her work on Shane Meadows has been published in *Scope: An Online Journal of Film and Television Studies*.

Melanie Williams is lecturer in film studies at the University of East Anglia. She is the author of *Prisoners of Gender* (2009) and *David Lean* (forthcoming), and co-editor of *British Women's Cinema* (2009), *Ealing Revisited* (2012) and *Mamma Mia!* (2013). She has also written on British cinema topics for a wide variety of journals and edited collections.

Faye Woods is lecturer in film and television at the University of Reading. Her research interests include popular music in film and television, youth representations, television industries and gender. She has published on popular music in teen television, the relationship between British and US teen television, and the teen dance film.

CHAPTER 1

Introduction: Shane's World

Martin Fradley, Sarah Godfrey and Melanie Williams

If any one moment marked Shane Meadows' indelible entry into the British cinema canon, it was the victory of *This is England* (2006) in the best film category at the 2008 BAFTAs. Just as *This is England* was a semi-autobiographical coming-of-age drama, this award-ceremony victory represented a parallel 'coming-of-age' in Meadows' filmmaking career. Triumphing over a particularly glossy roster of nominated films – David Cronenberg's *Eastern Promises*, rock biopic *Control*, the sweeping historical spectacle *Atonement* and political action thriller *The Bourne Ultimatum* (all 2007) – the low-budget *This is England* certainly stood out among its competitors. Moreover, as perhaps the only uncontentiously 'British' film among the nominees with a cast largely made up of unknown and non-professional performers, Meadows' 1980s period drama seemed particularly incongruous when the competition featured globally recognisable stars such as Naomi Watts, Keira Knightley, Viggo Mortensen and Matt Damon.

The success of *This is England* consolidated Meadows' pre-eminence among the younger generation of contemporary British directors, a cultural status only confirmed by the much-hyped television sequels *This is England '86* (2010) and *This is England '88* (2011), broadcast on Channel Four. The *This is England* series is also notable for managing to combine critical esteem with commercial success. *This is England*'s theatrical release in the UK comfortably recouped its budget of £1.5 million, while the domestic DVD of the film sold an extraordinary 785,000 copies. Moreover, the opening episode of *This is England '86* scored a Channel Four launch record for an original drama of 2.56 million viewers.[1] The growing recognition of Meadows' significance as a key twenty-first-century British filmmaker was underscored in more prosaic scholarly terms when the publishing imprint of the British Film Institute chose an image of Thomas Turgoose to adorn the cover of the third edition of their flagship anthology *The British Cinema Book* (2009), reaffirming *This is England* – and by extension, its director – as emblematic of British national cinema.

While the financial rewards and award-winning kudos gained from *This is England* were new experiences for Meadows, the film itself is best understood as the triumphant culmination of an already impressive and coherent body of work stretching back to the mid-1990s. This encompasses over fifty short films, his debut feature *TwentyFourSeven* (1997), the coming-of-age stories *A Room for Romeo Brass* (1999), *This is England* and *Somers Town* (2008), the 'tinned spaghetti Western' *Once Upon a Time in the Midlands* (2002), the dark vengeance drama of *Dead Man's Shoes* (2004) and the comic improvisation of *Le Donk and Scor-zay-zee* (2009). It also takes in advertisements, music videos and, most recently, the highly successful *This is England* television franchise. From the outset of his career to the present day, Meadows has continually returned to certain key themes, specific regional locales and distinctive character types: a recurrent set of motifs that several contributors to this book refer to as 'Meadowsian'. In order to explore Meadows' authorial identity in full – while also taking into account the input of his key collaborators – and to provide a broad explanatory context for the essays in this collection, it is necessary to return to the origins of Shane Meadows.

'This ain't fuckin' London!' Short films and 'small time' beginnings

Shane Meadows was born in the small Staffordshire market town of Uttoxeter on Boxing Day, 1972. Growing up in a semi-detached house on Westlands Road on the outskirts of the town, his early childhood was unremarkable until his father, Arthur, was propelled into the media spotlight in 1982 after discovering the dead body of an eleven-year-old girl, Susan Maxwell, during a routine journey up to Scotland working as a long-distance lorry driver (Harvey 2011). 'Arty' Meadows – after whom his son would later name his production company, 'Big Arty' – was, for a time, a key suspect in the murder case (Romney 2004). Although finally cleared of all suspicion (serial killer Robert Black would eventually be convicted for the murder), the stigma of association with the crime had inevitable repercussions for Arthur Meadows' young son. Shane Meadows has since testified to the centrality of paternal status in his formative years: 'I grew up in a very male-dominated town, where fathers were very important to kids. If you had a hard dad, then it gave you a ticket through certain doors. You probably weren't going to be bullied, you probably weren't going to get preyed on, and obviously expectation comes with that' (Wagstaff 2010). Little wonder, then, that his films often place at their centre a father figure of some kind, often malign or flawed but always profoundly influential.

As is well-established in promotional and interview material, after leaving school Meadows became involved in low-level petty crime. The director's own official website describes how, despite his desire to become Uttoxeter's very own 'infamous, criminal mastermind of legendary proportions', Meadows' formative adventures in juvenile delinquency culminated in a farcical criminal charge for the theft of – among other things – an egg custard tart and a breast pump from a chemist.[2] Such inept criminality finds its place in Meadows' films too, and his thematic interest in minor crime has its roots in the day-to-day economic pragmatism he saw necessitated by mass unemployment in 1980s Staffordshire. Known for little other than its dilapidated racecourse and economically sustained largely by its elephantine JCB manufacturing plant, the specificities of Uttoxeter directly underpin and inform much of Meadows' autobiographical early work. As Martin Fradley suggests, 'growing up on the social and geographical margins ... has directly shaped Meadows' creative sensibility and distinctive worldview', making him '[s]harply attuned to the daily rhythms and often unconventional lifestyles of these regional non-places' (2010: 290). Clearly class location, as well as geographical location, is absolutely crucial to Meadows' identity as a filmmaker. The focus of all his work falls almost exclusively on what Claire Monk terms the 'post-working class', created by 'the economic and structural damage wrought by globalisation, local industrial decline, the restructuring of the labour market and other legacies of the Thatcher era' (Monk 2000a: 274); indeed, as Meadows' career develops, his return to the 1980s, the 'primal scene' of Thatcherism, will become increasingly compulsive.

With hindsight, it is clear that Meadows' life changed irrevocably once he began studying at technical college in Burton-on-Trent in the early 1990s. This was where he met his friend and future collaborator Paddy Considine and where he made his first short films, borrowing video equipment from Intermedia, a film collective based in Nottingham. Making zero-budget films with friends, Meadows showcased his early shorts at local events and amateur film festivals (Fuller 2007). Filmed while claiming the dole, Meadows' early low-fi short films, such as *The Datsun Connection* (1994), *The Zombie Squad* and *Sneinton Junction* (both 1995), expressed both his autodidact talent and idiosyncratic worldview.[3] After several years of frugal guerrilla filmmaking, Meadows' first film to gain a wider public audience was *The Gypsy's Tale*, a bittersweet ten-minute documentary about Uttoxeter's bare-knuckle boxing champion Bartley Gorman. Forming part of the Channel Four season 'Tales of Battered Britain', *The Gypsy's Tale* was broadcast in June 1995 and marked the beginning of a long-term working relationship between Meadows and the broadcaster.

Melancholy and quietly poetic, *The Gypsy's Tale* is notable for the dignity it grants Gorman and his extended family. Alternating between static talking-head shots of Gorman reminiscing and impressionistic montages of the lush rural landscape in which he lives, Meadows' film marks an early foray into areas that would become hallmarks of his authorship: a preoccupation with the troubling relationship between masculinity and violence; an intuitive understanding of small provincial communities and their symbiotic relationship with the Midlands landscape; and an empathetic view of social marginality.

The following year, both *Where's the Money Ronnie!* and the 'featurette' *Small Time* helped to increase awareness of Meadows' work beyond the Midlands. Featuring an array of dissolute characters from the wrong side of the provincial tracks, the production of the two films was part-funded by the British Film Institute. With a running time of barely 12 minutes, *Where's the Money Ronnie!* is markedly more formally energetic than *The Gypsy's Tale*, featuring extensive hand-held camerawork, extreme close-ups, dynamic editing and striking, sometimes intrusive, use of music. The film also marks a shift from the bucolic idyll of Gorman's story to the bleak monochrome of Nottingham's working-class suburbs, all post-war concrete conurbation and anonymously sprawling terraced streets. It features Meadows as the titular Ronnie: a brash debt-collector involved in a murder inquiry following a botched robbery. Consisting of a series of police interviews with four suspects giving conflicting accounts of the event, the film makes obvious nods to *Rashomon* (1950) as well as the early crime films of Martin Scorsese and the contemporaneous work of Quentin Tarantino.

Small Time's expanded running time of an hour allowed for a more detailed and generous exploration of parochial criminality. Largely improvised with friends and shot on analogue video, *Small Time*'s gallery of underclass rascals and would-be hoodlums is a comically preposterous transposition of the Little Italy of *Mean Streets* (1973) onto Meadows' experiences of petty crime in 1990s Nottingham. The introductory monologue – spoken by Meadows' character, Jumbo – is as much a statement of creative intent as it is an expression of defiantly specific regional identity (even including a glancing reference to local hero Robin Hood):

> There's one thing you gotta understand, right? This ain't fuckin' London, this isn't even Nottingham, man. This is Sneinton, and all that matters in Sneinton is having a tenner in yer pocket, youknoworramean? It don't matter how you get it … We're

not into anything heavy: we rob from the rich and we sell it to the poor at half price. We're just small-time.[4]

With its colourful vernacular and raucous but quotidian dole-culture milieu, it is tempting to see *Small Time* as a virtual blueprint for the popular and much-discussed 'underclass' comedy-drama *Shameless* (Channel Four, 2004–13). However, Meadows' film, shot on location in the streets and terraced houses of Sneinton in which the director and his friends lived, is often as gleefully amateurish as the chancers it depicts. Meadows and his cast of mates burst into laughter at both their surreal improvised banter and the preposterous self-delusion of would-be gangsters whose criminal activities consist of stealing cans of dog food and raiding car boot sales. As Claire Monk points out, unlike most British social realism, *Small Time* 'had genuine origins in the (non-)working-class community it depicted rather than observing it with the gaze of the socially concerned outsider' (1999: 185). Perhaps the most significant of his early works, *Small Time* remains most impressive for being that rarest of things: a genuine grass-roots feature for, by and about the community it represents.

Meadows' early short films typify a working method which the film-maker has continued to mobilise throughout his career. Rejecting aesthetic purity and formal precision in favour of a buccaneering 'can do' attitude, Meadows' DIY approach makes the best use of the resources at hand, however derogated they might be. Meadows has been dismissive of purists' attachment to celluloid: 'There are people out there who won't make a film unless they can shoot on 16mm: well, I think "fuck off, then." Camcorders cost nothing' (in Macnab 1998: 16). If the reference to analogue video now seems quaintly anachronistic, Meadows' rhetorical point about the democratic possibilities of inexpensive technology remains forceful, and an ideal to which he has remained faithful: in 2005, he made *The Stairwell* (2005), a frantic 15-second short filmed on a mobile phone.

Even after he had made his feature debut, Meadows would still hark back to his original 'can do' approach to making films: the idea that 'anyone can make a film for £100 – and have enough left over to get legless with yer mates' (Macnab 1998: 14). The reference to 'yer mates' is important: Meadows' method consistently foregrounds improvisation and a strong collaborative ethos, and he has regularly highlighted the importance of communality in his filmmaking practice:

What I had with my short films was very much a family environment – I did a lot of the cooking and that sort of thing ... We used to play football every dinner time – a little match between the cast and the crew. It gave us something to focus on other than the film. A bad environment can hinder the performances. I try to create an

environment where anyone can deliver a really good performance. (Meadows in
Macnab: 14)

The parallel between film unit and family unit is evident from even the
briefest examination of Meadows' production methods. The director has
long surrounded himself with a trusted group of close friends and family
who function as the nucleus of his creative team, many of his friends from
the Midlands having worked for free on his early films. Paul Fraser,
Meadows' childhood neighbour, is a regular (co-)screenwriter, their
relationship forming the basis for characters in both *A Room for Romeo
Brass* and *Somers Town*. Other friends from the wastelands of 1980s
Staffordshire – including Paddy Considine, musician Gavin Clarke and
charismatic non-professional performers like Mat Hand and Gena
Kawecka – are also key collaborators without whom the colloquial texture
of Meadows' earliest work is practically unthinkable. Meadows has also
maintained a long-standing and highly productive association with the
Nottingham Central TV workshop where he discovered actors including
Andrew Shim and Vicky McClure. While the story of Thomas Turgoose
might be the most celebrated example of Meadows' practice of recruiting
actors from outside the drama school circuit, McClure has the distinction
of being one of the few women to feature prominently in Meadows' work.
Although she described working with Meadows while playing the role of
Lol in the *This is England* television series as a 'psychological nightmare'
(Petridis 2012), McClure also endorsed the director's working methods for
enabling her to access the rawest possible performance.

Making films 'from yer 'aart'

Shane Meadows was only twenty-five years old when he made his 1997
debut feature *TwentyFourSeven*, already having over thirty short films
under his belt. Originally conceived as another short, producer Stephen
Woolley convinced Meadows that the script for *TwentyFourSeven* was more
suited to a longer form and helped secure a comparatively vast £1.4 million
production budget from Scala Productions and BBC Films. Co-written
with Paul Fraser, *TwentyFourSeven* is a simple but self-evidently heartfelt
story about a group of disenfranchised lads and the middle-aged man who
restores their ability to believe in both themselves and each other. Meadows
and Fraser, unbeknown to each other, had very similar ideas for the central
character of Darcy. As Meadows explains, 'We had a discussion and it
turned out we were both writing scenes for Bob Hoskins' (Null 1998). They
decided to send a draft to Hoskins, who agreed to take part after being

'astonished at the compassion, the insight and the poetry' of the script (Miller 1998). Despite the fact that the five-week shoot in and around a notoriously deprived housing estate on the outskirts of Nottingham was a world away from his typical filmmaking environment, Hoskins' instinct about the film was proved right. Although the film struggled at the box office, *TwentyFourSeven*'s bleak but understated tale of social paralysis attracted the attention of critics and the film industry alike. Meadows' film was nominated for the Alexander Korda award for Best British Film at the 1998 BAFTA ceremony, won the British Independent Film Award's Douglas Hickox prize for directorial debuts and was garlanded with the prestigious FIPRESCI award at the Venice Film Festival.

The young director's acclaimed debut was followed by *A Room for Romeo Brass*, also co-written with Fraser and, like *TwentyFourSeven*, loosely inspired by events from their childhood. Filmed in Calverton in Nottinghamshire, the film is notable for many reasons, not least for offering the debut performances of frequent Meadows collaborators such as Andrew Shim, Vicky McClure and Paddy Considine. In particular, Considine's striking acting debut as the troubled Morell represents what might be termed a typically 'Meadowsian' form of masculinity, as he transforms from 'benign oddball to malevolent sociopath' (Godfrey 2010: 285). Despite critical acclaim and a widespread belief that Meadows was proving to be a unique new talent in British film, *A Room for Romeo Brass* suffered from catastrophically poor marketing and distribution, barely recouping £100,000 of its £3.2 million budget on its theatrical release in February 2000.

Perhaps bruised by the commercial failure of *A Room for Romeo Brass*, Meadows returned to a more familiar working environment with *Shane's World* (2000), a feature-length compendium of short films broadcast on Channel Four. Featuring a disparate collective of provincial hard-luck cases and oddball grotesques, *Shane's World* recaptures the lo-fi energy and brash charm of *Where's the Money Ronnie!* and *Small Time*. With many of the films featuring Considine – including an early outing for a breakdancing Le Donk in 'Chip Shop, Don't Stop' – the compilation serves as an impressive showcase of the duo as a comedic force. 'The Poppa Squeeze Affair', for example, features Considine as a sub-Scorsese hoodlum with a thick Lower East Side accent bizarrely harassing the residents of Nottingham suburbia. While humour is to the fore, *Shane's World* is equally notable for its evocative explorations of fractured male identity in both 'Macca's Men' and 'Three Tears for Jimmy Prophet'. Perhaps most significantly for those seeking to understand Meadows as an auteur, there is 'Tank's Top Tips', in which the director himself plays the mercurial Tank Bullock, a Uttoxeter farm labourer and amateur filmmaker-cum-pathological bully. Bursting with filmmaking tips for aspirant directors delivered in a preposterously exaggerated Staffordshire dialect, the bale-stacking, toupee-wearing Tank is a knowing self-caricature of Meadows' own working methods. While Tank's comic delivery could be read as a satire on making films 'from yer 'aart', the credo is nonetheless a noble one which seems to be sincerely held by Meadows.

This ideal of personal filmmaking would be tested when Meadows' growing reputation within the film industry meant that his next film, *Once Upon a Time in the Midlands*, was able to recruit an impressive array of British acting talent and a bigger budget than ever before, courtesy of Film Four. Despite its light-hearted and accessible romantic script (again co-written by Fraser and Meadows) and the presence of mainstream British stars including Robert Carlyle, Ricky Tomlinson, Kathy Burke and Rhys Ifans, *Once Upon a Time in the Midlands* was, and continues to be, almost uniformly perceived as Meadows' weakest and least distinctive feature to date. The director later described the experience of making it as a painful learning curve:

> I've grown to realise that my films don't necessarily come together according to a strict plan. That's what I learned from *Once Upon a Time in the Midlands* and I'm never again going to be involved in something where someone gives me a load of money to make a film I don't care about. You have to really want to do it. If I'm on my way to the set and I see something I want to include I will, or if someone comes up with a brilliant idea then I'm going to use it. Film-making can't be a precise thing anyway – you can start a shot in brilliant sunshine then a cloud comes over and changes it all. (Meadows in James 2007: 41)

If *Once Upon a Time in the Midlands* has been widely interpreted as one of Meadows' most disappointing films, its follow-up has been hailed as perhaps his finest achievement. The low-budget and heavily improvised *Dead Man's Shoes*, co-written with its star Paddy Considine, was again grounded in personal experience. This time, Meadows' inspiration came from returning to Uttoxeter and discovering that the town – and many of his old friends and acquaintances – had been ravaged by a drug scene that he himself had abandoned years before. 'I think you don't draw on the darker recesses of your experience until further on in life,' he told *Sight & Sound*. 'I didn't take acid with hippies – I took it with rough lads who would smash you round the head with a hammer when they were off their heads' (in Lawrenson 2004: 36). A disturbing revenge drama shot on location in and around Matlock in north Derbyshire, Meadows' astute sense of place has rarely felt more atmospheric or intimidating. Attentive to the bleak landscape's resonant spaces and rain-sodden textures, *Dead Man's Shoes'* isolated rural backwater is as haunted as any of its troubled denizens. Despite the sparse plot, *Dead Man's Shoes* is dominated by a palpable sense of stasis and social decay. Understated montages of agricultural debris and rotting council houses underscore its hermetically sealed depiction of life on the social and economic peripheries, imbuing this unloved, gothicised double of Uttoxeter with a sense of the uncanny. Both brutal and darkly comic, the film has acquired a substantial cult reputation. As numerous contributors to this volume argue, *Dead Man's Shoes* marks something of a watershed for Meadows in terms of both formal accomplishment and thematic complexity. It also began his productive and mutually beneficial association with Mark Herbert's Sheffield-based Warp Films. Their support has been instrumental in establishing Meadows as a leading light of new British cinema, while Meadows' growing reputation has enabled Warp to grow into a 'creative powerhouse' of distinctive 'innovative and uncompromising' films (Youngs 2011), including *Submarine* (2010), *Four Lions* (2010), *Kill List* (2010), Paddy Considine's directorial debut *Tyrannosaur* (2011) and *Berberian Sound Studio* (2012). His alignment with Warp also seems to confirm Meadows' genuine and ongoing commitment to the media industry which exists beyond London.

Following on from the critical success of *Dead Man's Shoes* came the film with which Meadows has become most readily associated; *This is England* once more saw the director return to his 1980s youth for direct inspiration. The autobiographical elements of the film are more explicitly rendered than ever before: the name of *This is England*'s grieving adolescent protagonist – Shaun Fields – is an obvious echo of the director's own. As played by Thomas Turgoose, *This is England*'s bullied and alienated young hero initially finds solace and comfort in a group of skinheads, but what appears to be a warm, accepting and non-judgemental community is thrown into disarray when one of its former members, Combo, returns from prison spouting ugly but eloquent right-wing rhetoric. Perhaps Meadows' most explicitly political film, *This is England* drew much comment for its self-conscious mirroring of contemporary issues. Set in 1983 against the backdrop of a politically divisive war in the Falklands and a rise in National Front membership, the film could not help but resonate on its theatrical release in 2007 as the far-right British National Party gained election victories while British troops remained firmly entrenched in the Middle East.

Despite the critical and commercial triumph of *This is England*, Meadows' subsequent features were two frugal, low-profile affairs with limited theatrical distribution. A return to his collaboration with Paul Fraser, *Somers Town* is in many ways a slight film, running at little over an hour. But despite its brevity and wafer-thin plot, it is perhaps one of the richest and finely nuanced of Meadows' films. Detailing the developing friendship between two adolescent boys hopelessly dislocated in the vast expanse of London, *Somers Town* was Meadows' first film set entirely outside the Midlands. Offering an optimistic counterpoint to *This is England*'s bleak depiction of racism, xenophobia and ugly nationalist politics, *Somers Town* provided a gentle endorsement of transnationalism and the progressive dissolution of national boundaries. Equally, however, *Somers Town* begs to be read on an allegorical level. Like his dole-funded early films (and, indeed, like Tomo and Marek in the movie), Meadows makes the best of what is to hand, using creative lateral thinking to construct small wonders out of ostensibly worthless materials. Its funding from Eurostar, with the intention that the film would act as a partial advertisement of the company's intercontinental rail services, did not prevent it from treading its own idiosyncratic and highly personal path (Brouillette 2009). Just as the adolescent waifs of the story find magic in a social world characterised by frugality and limitation, so too does Meadows, with a deliberate return to his founding spirit after the triumph of *This is England*. Similarly, Meadows' next film, the largely improvised 'Five Day Film' project *Le Donk and Scor-zay-zee*, a free-wheeling mockumentary starring Considine as a would-be rap impresario, clearly demonstrates how the director remains firmly committed to the improvisational ethos of his earliest filmmaking experiments.

'A richer time to draw on for me than any other': memory, the 1980s and screening nostalgia

If the semi-autobiographical *This is England* was unquestionably a significant film in its own right, it was also important for instigating a successful, BAFTA-winning series of television sequels. Set at periodic intervals – 1983, 1986 and 1988, with a third instalment set in 1990 anticipated at the time of writing – the *This is England* saga's compulsive exploration of the experience of growing up in the Midlands in the 1980s could easily be read as morbidly nostalgic. These accusations might also be levelled at Meadows in relation to what is, at the time of writing, his latest backward-looking project: a film about the re-forming of The Stone Roses.

On 18 October 2011, the four original members of the revered Manchester rock band held a press conference to announce their long-rumoured re-formation. The event was filmed by Meadows, and a few weeks later it was confirmed that the director's eighth feature would be a documentary film about the iconic band. Aged seventeen when their debut album was released in 1989, Meadows described The Stone Roses as 'my favourite band ever that there ever was, has been or ever will be'.[5] He was also candid about the dimension of nostalgic revisitation in his attachment to the project:

> I missed the famous Spike Island gig because I had a bad acid trip. You had to be there ... I wouldn't have cared if they'd come back and smacked me with a sandwich, I just wanted to be there and I missed it, so this is me going back to Spike Island at about 40 and with no hair. (Meadows in Miller 2012)

The Spike Island concert on 27 May 1990 marked the popular highpoint of the interconnected youth movements of acid house and 'Madchester' which – with their distinctive homology between specific types of music, fashion and drugs – signifies for some the last hurrah of post-war, pre-digital British youth culture. The pivotal years 1988–92 marked the gradual erosion of the egalitarian DIY ethos, anti-metropolitan ideology and Leftist political thrust of the 1980s independent music scene, as exemplified by the implosion of Manchester's celebrated Factory Communications (Harris 2003; Nice 2010; King 2012) as documented in Michael Winterbottom's *24 Hour Party People* (2001).

For some, The Stone Roses' much-hyped re-formation could be seen to typify what Simon Reynolds (2011) dubs twenty-first-century 'retromania'. 'Instead of being about itself,' Reynolds argues, 'the 2000s have been about every other previous decade happening again all at once: a simultaneity of pop time that abolishes history while nibbling away at the present's own sense of itself as an era with a distinct identity and feel' (x–xi). Yet while heady 1980s and '90s nostalgia undoubtedly motivated the thousands of people who bought tickets to watch the band play together for the first time in over two decades, and motivated Meadows' own enthusiasm for making a documentary about them, this return to the past should not be dismissed as mere hankering after old times or conveniently lucrative revivalism. Rather, *The Stone Roses: Made of Stone* (2013) offers just another example of Meadows' obsessive return(s) to the 1980s, combining nostalgia and melancholia in a look back at the era which remains the point of origin for the state of contemporary Britain.

Born in 1972, Meadows himself is – like the editors of this volume – a member of the generation known as Thatcher's children, 'the aphorism that describes an entire generation who has grown up knowing nothing but the aftermath of Thatcherite policies' (Hadley and Ho 2010: 3). Meadows' would-be 'nostalgic' interventions are thus both timely and symptomatic in an era of neoliberal consensus. As Louisa Hadley and Elizabeth Ho suggest, the triumph of market fundamentalism and the 'end of history' is registered all too clearly in the truism that, for a post-Thatcherite generation – Thatcher's grandchildren, if you will – 'there is nothing in the present to suggest, and little urgency to understand, that there was a "break" at all' (2). In their view, memories of the Thatcherite 1980s continue to serve as 'traumatic flashbacks' to an era which continues to haunt the present. If we can consider the entire *This is England* saga to form part of this continuum, these flashbacks are perhaps most clearly located in the evocative period montages which open each instalment. Refusing to indulge nostalgic reveries or cultural amnesia, the ongoing *This is England* series does not hesitate to interrogate the gulf between period kitsch and the often brutal socio-political schisms of the period; nor does it shy away from drawing explicit parallels between the 1980s and the various social and economic crises of the present.

In both its reactionary and its radical manifestations nostalgia is always political, characterised as it is by a profound dissatisfaction with the present. More complex than is generally imagined, nostalgia, argues Stuart Tannock (1995), creates a narrative which 'responds to a diversity of personal needs and political desires' and which 'may embody any number of different visions, values and ideals' (454). For Tannock, nostalgia cannot be dismissed as either naively sentimental or simply reactionary:

> We need to separate out, in the critique of nostalgia, the critique of the content, author and audience of a nostalgic narrative – who is nostalgic for what, and in the names of which community – from the critique of nostalgia itself – the positive evaluation of the past in response to a negatively evaluated present. (456)

To this end, invocations of nostalgia and popular memory are absolutely key to understanding Meadows' work. Although the *This is England* cycle remains Meadows' only period piece to date, nearly all the director's work is grounded in some way in autobiography and social memory. *Twenty-FourSeven*, *A Room for Romeo Brass* and *Dead Man's Shoes* are all firmly rooted in Meadows' personal experiences growing up in 1980s Uttoxeter. Moreover, as Paul Dave (2011) has noted, Meadows repeatedly uses children and adolescents as figures through which to explore long-term social fallout. When asked by *Sight & Sound* about this apparently compulsive return to his childhood, Meadows remarked:

> I seem to have cornered the market where kids are hanging out with psychopaths. I was thinking about it when I saw *The Devil and Daniel Johnston* and they were saying the songwriter only had three themes. I think my 1980s is a richer time to draw on for me than any other. (Meadows in James: 41)

Yet at the same time as it mourns the decline of Leftist politics as a genuine force in British culture, Meadows' work remains nostalgic for the 1980s' powerful sense of genuine political oppositionality. In this way, Meadows' work is – to borrow Jacques Derrida's (1994) aphorism – *haunto-logical*; that is, it retains spectral traces of a recent political past. Meadows' films are often haunted both thematically and textually, displaying post-traumatic symptoms of repetition and a therapeutic working-through of histories both personal and socio-political. The recurrence of the spectral trope is telling; as Andrew Smith (2007) points out, ghosts 'are messengers about the preoccupations of a personal age ... Ghosts are never just ghosts; they provide us with an insight into what haunts our culture' (153).

As Owen Jones has recently argued in *Chav: The Demonization of the Working Class* (2011), over the last ten years a legitimised hatred of people existing at the lower end of Britain's socioeconomic scale has become a *de facto* ideological norm in British culture. 'Politicians, particularly in the Labour Party', argues Jones, 'once spoke of improving the conditions of working-class people':

> But today's consensus is about *escaping* the working class ... 'Aspiration' has been redefined to mean individual self-enrichment: to scramble up the social ladder and become middle-class. Social problems like poverty and unemployment were once understood as injustices that sprang from flaws within capitalism ... [But] today they have become understood as the consequences of personal behaviour, individual defects and even choice. (10)

In contrast with the insidious neoliberal rhetoric outlined by Jones, Meadows' work emphatically refutes the idea that poverty and social marginalisation are, in any way, the 'choice' of his characters. Indeed, the opening monologue in *TwentyFourSeven* makes the point that the characters have no choice: they are the trapped recipients of supposed 'development' and forgotten victims of social and economic 'progress'. Both Meadows' early crime films and *TwentyFourSeven* are notable for the way they rejected the voguish tide of underclass crime films inspired by 'lad culture' in the late-1990s, such as *Lock, Stock and Two Smoking Barrels* (1998) and *Twin Town* (1997), by offering a considerably more socially aware and far less celebratory representation of male disenfranchisement (Monk 1999; Godfrey 2010). As reiterated later in *Dead Man's Shoes*, *This is England* and *Somers Town*, widespread unemployment and expedient survivalism is a taken-for-granted state of being for the characters inhabiting his narratives. Meadows' work thus offers an empathetic depiction of communities left bereft by neoliberal consensus and complicates the dominant stereotypes of the British poor in the late twentieth and early twenty-first centuries. In spite of what Heather Nunn and Anita Biressi describe as 'the inexorable momentum of the individualist ethos, championing the benefits of consumption, flexibility and entrepreneurial zeal' (2010: 144), repeatedly in Meadows' films it is social groupings based on mutuality and inclusively collective public spaces that are celebrated. In the no-income worlds of *TwentyFourSeven*, *Somers Town* and *This is England* it is subway tunnels, swimming baths, parks, overcrowded living rooms and small cafes which are quietly eulogised as democratic micro-spaces of belonging for those eternally outside the sacred property ladder. Rarely didactic in tone, Meadows nonetheless defends what Paul Dave calls 'the protective, reciprocal and collective aspects of working-class culture' (2006: 85). For Meadows, there *is* such a thing as society, *contra* Thatcher, and present-day atomised consumer society compares unfavourably to a more authentically interactive past. 'If you were a kid in 1983,' he has remarked, 'you wouldn't have a PlayStation to sit indoors alone with':

> You got your entertainment from mixing with a variety of different people. While making the film, I realised that all of my fondest childhood memories surrounded human contact: mucking about with mates or going camping. In 2007, people put less emphasis on that sort of thing and more on planning their careers and their TV viewing. As far as I'm concerned, if you're working from nine to five then coming home to watch shows that your Sky box has recorded for you while you were out, you might as well be on a fucking drip. (Meadows 2007)

Of course, this kind of middle-aged nostalgia for a vanished golden age inevitably leaves Meadows open to accusations of (reactionary) sentimentality and conservatism. There is also an undeniable irony in romanticised depictions of Meadows' creative practice and working-class-lad-made-good persona. Unquestionably a product of conflicting ideologies, Meadows is both creative artist and pragmatic businessman whose successful career can easily be understood as a late flowering of Thatcherite enterprise culture. Indeed, the director's unapologetic sense of commercial expediency is evident in his acceptance of advertising assignments for, among others, Barclaycard, NatWest, McDonald's and Quorn, as well as the sponsorship of Eurostar for *Somers Town*.

Beyond The Stone Roses: Made of Stone and *This is England '90*, Meadows' future projects (according to his official website) include a tale of demonic possession, *Beware the Devil* – plenty of hauntological potential there – as well as a return to the story of Bartley Gorman, thus taking Meadows' directorial career full circle. But even while it revisits the past, the director's work will also undoubtedly develop and change, moving forward into new areas and forms of expression.

Critical essays on Shane Meadows

This book emerges from a two-day conference held at the University of East Anglia in April 2010. Entitled 'Straight Outta Uttoxeter' (named in self-mocking homage to the seminal gangsta rap album *Straight Outta Compton* by Los Angeles's NWA), the rationale for the event was straight-forward: despite Meadows' popularity and growing critical reputation, there was still a dearth of sustained academic engagement with his work. Some of the chapters that follow stem directly from papers first given at that conference, while others have been specially commissioned for this collection. In bringing together these very different, often markedly diver-gent, critical voices on Meadows' work, we have not attempted, to borrow Robert Murphy's words, 'to impose an orthodox view, nor suppressed contradictions' (Murphy 2000: xi). We also hope that this will be the first of many scholarly investigations into the still-burgeoning directorial career of Shane Meadows.

Beyond this introductory chapter, the anthology opens with three essays providing broader overviews of specific aspects of Meadows' career. The epithet 'straight outta Uttoxeter' may serve as parodic shorthand for Meadows' striking emergence from the Midlands to become a leading contemporary British director, but this 'origin myth' hardly tells the whole story. In his essay, Jack Newsinger carefully outlines the complex indus-trial foundations which provided support for Meadows' distinctive working methods and an economic platform for the director's rise 'outta' the provin-cial hinterlands. In emphasising the economic determinants for Meadows' emergence, Newsinger's empiricist account of the importance of Regional Screen Agencies underlines the continued centrality of public funding to sustain young British talent. Concluding with the announcement in July 2010 that the UK Film Council was to be abolished, Newsinger ends with a bleak prognosis for the creation of any future Shane Meadowses.

While Newsinger provides the industrial context in which to under-stand Meadows' work, Dave Forrest situates the director within the national tradition of cinematic social realism. Comparing the director with contemporaries such as Lynne Ramsay, Andrea Arnold and Paweł Pawlikowski, Forrest offers a more nuanced understanding of twenty-first-century British realism. Emphasising Meadows' mobilisation of abstract image-led narration, Forrest reads the director's work as moving beyond a more didactic model towards a hybrid of art cinema and oblique socio-political commentary.

The social and political dimensions of Meadows' work are also at the heart of Martin Fradley's chapter on abjection. Here, Fradley finds in the gleeful scatological excesses and insistent bodily humour of Meadows' work a nostalgic longing for the democratic – and significantly oppositional – folk culture of Bakhtin's carnivalesque.

The next six chapters provide detailed analyses of particular examples of Meadows' film work from *TwentyFourSeven* to *Le Donk and Scor-zay-zee*. First, in an echo of some of the points raised in Forrest's chapter, Jill Steans locates the latent social criticism of Meadows' debut feature *TwentyFour-Seven* in the potency of its affect. Drawing on debates within political science and sociology, Steans reiterates that Meadows' employment of sentiment is not without its uses. Her close analysis of Darcy – a character who she sees as a charismatic hero in a world entirely disengaged with the processes of party politics – draws on parallels with *This is England*'s Combo, and that later film's more explicit engagement with the politics of the Thatcher era.

Paul Elliott's chapter on *Dead Man's Shoes* and *TwentyFourSeven* draws extensively on Freud's work on memory and repetition. Although a psycho-analytic approach may initially seem slightly incongruous, Elliott's careful examination of Meadows' compulsively mournful engagements with the recent past and his deft exploration of recurrent psychological themes serves as a useful synopsis of 'Meadowsian' tropes which recur throughout the director's work (and the essays in this collection). Clair Schwarz also uses *Dead Man's Shoes* to interrogate Meadows' depiction of atavistic male enclaves. Like Forrest, Schwarz finds an orthodox social-realist model inadequate to explicate the thematic complexity and generic hybridity of Meadows' work. Instead, she argues, *Dead Man's Shoes* fuses a dense array of mythic tropes with the conventions and motifs of genre cinema, combin-ing them in a gothicised critique of homosociality.

Many of Meadows' films are either implicitly or explicitly about memory, and Tim Snelson and Emma Sutton's chapter draws on subcultural theory and the affective power of popular music to examine the politics of 1980s youth culture in *This is England*. While Snelson and Sutton discuss the film in terms of Meadows' own experiential connection to skinhead culture, Sarah Petrovic examines *This is England* and its successor *Somers Town* in relation to the director's acute sense of place. From the pastoralism of *The Gypsy's Tale* and mean streets of Sneinton in *Small Time* onwards, Meadows' work has often dwelt on the resonance of regional locale. Drawing on concepts of psychogeography, Petrovic traces the significance of the relationship between physical location and mental dislocation in these two key films.

Despite the often disturbing content of his films, comedy nonetheless remains one of the most distinctive aspects of Meadows' work. In his chapter on *Le Donk and Scor-zay-zee*, Brett Mills offers a sustained analysis of a film dismissed in some quarters as little more than an extended in-joke between the director and his old friend Paddy Considine. Stressing that comedy always has its roots in social commentary, Mills examines this mockumentary in that light, finding in *Le Donk* another of Meadows' dissections of masculinity and its discontents.

Gender provides the basis for the next two chapters in the book. Familial relations are invariably at the heart of Meadows' work, and the penultimate section of the book offers a twinned investigation of the sexual politics at play in Meadows' world with chapters on representations of motherhood and fatherhood in his work. Firstly, Louise Fitzgerald and Sarah Godfrey provide a feminist critique of the director's largely androcentric terrain. Casting a sceptical eye over the homosocial emphasis of Meadows' work, Fitzgerald and Godfrey argue that his films' insistent marginalisation of women leads to a repression – even negation – of the maternal which necessarily limits the efficacy of Meadows' working-class political agenda. Conversely, Martin Fradley and Seán Kingston offer a comprehensive survey of paternal themes throughout Meadows' career. Contextualising their essay with an overview of contemporary critical debates about fatherhood and the so-called 'crisis of masculinity', Fradley and Kingston argue that the innumerable flawed fathers, 'bad dads' and symbolic father-figures in Meadows' work provide a detailed critique of normative masculinity and suggest, by extension, the impossibility of sustaining traditional male authority.

The final section of the book looks in more detail at Meadows' television work, specifically the *This is England* franchise. Dave Rolinson and Faye Woods highlight challenging television drama – including the work of Alan Clarke, Ken Loach, Mike Leigh and Stephen Frears – as a key formative influence on Meadows. Post-*Big Brother,* Channel Four sought to position itself as the inheritor of that tradition, commissioning a number of one-off dramas and series, including the first of Meadows' extensions of *This is England*. However, Rolinson and Woods stress the hybridity of Meadows' television work, which fuses the social drama of an earlier epoch with the formally energetic teen-oriented world of Channel Four's *Skins* (2007–present) and other youth dramas. In their concern with memory and their 1980s focus, *This is England '86* and *'88* are characteristically Meadowsian, but being co-written by Jack Thorne and co-directed by Tom Harper, the collaborative end product challenges a straightforwardly auteurist reading.

The final word in this collection of essays belongs to Robert Murphy, whose chapter focuses on *This is England '88*. While providing a detailed examination of the latest instalment in the lives of Shaun, Lol, Woody, Smell, Combo, Milky et al., Murphy also notes a markedly spiritual turn in Meadows' latest television work. Continuing on this theme, he concludes by making the case for taking Shane Meadows seriously as 'an extraordinarily sophisticated and complex filmmaker' whose evocations of religion might bear comparison with revered auteurs such as Carl Dreyer and Ingmar Bergman, if only the director 'looked more like an intellectual and didn't come from Uttoxeter'.

Unheard melodies

Shane Meadows' use of music, as many contributors to this volume attest, is one of the crowning glories of his films. The ending of *This is England* offers a superb example. Jettisoning his flag of St George in the sea, Shaun finally meets the audience's gaze in a freeze frame that deliberately invokes the conclusion of Truffaut's autobiographical *Les quatre cents coups* (1959). Both Truffaut's Antoine Doinel and Meadows' Shaun Fields face uncertain adult futures; in Shaun's case, he has abandoned his previous convictions but is left with nothing to replace them. The sequence is immeasurably enriched by its music, Gavin Clarke's mournful cover version of the Smiths' 'Please, Please, Please Let Me Get What I Want', with its delicately chiming melody and imploring lyrics, perfectly capturing the yearning, bereaved child at its centre.

The great sadness of completing this book is that it lacks Mark Brownrigg's planned chapter on music as a storytelling device in Meadows' films. Mark's death in 2010 was an enormous loss not only to everyone who knew and loved him, but also to the students who will never benefit from his endless warmth and enthusiasm, and to film and television scholarship more broadly. We dedicate this book to his memory.

Notes

1. Source: www.guardian.co.uk/film/shane-meadows.
2. Source: http://www.shanemeadows.co.uk/who.htm.
3. The Shane Meadows official website lists a total of fifty unique short films – as well as a number of other films which rework the same story (three versions of *Where's the Money Ronnie!*, for instance) – lasting in duration from just 15 seconds to 30 minutes. Meadows continues to produce short films, seeing them not as calling cards or stepping stones necessary for the development of his feature career but as an integral part of his filmmaking practice. More recent examples have included the gentle tragicomedy *Northern Soul* (2004),

featuring Toby Kebbell as a delusional young man with a quixotic longing to become a professional wrestler, its humour and mockumentary style serving – alongside several of the shorts in *Shane's World* – as dry runs for *Le Donk and Scor-zay-zee*, and *The Living Room* (2009), a documentary about the musician Gavin Clarke. Meadows' enthusiasm for the short film format remains undiminished: a 'masterclass' contained on the *Somers Town* DVD extras sees Meadows regale an audience in New York with an account of *The Burgernator*, an ad hoc film shot earlier in the day about Paul Fraser's insatiable appetite for American fast food. The sheer scale and variety of Meadows' work in short film demands more attention than we have been able to pay it in this volume, and we hope that many of his currently unavailable short films will be made publicly accessible soon.

4. This insistence on the specificities of places-within-places is also evident in Meadows' later film *Somers Town*, when Londoner Graham (Perry Benson) asks Tomo (Thomas Turgoose) where he's from. He replies 'Up north' before correcting himself: 'Well, the Midlands. Nottingham. East Midlands.' A bemused Graham merely feigns comprehension, but it is clear that for Meadows these geographical distinctions are far from trivial.

5. Source: www.shanemeadows.proboards.com/index.cgi?board=stone&action =display&thread=4765&page=1.

References

Brouillette, S. (2009), 'Creative labour and auteur authorship: reading *Somers Town*', *Textual Practice*, 23: 5, 829–47.

Dave, P. (2006), *Visions of England: Class and Culture in Contemporary Cinema*, Oxford and New York: Berg.

Dave, P. (2011), 'Tragedy, ethics and history in contemporary British social realist film', in D. Tucker (ed.), *British Social Realism in the Arts since 1940*, Edinburgh: Edinburgh University Press, pp. 29–52.

Derrida, J. (1994), *Spectres of Marx: The State of the Debt, the Work of Mourning, and the New International*, trans. by P. Kamuf, Cambridge: Polity Press.

Fradley, M. (2010), 'Shane Meadows', in Y. Tasker (ed.), *Fifty Contemporary Film Directors*, London: Routledge, pp. 280–8.

Fuller, G. (2007), 'Boys to men', *Film Comment*, 43: 4 (July–August 2007), 44–7.

Godfrey, S. (2010), 'Nowhere Men: Representations of Masculinity in 90s British Cinema' (unpublished PhD thesis).

Hadley, L. and E. Ho (2010), 'The Lady's not for turning: new cultural perspectives on Thatcher and Thatcherism', in Hadley and Ho (eds), *Thatcher and After: Margaret Thatcher and Her Afterlife in Contemporary Culture*, London: Palgrave Macmillan, pp. 1–26.

Harris, J. (2003), *The Last Party: Britpop, Blair and the Demise of English Rock*, London: Harper Perennial.

Harvey, C. (2011), 'Shane Meadows and Vicky McClure on This Is England '88: Interview', *Daily Telegraph*, 13 December: http://www.telegraph.co.uk/culture/tvandradio/8950839/Shane-Meadows-and-Vicky-McClure-on-This-Is-England-88-interview.html.

James, N. (2007), 'At the edge of England', *Sight & Sound*, 17: 5, 41.

Jones, O. (2011), *Chavs: The Demonization of the Working Class*, London: Verso.

Kermode, M. (2004), 'Dead Man's Shoes', *Sight & Sound*, 14: 10, 51.

King, R. (2012), *How Soon Is Now? The Madmen and Mavericks Who Made Independent Music 1975–2005*, London: Faber & Faber.

Lawrenson, E. (2004), 'Getting personal', *Sight & Sound*, 14: 10, 35–6.

Macnab, G. (1998), 'The Natural', *Sight & Sound*, 8: 3, 14–16.

Meadows, S. (2007), 'Under my skin', *The Guardian*: http://www.guardian.co.uk/film/2007/apr/21/culture.features.

Miller, P. (1998), '*TwentyFourSeven*: interview with Bob Hoskins': http://www.angelfire.com/celeb/bobhoskins/interviews/twentyfourseven.html.

Monk, C. (1999), 'From underworld to underclass: crime and British cinema in the 1990s', in S. Chibnall and R. Murphy (eds), *British Crime Cinema*, London: Routledge, pp. 172–88.

Monk, C. (2000), 'Men in the 90s', in R. Murphy (ed.), *British Cinema in the 90s*, London: BFI, pp. 156–66.

Murphy, R. (2000), 'Introduction', in Murphy (ed.), *British Cinema of the 90s*, London: BFI.

Murphy, R. (2009) (ed.), *The British Cinema Book* (3rd edn), London: BFI-Palgrave Macmillan.

Null, B. (1998), 'An interview with Shane Meadows', *AMC Blog*, 25 April 1998: http://blogs.amctv.com/movie-blog/1998/04/an-interview-wi.php.

Nunn, H. and A. Biressi (2010), 'Shameless? Picturing the "underclass" after Thatcherism', in L. Hadley and E. Ho, *Thatcher and After: Margaret Thatcher and Her Afterlife in Contemporary Culture*, London: Palgrave Macmillan, pp. 137–57.

Petridis, A. (2012), 'Vicky McClure: "I cannot see her taking any more damage"', *The Guardian* (online), 11 June 2012: http://www.guardian.co.uk/tv-and-radio/2012/jun/11/vicky-mcclure-interview.

Pook, L. (2012), 'Interview: Vicky McClure', *Stylist*, 6 June: http://www.stylist.co.uk/people/interviews-and-profiles/interview-vicky-mcclure.

Romney, J. (2004), 'Shane Meadows: Shane's world', *Independent*, 3 October 2004: http://www.independent.co.uk/arts-entertainment/films/features/shane-meadows-shanes-world-6160552.html.

Smith, A. (2007), 'Hauntings', in C. Spooner and E. McEvoy (eds), *Routledge Companion to Gothic*, London: Routledge, pp. 147–54.

Tannock, S. (1995), 'Nostalgia critique', *Cultural Studies*, 9: 3, 453–64.

Wagstaff, L. (2010), 'Creator can see today's town in stories for TV series set during 1986': http://www.thisisuttoxeter.co.uk/news/Creator-todays-town-stories-TV-series-set-1986/article-2551436-detail/article.html.

Youngs, I. (2011), 'Warp Films' new breed of Brit flick', BBC News website, 7 October 2011: http://www.bbc.co.uk/news/entertainment-arts-15196509.

CHAPTER 2

Structure and Agency: Shane Meadows and the New Regional Production Sectors

Jack Newsinger

> The way that things have spurted and grown in the industry in the last sort of two
> or three years, I'm definitely a beneficiary of all of that. Ten years previous the world
> probably wouldn't have accepted me in the same way, or I probably wouldn't have had
> as many opportunities, so I have probably landed at just the right time. Ten years ago
> I think I'd have been making television pieces.
>
> Shane Meadows in Applebaum 2008

What is it that changed in the British film industry in the mid-1990s that
allowed a working-class young man with a regional accent to develop a
career making films almost exclusively set and shot in the Midlands? Part of
the answer to this question must, of course, include Shane Meadows' personal
agency: his determination, his creativity, his proficiency as a director, and
so on. However, while these qualities should not be underestimated, they are
only half the answer. While Meadows and his collaborators have utilised
very effectively the opportunities and resources available to them, this
chapter focuses on what created those opportunities and what this means
for British cinema. As such, it takes an approach to Meadows' filmmaking
that is different to many of the other contributions to this volume by
seeking to understand it within an institutional–industrial context.

The first contextual framework to note is overall growth in the British
film industry from the mid-1990s. For example, in 1994 there were 32,000
people employed in the film and video industries. From a high-point of
57,000 in 2003, by 2009 the figure was 42,500 (Steele 2004: 14; UKFC 2010).
Likewise, in 1994 total production investment in the UK was £242m; in the
2000s annual production spend was often twice or three times this amount
and reached well over £1bn between 2008 and 2011 (BFI 2012: 158).
However, most of this growth has been in foreign-based companies, particularly in Hollywood, investing in co-productions with UK-based companies
in order to take advantage of tax breaks. Independent UK production –
defined as films made by a UK-based production company that are

produced wholly or partly in the UK – remained relatively constant up to 2002 and then declined steadily from 162 films in 2003 to 94 films in 2009. Furthermore, the median budgets of UK films steadily fell during the same period from £3.1m in 2003 to £1.9m in 2009.[1] While growth in inward investment can help to develop filmmaking infrastructure and expertise, it cannot alone account for the opportunities afforded to regionally based filmmakers. More important in transforming the structure of the British film industry were policy initiatives designed to encourage a regionalisation of film and media production. There was a steady growth of regional film infrastructure, up to the point where the English regions could be described as significant components of the commercial film industry in Britain for the first time since c. 1914. This directly benefited regionally based filmmakers who were more able to resist the gravitational pull of London or Los Angeles and sidestep the traditional route of film school or long, London-based apprenticeships. Meadows is the most successful filmmaker to emerge from this system and, as such, his career can tell us a great deal about the new regional production sectors.

Why and how did regional infrastructure develop? How did this affect Meadows' career? And what might this mean for British cinema? These are the questions that will be addressed in what follows. The first part of the chapter will outline the development of regional production sectors. From there, how this system worked in practice will be explored by mapping it onto Meadows' career. The chapter finishes by looking at the most recent changes to the structure of the British film industry. Much has changed since Meadows began his career in the middle of the 1990s, and these industrial and economic shifts are sure to impact on the potential prospects for emerging regional filmmakers looking to follow in Meadows' footsteps.

The old regional production sectors

In what way is regional film production new? Since c. 1914 the commercial film industry in Britain has been concentrated in London and the wider South-East, in terms of studio space and post-production facilities, production finance and company offices. While there are notable exceptions – John E. Blakely's Mancunian Films studio,[2] for example – and while the regions have a long history as a location for British films, particularly within the social realist tradition, for most of its history the British film industry has been London-centric. In this context, filmmaking in the English regions developed outside the commercial industry under an 'arts' or cultural film paradigm supported by cultural institutions such as the British Film Institute, the Regional Arts Associations (renamed Regional Arts Boards during the 1990s) and, from the 1980s, Channel Four.

The development of regional filmmaking can be traced back to the regional film society movement of the 1960s, the regional Film Theatre Movement of the 1970s and, most significantly, the film workshop movement of the 1970s and 1980s. By the end of the 1980s, years of campaigning and debate had resulted in a publicly funded regional network of workshops, organisations, groups and filmmakers in cities such as Newcastle, Sheffield, Birmingham, Leeds, Liverpool, Manchester and, of course, Nottingham. While these groups were very different, they often maintained links with local communities and placed an emphasis on film and video production as a form of community and working-class empowerment and expression (see Dickinson 1999). It was this network that formed the basis of the structure of the new regional production sectors.

The 1980s also marked a change in regional audiovisual policy. Local authorities began to recognise film and media development as a key area of economic regeneration in the face of a decline in traditional manufacturing sectors. Regional Film Commissions were set up in order to attract outside investment from film and television companies. For local authorities eager to encourage investment in local facilities – not only production but also hotels, catering, spending on materials and so on – Screen Commissions could also help wrest film and television productions away from London and the South-East. Liverpool City Council opened a Film Liaison Office in 1989 with the support of Merseyside Television; other cities followed suit. In 1991 a national organisation – the UK Film Commission – was set up to co-ordinate these activities and thereby attract foreign and outside investment. Its initial budget was £3.5m over the first four years (Marris 1991: 29). The first regional Media Development Agency was formed in the North-East in 1984; other regions followed. For example, a Comedia feasibility study recommended that Birmingham City Council set up an Agency in 1987, a Manchester-based organisation produced a similar report in 1989 and in Nottingham the local authority began a strategy to develop the city as a media centre at around the same time (Comedia 1987; Centre for Employment Research 1989). Over the next few years Liverpool, Bristol, Leeds, Sheffield and Leicester also undertook media/cultural industries mapping exercises (McIntyre 1996: 224). By 1991 Paul Marris could argue:

> While London and its geographical surround continue unquestionably to hold the foremost place in the UK industry, there is now a second tier, comprising Bristol, Birmingham, Cardiff, Glasgow, Leeds, Manchester and Newcastle upon Tyne, and

a third including Belfast, Edinburgh, Liverpool, Nottingham, Norwich, Sheffield and Southampton. Each region of the UK has a labour and technical facilities infra-structure in the audiovisual production industry concentrated in major urban centres. (Marris 1991: 27–8)

All of this increased the levels of expertise and infrastructure in the regions, and by the middle of the 1990s regional cultural industries were being hyped as key drivers of employment, with added bonuses such as increased tourism, higher property values, better quality of life and other multiplier effects. However, there was a perception of disorganisation and fragmen-tation across the sector.

The new regional production sectors

After the election victory of New Labour in 1997, the new Department of Culture, Media and Sport launched a consultation process which led to the policy statement 'Film in England: A Development Strategy for Film and the Moving Image in the English Regions'. The report recommended the creation of nine Regional Screen Agencies (RSAs) intended to form 'an integrated planning framework between the "centre" and the regions, and between industrial and cultural priorities' (UKFC 2000: 37). The RSAs were formed through the amalgamation of the agencies that charac-terised regional film sectors previously: the film activities of the Regional Arts Boards, regional Media Development Agencies, Screen Commissions and other investment funds, training funds and production schemes.

So what were the features of the new regional production sectors? With increased funds, the RSAs consolidated and expanded regional film activity in two main ways. Firstly, there was a massive growth in regionally based short film schemes funded under a training and development remit. In contrast to the uneven provision that existed previously, under the UKFC each RSA administered a 'Digital Shorts' short film production scheme to identify and nurture would-be writers and directors, to develop skills and to provide a calling card to enable the transition to more ambitious work. Short film schemes were organised as a series of 'stepping stones' to facili-tate a line of career progression, through the regional schemes, to the nationally administered short film schemes such as Cinema Extreme, and ultimately to feature film and television work. Digital Shorts – described by the UK Film Council as 'the largest digital shorts scheme ever devised' – supported the production of nearly three hundred short films between 2001 and 2004, representing a substantial growth of institutionally funded film-making in the regions (UKFC/Digital Technology Strategy Group 2003: 8).

Secondly, RSAs invested in low-budget feature film production, often utilising digital production technology, produced by small independent production companies and funded through co-production deals, most often between an RSA and a broadcaster. Although no comprehensive official data exists, these initiatives undoubtedly helped to stimulate a substantial growth in regional filmmaking.[3]

Regional film funding had two objectives: on the one hand, to 'develop a sustainable UK film industry by developing the pool of creative skills and talent; developing entrepreneurial acumen and business clusters; and developing an industrial infrastructure' (Holden 2006: 37), and on the other, 'to help capture the many facets of British communities':

> To encourage the growth of a sense of community and identity, to identify and empower under-represented and marginalised voices, give support for different forms of distribution, and ensure diversity of access and participation. (Holden 2006: 20, 17)

In this way, the new regional production sectors were given a particular role within film culture: that of representing Britain in a way that was more in line with contemporary ideas of national identity, of providing pathways into the industry for social groups traditionally excluded, and of injecting some new life and vibrancy into the cinematic canon.

This regionalisation of British film production can be mapped onto Meadows' career, which follows the development of the new regional production sectors very closely, in both structural and ideological terms. Meadows' career reflects and even pre-empts many of the features of the emerging regional sectors which became institutionalised in the funding structures of the RSAs and their partners.

From shorts to features

According to Kate Ogborn, Meadows appeared to be 'a film-maker who came from nowhere, who proved that you didn't need to go to film school, that all you needed was a strong enough desire to make films and the gift of the gab'. She continues:

> The interesting aspect to Meadows' progression and development as a film-maker is that he paid no attention to the kinds of films he was supposed to make, and didn't waste time trying to second guess the successful formula for getting funding. Instead he concentrated on the resources that were available to him on his doorstep, and on telling the stories he and his friends wanted to hear. (Ogborn 2000: 65)

In this way, Meadows is often characterised as an instinctive filmmaker, part of a new breed drawn from outside the established film and television industries as well as the theoretically informed intelligentsia. As such a kind of origin myth surrounds his move into features, from his beginnings in homemade short films in which he played all the characters (sporting different trademark wigs), to *Small Time* (1996), funded through ingenuity with non-professional actors improvising their performances, to the commercial and critical success of his subsequent feature films. However, Meadows' development as a filmmaker also depended on the expansion of regional filmmaking in this period. He began making films in the mid-1990s at a transitional time. Film workshops and community-based initiatives co-existed and competed with the more commercially orientated organisations which eventually supplanted them. Film workshops active during the 1980s in Nottingham included the Other Side Video Collective, Astrodam, Isthmus Productions, the New Cinema Workshop and Nottingham Video Project, which later became Intermedia Film and Video. Intermedia, an institution with a long-standing reputation in Nottingham's independent film scene,[4] was particularly important to Meadows' early development, lending equipment and offering support. As is well known, Meadows got his first experience through a film production scheme for the unemployed run by Intermedia in the mid-1990s and began making films with borrowed equipment in Sneinton, a predominantly working-class suburb of Nottingham. Between 1994 and 1997 Meadows made some twenty-five short films, including the short documentary *The Gypsy's Tale* (made in 1995 for Channel Four's 'Tales of Battered Britain' series), the award-winning *Where's the Money Ronnie!* (1996) and the 'featurette' *Small Time.*[5]

With the exception of *The Gypsy's Tale*, all the films were made without direct production funding. They feature Meadows and friends and, with the exception of those mentioned above, are probably best understood as practice pieces. However, they are notable for two reasons: firstly, because they show the development of themes and working methods that inform all Meadows' subsequent feature filmmaking; and secondly, because they demonstrate the willingness of funding bodies to support 'no-budget' regional filmmakers on the basis of such 'homemade' work during the period.

Take *Small Time* as an example. The film centres on two unemployed petty criminals, Malcolm (Mat Hand) and Jumbo (Meadows), their relationships with their respective girlfriends, Kate (Dena Smiles) and Ruby (Gena Kawecka), and how these relationships interfere with their gang's criminal activities. The narrative is a series of episodic comic sequences: the gang engaging in various and mostly unsuccessful robberies, the domestic lives of the two couples and the social activities of the group, ending with the gang's farcical attempt to rob a 'hippie shop'.

The film follows the thematic concerns of Meadows' other early films: broad satirical comedy centred on a group of young, working-class men and women in the Midlands. The humour is based on an ironic detachment from the provincialism and ignorance of the characters juxtaposed with some of the generic motifs of the crime or gangster film. As Jumbo's opening voiceover explains: 'There's one thing you've got to understand, right? This ain't fucking London, this ain't even Nottingham. This is Sneinton. And all that matters in Sneinton is having a tenner in your pocket, it don't matter how you get it.' In this vein the gang's activities are ludicrous parodies of provincial criminality such as stealing tins of dog food from behind a shop or robbing a car-boot sale.

Small Time was shot over nine days with the actors, mostly Meadows' friends, improvising the dialogue and scenes from a rough script. Thirteen hours of footage were then edited into the final 60-minute film.[6] It was shot in the streets and houses that Meadows and his collaborators lived in at the time, which works to authenticate the film.

Meadows has repeatedly emphasised the link between his own working-class background and the themes and preoccupations of his films. For example:

> Both *Small Time* and *Where's the Money Ronnie!* are about the people I grew up with in Uttoxeter. It's as working class as it gets – full of Irish, Scots, Brummies and Stokies who came to work for JCB in the sixties. My memories of the men I grew up around were of small-time crooks, good people who had been shat on during the recession, trying to get by by skimming a bit off the top ... When I started doing filming, I used these characters. (Fraser and Meadows 1998: ix–xiv)

Meadows' sense of belonging and access to the social groups which form his films' subjects are thus inscribed in the production practices and stylistic choices that were developed in his early filmmaking. This means that despite the use of farcical comedy alongside motifs drawn from American and British popular culture, *Small Time* works as an authentic representation of a regional working-class community.

Small Time received completion funding from BFI Production to transfer it from video to 35mm film for a theatrical release. It was screened at the Edinburgh Film Festival, where, according to Ogborn, it 'created a huge buzz' (Ogborn 2000: 65). At around the same time *Where's the Money Ronnie!* won the Channel One short film prize and put Meadows in contact with Steve Woolley, a member of the jury, who encouraged him to develop a feature film project which became *TwentyFourSeven*. All Meadows' subsequent film and television works, in different ways, take up the themes, aesthetics and working practices developed in his early filmmaking. They were made on relatively low budgets and were funded by the range of agencies that invested in the emerging regional sectors in the period: Channel Four, the BBC, the British Film Institute, the UKFC and RSAs, specifically EM Media and Screen Yorkshire.

However, while on the surface his films demonstrate the steady development of regional production in the period, a more detailed analysis reveals this as characterised by a number of different strategies with varying levels of critical and commercial success. For example, *Twenty Four Seven* featured Bob Hoskins, Bruce Jones and Frank Harper, with the majority of the cast made up of non-professional actors. The film was funded by the BBC and produced by Scala, a British production company specialising in low- to medium-budget British features and British-American co-productions. Along with its budget of £1.5m, the use of actors from British film and television alongside unknowns would suggest it was intended primarily for a domestic audience but with the potential to cross over into international markets, in common with other Scala productions.[7] It was, however, a commercial failure, grossing just £236,000. Similarly, *A Room for Romeo Brass* was funded by the BBC and the National Lottery via the Arts Council. The film received a cinema release of just ten prints in the UK and grossed less than £100,000, making it Meadows' poorest box-office return.

Once Upon a Time in the Midlands, on the other hand, can be seen as an attempt to court widespread commercial success more directly and represents a distinct change of emphasis within Meadows' established practice. It was funded by the UK Film Council and the East Midlands Media Initiative (EMMI) and produced by Film Four and EM Media, the RSA for the East Midlands. Budgeted at £3.5m, it featured a cast of British stars, several of whom have appeared in Hollywood films: Robert Carlyle, Kathy Burke, Ricky Tomlinson, Rhys Ifans and Shirley Henderson, apparently working for reduced wages on the basis of Meadows' critical reputation. *Once Upon a Time in the Midlands* received widespread mediocre reviews. Meadows later distanced himself from the film, putting its perceived failures down to outside interference and lack of editorial control. In particular, the commercial pressures associated with 'mainstream' casting practices forced a departure from his established production techniques during filming:

> Having famous people in your films makes a difference to your box office, but it's not something I'd do regularly because it doesn't fit with how I work. It wasn't my choice in the first place to fill the cast with lots of big names … the problem with working [with] successful actors is that it's totally different to the way I normally like to work … Usually we all live together for six months before I start shooting, so I'm

getting to know the cast. When you're working with famous people they're so busy that they can only turn up for the odd week here and there. (Wilson 2004)

The budget, casting and content of *Once Upon a Time in the Midlands* would suggest an attempt to appeal to a broader domestic and international audience, in common with other Channel Four productions of the period and as part of an attempt to emulate the international commercial success of films like *The Full Monty*, also starring Robert Carlyle.[8] While more than doubling Meadows' previous box-office returns, it still made only a minor impact in cinemas, grossing £496,000.

Dead Man's Shoes and *This is England* were made under entirely different conditions. They represented a significant reduction in production budgets (*Dead Man's Shoes* cost just £750,000 to make) and feature largely unknown and non-professional actors, suggesting they were aimed at specialised niche audiences. Both were joint-funded by EM Media, Screen Yorkshire and Film Four and produced by Sheffield-based Warp Films. It was these films that turned out to be Meadows' biggest commercial successes, simultaneously confirming his critical reputation as a young filmmaker of great promise.[9] This model informed the production of the micro-budget films *Somers Town* (2008) and *Le Donk and Scor-zay-zee* (2009), and the subsequent move into television with *This is England '86* (2010) and *'88* (2011).

Meadows' films demonstrate a number of strategies for regional production during the period. These range from larger-budget attempts to reach broad and even international audiences to more innovative low-budget, niche strategies. The production strategy first championed in Meadows' collaboration with Warp Films is particularly noteworthy. Concentrating on micro- to low-budget productions, Warp Films works as a regional mini-studio, integrated with distribution partners (Optimum Releasing for theatrical and DVD, Channel Four for broadcast) and regional funding agencies (EM Media and Screen Yorkshire). It represents a new kind of small, independent, regionally based film production company that was formed to take advantage of the beneficial film- funding arrangements in the new regional production sectors. It is Warp Films' regional basis, vertical and horizontal integration – across finance, production, distribution and in ancillary markets such as music and publishing – and strong brand identity that provide the most successful business and production model for regionally based film to emerge from the new regional production sectors. It is a particularly flexible approach that has enabled Meadows to retain creative independence while combining finance from various public and private organisations (for a discussion of this in terms of a pan-European independent film practice, see Scott forthcoming 2013). Furthermore,

Warp's financing structure through EM Media and Screen Yorkshire demonstrated an increasing inter-regional integration as well as an increasing regional autonomy from the London-based industry in the period. This was mirrored by developments in other regions. For example, Digital Departures was launched by North-West Vision and Media in 2008 in Liverpool to produce low-budget, commercially orientated feature films financed, shot and produced in the region. In a similar fashion, Northern Film and Media's Atomic Pictures supported a slate of film production by Pinball Films in the North-East from 2008, and the Bristol-based iFeatures initiative is, at the time of writing, in its second production cycle. It is too early to say what the long-term effects of these initiatives might be, but they certainly suggested a workable strategy for the future of regional film production as the first decade of the twenty-first century came to a close.

Conclusion

The period since the late 1990s has seen a transformation in the structure of the film industry in Britain. There is evidence of a growing division in this period between a larger-budget inward investment sector and a lower-budget, indigenous production sector that was increasingly regionally based. Film policy initiatives directly contributed to this regionalisation.

However, as Meadows' career demonstrates, regional film production in this period was complex, characterised by different local and national agencies, different production strategies and aimed at different markets and audiences. Meadows' career began during a time of competing models for regional filmmaking. The older workshop and community filmmaking sector co-existed with new, more commercially orientated institutions best represented by organisations like EM Media and the other RSAs. Funding structures formed a 'stepping stone' system designed to identify and nurture regionally based filmmakers, allowing them to progress onto more ambitious projects. This system was institutionalised in the new regional production sectors as the accepted way that regionally based filmmakers could pursue a career. As Meadows' short films demonstrate, this was an important site for the development of working practices, thematic concerns and aesthetics, and a key source of innovation in British cinema.

Mike Wayne makes the argument that in the mid-1990s 'British Northerners increased their stock as a visible and viable category within the American market'. He looks at films such as *Brassed Off*, *The Full Monty*, *Little Voice* (Mark Herman, 1998) and *Billy Elliot* (Stephen Daldry, 2000) as a cluster of British product representing 'the recently acquired viability within the North American market of a certain kind of British film (low budget) offering a specific regional focus within Britishness (they are all set "up north")'. For him, this demonstrates that

> while it is widely recognised that English heritage films are shaped according to the pressures of the international and especially American market, it is now the case that the CTNCs [Cultural Transnational Corporations] are today shaping the kinds of 'realist' films that were once thought to be the authentic representations of a national film culture. (Wayne 2006: 296)

Arguably, Meadows' films show the operation of this international market on regional production sectors during the period, of which *Once Upon a Time in the Midlands* is the clearest example. However, there were also attempts to utilise and experiment with other finance and production models which demonstrate an increasing regional autonomy, particularly through organisations like EM Media and Screen Yorkshire. The most successful to date has been the low- to micro-budget production strategy adopted by Warp Films. As Meadows' work shows, these sorts of initiatives can provide a space for regional working-class experience in British cinema made by filmmakers with genuine roots in regional communities. This suggests one possible future for British film.

If the development of the new regional production sectors sounds very positive and optimistic, there are a number of caveats that need to be mentioned. On 26 July 2010 the Conservative-Liberal Democrat coalition government announced that the UK Film Council was to be abolished. This was followed by the closure of the nine RSAs, replaced by three agencies with reduced budgets. The structures that developed over the previous fifteen or so years to support regional filmmaking were dismantled (for a more detailed discussion of this, see Newsinger 2012).

If Meadows' career demonstrates one thing, it is the continuing dependence of regional filmmaking on public investment in various forms. The subsidisation of regional film sectors provided a basis for low-budget indigenous production that could be maintained even if inward investment from Hollywood stopped flowing, as it periodically does. The danger is that the support for the sort of grassroots-based filmmaking that was central to Meadows' development is forced into decline. To take one example: Intermedia, a Nottingham institution that gave Meadows and many other local filmmakers their first production experience, was effectively closed when EM Media shifted funding to another organisation. Across the sector, older workshop groups that developed within an 'arts' remit, funding film for cultural and social reasons and not simply as economic development, have had their funding cut or removed altogether. Put another way, if regional film sectors provided a ladder for first-time filmmakers to climb, the ladder is now being pulled up behind them. If Meadows is to be the first of a new breed of young, innovative, regionally based filmmakers, then these support structures need to be protected.

Notes

1. Figures are taken from the UKFC 2009 Full Year Production Report (2010). This data only covers films with budgets over £500,000 and is therefore taken to be indicative of production trends as opposed to comprehensive.
2. Mancunian Films operated from 1933 to 1953 and made twenty-five low-budget films featuring leading Lancashire comics. See Russell (2004).
3. The UK Film Council does not record the geographical location of production companies or shooting locations of individual films. However, Nick Redfern's research suggests that between 2003 and 2007, approximately 20 per cent of UK film production took place in the English regions (Redfern 2009).
4. Intermedia has produced many short films and documentaries for various broadcasters and was the delivery company for the East Midlands region Digital Shorts film scheme, 2002–4. In 2002 it produced Metin Huseyin's *Anita and Me*, in 2003 it produced Chris Cooke's debut feature film *One for the Road*, and in 2004 it co-produced Annie Watson's BAFTA-nominated short *Knitting a Love Song*.
5. *Small Time* and *Where's the Money Ronnie!* were commercially released on video by Polygram in 1998. Thanks are due to Dave Clarke of www.shane-meadows.co.uk for providing exhaustive information on Meadows' early unavailable films and for help tracking down some of the others.
6. The improvisation can be identified by looking at the difference between the shooting script and the finished film. The twenty-five-page script features extended sequences of dialogue but has no ending. The only scene to make it into the finished film in a relatively similar fashion to the script is the opening one featuring the aforementioned dog food theft. By way of explanation, Meadows notes that he 'was simply going to use this structure to ensure that the film wasn't a sloppy lump of shite that ran on for fourteen hours' (Fraser and Meadows 1998: 165).
7. Scala's notable production credits include *Backbeat* (Iain Softley, 1994), *Fever Pitch* (David Evans, 1997), *Divorcing Jack* (David Caffrey, 1998), *Little Voice* (Mark Herman, 1998) and *Last Orders* (Fred Schepisi, 2002). Mike Wayne describes Scala as 'a regular vehicle by which the Disney/Miramax CTNC "plug in" to British culture and talent' (Wayne 2006: 291). All information on production budgets, production companies, grosses and prints has been sourced and cross-checked from the BFI Film and Television Database, The Internet Movie Database, Grant (2007) and Spencer (2002).
8. *The Full Monty* cost £2.2m and grossed £134m.

9. While *Dead Man's Shoes* made under £200,000, it reportedly went on to sell 100,000 copies on DVD release. *This is England* grossed a healthy £1.5m at the UK box office.

References

Applebaum, S. (2008), 'Interview with Shane Meadows', retrieved 15 January 2008 from http://www.britmovie.co.uk/features/applebaum/meadows00.html.

BFI (2012), *Statistical Yearbook 2012*, London: British Film Institute.

Centre for Employment Research (1989), *The Culture Industry: The Economic Importance of the Arts and Cultural Industries in Greater Manchester*, Manchester: Manchester Polytechnic.

Comedia (1987), 'Birmingham Audio-Visual Industry Report – Mechanisms for Intervention: Feasibility Study', London: Comedia.

Dickinson, M. (ed.) (1999), *Rogue Reels: Oppositional Film in Britain, 1945–90*, London: BFI.

Fraser, P. and S. Meadows (1998), *TwentyFourSeven* (including Shane Meadows, *Where's the Money Ronnie!* and *Left* [*Small Time*]), Suffolk: Screen Press Books.

Holden, J. (2006), 'The big picture: the Regional Screen Agencies building community, identity and enterprise', London: DEMOS.

Marris, P. (1991), 'UK Film Commission', in R. Lewis and P. Marris, *Promoting the Industry*, London: BFI, pp. 22–42.

McIntyre, S. (1996), 'Art and industry: regional film and video policy in the UK', in A. Moran, *Film Policy: International, National and Regional Perspectives*, London: Routledge, 215–33.

Newsinger, J. (2012), 'British film policy in an age of austerity', *Journal of British Cinema and Television*, 9: 1, 133–44.

Ogborn, K. (2000), 'Pathways into the industry', in R. Murphy, *British Cinema of the 90s*, London: BFI, 60–7.

Redfern, N. (2007), 'Defining British Cinema: Transnational and Territorial Film Policy in the United Kingdom', in *Journal of British Cinema and Television*, 4:1, 150–64.

Russell, D. (2004), *Looking North: Northern England and the National Imagination*, Manchester: Manchester University Press.

Scott, J. (2013), 'The "local" films of Shane Meadows', *Journal of British Cinema and Television* (forthcoming).

Steele, D. (2004), 'Developing the evidence base for UK film strategy: the research process at the UK Film Council', *Cultural Trends*, 13: 4, 5–21.

UKFC (2000), 'Film in England: a development strategy for film and the moving image in the English regions', London: UK Film Council.

UKFC (2010), *Statistical Yearbook 2010*, London: UK Film Council.

UKFC/Digital Technology Strategy Group (2003), 'Digital technology strategy: an interim position paper', London: UK Film Council.

Wayne, M. (2006), 'The performing Northern working-class in British cinema:

cultural representation and its political economy', *Quarterly Review of Film and Video*, 23: 4, 287–97.

Wilson, J. (2004), 'Interview with Shane Meadows', retrieved 1 October 2010 from http://www.leftlion.co.uk/articles.cfm?id=213.

CHAPTER 3

Twenty-first-Century Social Realism: Shane Meadows and New British Realism

David Forrest

When we think of British realist cinema we think of Ken Loach, Mike Leigh, Alan Clarke and the British New Wave, among others, and it is testament to the importance of the subject of this collection that – for someone who has only been making feature films since the late 1990s – we now think of Shane Meadows. Meadows has emphatically continued the progression and diversification of arguably Britain's richest cinematic tradition. He is a unique filmmaker who can be understood both within the lineage of the realist mode and as a maverick who breaks as many moulds as he shapes. By analysing these two characteristics in unison, we are able to assess more clearly the director's influence on British cinema, and British culture more generally. Meadows retains key aspects of Britain's realist heritage while redrawing the mode's stylistic and thematic boundaries, practices which can be understood more clearly by investigating the work of other contemporary filmmakers whose films have parallels with those of Meadows, and who together illustrate the emergence of this new British realist address.

Since Shane Meadows' feature film debut in 1997, the likes of Lynne Ramsay (*Ratcatcher* [1999] and *Morvern Callar* [2002]), Paweł Pawlikowski (*Last Resort* [2000] and *My Summer of Love* [2004]), Andrea Arnold (*Red Road* [2006] and *Fish Tank* [2009]), Duane Hopkins (*Better Things* [2009]), Samantha Morton (*The Unloved* [2009]) and Joanna Hogg (*Unrelated* [2007] and *Archipelago* [2010]) have produced films that have marked the reconfiguration of the realist paradigm in Britain. Therefore, to speak of Shane Meadows as a lone voice in Britain's realist renewal is inaccurate; while each of the aforementioned directors has unique signatures and characteristics, the formal and thematic aspects that unite the films tell us much about the continued relevance of realism in British cinema.

A focus on marginalised young protagonists, disconnected from their environments and searching haplessly for meaning and structure in their lives, broadly unites the filmmakers and subsequently defines the thematic preoccupations of contemporary British realism. While these characteristics may not seem out of step with the traditions of the mode, their deployment within aesthetic and structural systems which foreground space and place as the primary signifiers of meaning – alongside a rejection of the explicit sociopolitical emphasis that pervades the critical perception of realism in Britain – represents a clear departure from hitherto dominant modes of realism in Britain. James Leggott talks of this move away from long-standing thematic characteristics as illustrative of an 'opposing trend for films that instead foreground the minutiae of human interaction' (Leggott 2008: 45), and it is this emphasis, communicated through a formal approach that privileges aesthetically the 'inter-relationship of character and landscape' (Leggott 2008: 75), that underpins the new British realism.

For example, Paweł Pawlikowski's *My Summer of Love* observes the burgeoning relationship between two teenage girls, Mona (Natalie Blunt) and Tamsin (Emily Blunt), over a summer in a West Yorkshire village. While the two protagonists come from different social classes, *My Summer of Love* is not concerned directly with the authentic representation and explication of class difference. Rather, it operates on a broader thematic platform, using sustained and recurring images of the characters framed starkly against their picturesque but unforgiving landscape to proffer ambiguous and non-prescriptive interrogations of claustrophobia, stasis and unfulfilled emotion. For Pawlikowski, this turn from the 'social' detail in realism towards the poetic marks a break from the traditions of British cinema:

> British cinema is drowning in sociology – how people speak, everyone is so self-conscious. In this story it is clear: one is working class, one isn't. That goes without saying, it's no big deal. Let's now concentrate on the story and the psychology, let's make it universal and slightly abstract. (Foley 2004)

Meadows' own *Somers Town* (2008) can be viewed in similar terms. While its focus on a working-class English teenage runaway and the similarly aged son of a Polish migrant worker suggests sociological interpretation, the film departs consciously from these associations to allow for a more nuanced thematic programme to emerge instead. The film's striking visual emphasis on marginalised urban spaces – shot in black and white – is given added significance by its deployment within a minimal and simple plot. Narrative information is sparse and often eschews taut causality: Tomo (Thomas Turgoose) runs away from home for an unspecified reason; he is beaten up and mugged when he arrives in London; he makes friends with Marek (Piotr Jagiello); the pair develop a friendship with and attempt amusing advances towards a glamorous French waitress, Maria (Elisa Lasowski); they befriend and work for a spiv-like 'cockney', Graham (Perry Benson); Marek's father, Mariusz (Ireneusz Czop), catches the pair drinking and Marek is disciplined; Tomo moves in with Graham; Marek and Tomo go on a holiday to Paris. This episodic organisation of events places greater interpretative focus on the image, and more specifically the representation of space as a more opaque signifier of meaning, than on the thematic potentials – on socioeconomic grounds – of the protagonists' racial or social backgrounds.

Such an emphasis is typical of Meadows' films and the work of his contemporaries. Lynne Ramsay, whose debut feature *Ratcatcher* conveys the feelings of loss and isolation of a young Glasgow boy in the 1970s through a highly conspicuous and arresting *mise-en-scène*, articulates this sentiment succinctly: 'I wanted to make a film that was driven by emotion and images rather than narrative' (Spencer 1999: 18). While the authentic location, rejection of star actors, eschewal of cause-and-effect and goal-driven structures, and focus on the marginalised still mark the new realist films as heirs to a long tradition in British visual culture, the move towards an image-led narration in which the specificities of social and political detail are sidelined in favour of a more liberated textual approach suggests a genuine change in the heritage of British cinematic realism.

Realist moments

In order to understand the characteristics of the new British realist cinema, it is vital to explore the relationship that its exponents have with their antecedents. As the most prolific and prominent of British realist directors, Ken Loach makes for a pertinent example. For many, the director's work is viewed as a paradigm of realist cinema, and on the surface we can locate tangible similarities between his films and those of Meadows: naturalistic dialogue, the use of authentic environments, and an emphasis on families and their relationship to wider communities, to cite some examples. However, these similarities are largely cosmetic: while the pair can be understood as operating broadly within a defined British cinematic tradition, the manner in which Meadows and his contemporaries depart from the kind of methodological and ideological approach to realist cinema exemplified by Loach underlines Meadows' role – in particular – in reframing the realist tradition.

This is not to say that Meadows repudiates explicitly the influence of established realist practitioners in his own work, and indeed he is on record stating his admiration for their work:

In England in the '80s it was hard for the likes of Mike Leigh, Ken Loach, Alan Clarke and Stephen Frears to get funding for feature films [...] So they made films especially for the BBC or Channel 4. As a kid my cinema was the TV in the living room. Films that I might have been too young to see at the cinema were accessible to me at nine o'clock at night at home. (Raphael 2010)

By identifying himself within a tradition of realist filmmaking and emphasising implicitly the universal and prescient qualities of the mode, Meadows simultaneously 'pays his dues' to his forebears and suggests a point of departure. As mentioned, undoubtedly the defining and unifying characteristic of Meadows' work and that of his contemporaries in relation to the realist tradition is their heightened emphasis on the poetic potential of the everyday, in the process rejecting direct engagements with social issues and instead deploying a more aesthetically rooted engagement with space and place.

In keeping with Meadows' citation of Loach as an influence, it would be unfair to suggest that the latter director is averse to the lyrical treatment of location. The shots of Greenock rooftops in *Sweet Sixteen* (2002) and the high-rise flats of Sheffield in *Looks and Smiles* (1981) are both examples of sustained compositions of urban space in Loach's work which function to add figurative layers to the narrative concerns of the films. Perhaps most famously, Loach's almost stylised treatment of Billy Casper (David Bradley) as he flies his kestrel high above the coal mine that looms conspicuously in the foreground could be regarded as congruent with the kind of 'image-led narration' that is associated with the new realist filmmakers. Indeed, the focus on Billy's simultaneous – but paradoxical – self-sufficient alienation chimes with similar figurative representations of adolescence in Ramsay's *Ratcatcher*, Pawlikowski's *Last Resort*, Morton's *The Unloved*, Arnold's *Fish Tank* and Meadows' *This is England* (2006). However, what distinguishes Loach's *mise-en-scène* from that of the contemporary filmmakers is the codified organisation of the images into fixed and narrativised thematic discourses. The conflicting notions of freedom and entrapment that Loach so emotively communicates in the shots of Billy are tied to the film's explicit placement of the character within a sociopolitical dialectic. This works to locate Billy in relation to the limitations of working-class life in the period, and more specifically as an agent by which the social structures depicted as suppressing the freedom and creative intelligence of the protagonist can be revealed.

In this sense, Loach conforms to Raymond Williams' assertion that realism traditionally works to go 'below' the 'surface to the essential historical movements, to the dynamic reality' (Williams 1977: 65). In the case of Loach, this can be understood as the realist text working to authenticate a revelation of the systems and mechanisms that perpetuate – and by extension generate – the immovable socioeconomic machinery that the narrative observes. For Loach, this manifests itself through the use of debates, question–and–answer exchanges, and discussions that clearly mark out the social and/or political discourses that underpin the 'issues' at the heart of the films, with the narrative itself privileging a particular side of the relevant dialectic. By eschewing this prescriptive element of the realist mode, the contemporary realist filmmakers are able to circulate the poetic dimensions of their films within a less restrictive thematic sphere, moving away from rigid expectations of naturalistic veracity or sociological revelation.

In surveying the critical perceptions of realism as a mode of representation, Gill Brandon and Roy Stafford conclude with two defining principles:

> the film-maker is concerned to capture something about the experience of one event, to represent it as faithfully as possible for the audience and to mediate it as little as possible; or
> the film-maker has something specific to say about the real world and has developed a specific style, using realist conventions. (Brandon and Stafford 1996: 161)

While these conditions seem purposefully generalised, it is fair to suggest that the new British realist films still fail to conform to them. The first principle is confounded by the level of stylisation that makes conspicuous authorial presence across the work of Meadows and his contemporaries: slow motion (*This is England*, *The Unloved*, *Morvern Callar*); subjective narrative technique and distortions of temporality (*Dead Man's Shoes* [2004], *Ratcatcher*, *TwentyFourSeven* [1997]); expressionistic manipulations of sound (*Better Things*); and static long takes in Joanna Hogg's work (*Unrelated* and *Archipelago*), for example. Secondly, the sense of saying 'something specific about the real world' clearly chimes with the didactic impulse in Loach, whereas the new realist films refuse to adopt a specific condition. This distinction is worth observing in closer detail.

'Social' realism?

It is too extreme to suggest that Meadows, for example, rejects the socio-political potential of his work. As Martin Fradley rightly points out: 'his *oeuvre* has from the outset insistently registered the long-term social costs of Thatcherite policies upon peripheral working-class communities' (Fradley 2010: 281). However, to return to Stafford and Brandon's definitions, Meadows' treatment of these themes is by no means specific. Instead, the sociopolitical dimension is deployed in a complex and non-linear manner, inviting the viewer to engage with such themes alongside more diffuse textual and thematic elements.

To illustrate this notion, I want to look briefly at some examples of sociopolitical references in Meadows' films. Early on in *TwentyFourSeven*, Darcy (Bob Hoskins) begins a voiceover in which he describes the time 'when our town died' and laments the way that 'the lads and the people in this town have been living in the same day the whole of their lives'. The overtly political nature of Darcy's comments suggests the location of the film's action within a recognisable social context, namely the establishment of a narrative space that bears the scars of Thatcherism. Darcy's words are accompanied by a series of external images of a council estate, and then a single council house, before the camera goes inside to survey its 'demoralised inhabitants'. Viewed as a standalone entity, this extract may suggest a continuation of the Loachian practice of utilising realism as a means by which sociopolitical discourses can be communicated effectively, as Darcy explicitly frames the film's subjects in the light of a clearly established political sphere. Yet if we consider the other elements at work within the film, even at this early stage, such an understanding is compromised.

In the first instance, temporal and, by extension, narrative ambiguities cloud the delivery of the images and the voiceover. At the film's outset, Tim (Danny Nussbaum) finds a bedraggled tramp-like figure in an abandoned train carriage. He takes him home, puts him to bed, and begins to read from a notebook. It is at this point that Darcy's voiceover begins, as we cut to a shot of him clean-shaven, chirpily occupying the same train carriage in which we have seen him, confused and incomprehensible, just a few moments earlier. Tim, as the facilitator of the framing story, is both described and visually established in two separate temporal spheres, complicating the apparent primacy of the aural narration: we see him at the beginning of the film and during Darcy's voiceover commentary, itself a retrospective device. Indeed, in the space of a few minutes the viewer is faced with two or – if we are to include Darcy's reflective evocation of the 1980s – three separate temporal periods, periods that are occupied and exchanged by both characters. Thus, Meadows' marks of authorship – these manipulations of temporality and narrative – rapidly complicate the sense in which the film can be understood as politically inclined polemical realism: the delivery of a 'message' is undercut by multiple elements which draw our attention and undermine the potential for a single thematic motif to emerge. In addition, the visual composition of the sequence is, in part, distinguished by the lingering treatment of location: two static aerial shots of a row of houses and the town (lasting seven and six seconds respectively) preface a move inside Tim's family home. The shots' placement transcends mere exposition, with their length and ambiguous sequencing (medium shot of house – longer shot of houses – close shot in the yard outside a house) encouraging a more contemplative perspective.

Indeed, this facet of Meadows' visual armoury is evidenced in another of his films that may at first glance be located within a Loachian tradition of primarily *sociopolitical* realism, *This is England*. Despite its historical setting, the film's backdrop of an unpopular war and its focus on the rise of the Right in working-class communities and tribalism in youth cultures can and have been read as contemporary social allegory. Indeed, in the midst of the global economic downturn, the television sequels *This is England '86* (2010) and *This is England '88* (2011) continue to maintain and strengthen such parallels. Yet, unlike Loach's historical films such as *Land and Freedom* (1995) and *The Wind that Shakes the Barley* (2006), the past is not evoked primarily as a means of illuminating the marginalised sociopolitical realities of the present. As in *TwentyFourSeven*, textual and formal elements are at play which complicate this.

Early on in *This is England*, we witness Shaun (Thomas Turgoose) – in an extended sequence – riding his bike, washing cars, playing with a sling-shot, walking on the beach, and throwing stones into the sea. Meadows presents Shaun and his environment in a manner which is conspicuously directed towards a figurative rendering of his feelings of alienation and disconnection: an aerial shot shows Shaun sitting alone on an old rowing boat; a static medium shot surveys Shaun riding his bike through an abandoned warehouse, before the camera follows him as he plays in the building. While these compositions serve narrative functions by emphasising Shaun's solitude and self-reliance, the sustained placement of Shaun in spaces that are explicitly disused and empty may encourage a multiplicity of interpretations based on numerous political, social and/or emotional understandings. Crucially, Meadows resists the temptation to elicit these responses in prescriptive or didactic terms by eschewing the explicit commentary of voiceover or dialogue – ensuring that the images do not become singularly narrativised – as long shots of Shaun alone on the beach open up the symbolic spectrum of the film.

When the sequence comes to an end – with the soundtrack fading out as Shaun throws another stone seawards – the sounds of a speech by Margaret Thatcher can be heard. The almost violent appearance of Thatcher's non-diegetic voice on the soundtrack comes in the midst of this collage of poetic imagery. This is continued in the next three shots as

Meadows moves from the beach to two shots of a housing estate from
varying angles, with a third shot showing a window as Meadows returns to
the kind of static treatments of living space that we have already seen in
TwentyFourSeven. An understanding of Thatcher's introduction as solely
a move to politicise the shots is resisted by their lingering and ambiguous
deployment, suggesting again the disjunction of narrative, and by extension the complication of a linear thematic message.

Meadows' deployment of symbolically fertile imagery is typical of
contemporary realist films. Specifically, landscape is not used simply to
punctuate and augment narrative, but to offer an alternative means of
connoting the thematic structures of the films. André Bazin's seminal
analysis of Rossellini's *Paisà* (1946) develops this notion:

> The unit of cinematic narrative in *Paisà* is not the 'shot,' an abstract view of reality
> which is being analyzed, but the 'fact.' A fragment of concrete reality in itself
> multiple and full of ambiguity, whose meaning emerges only after the fact, thanks
> to other imposed facts between which the mind establishes certain relationships.
> Unquestionably, the director chose these 'facts' carefully while at the same time
> respecting their factual integrity. (Bazin 1971: 37)

The new British realist films, with their aesthetic foundations rooted
firmly in actuality, benefit from the ambiguous signification and figurative
potentiality of external space. The viewer engages with the 'realism' on an
entry level (and the inherent narrative 'issues' presented therein), before
allowing the multiple interpretative qualities of the image to emerge
without recourse to a clearly structured sociopolitical template, in line with
Bazin's endorsement of the poetic potential of the realist image.

This less prescriptive emphasis on the relationship between narrative
and aesthetics in the new realist films requires more attention. Meadows'
Dead Man's Shoes and Duane Hopkins' *Better Things* both adopt similar
strategies that illustrate this tension. *Better Things* begins with the sound
of wind which reaches a crescendo before abruptly falling silent as a static
shot of trees in a field initiates the diegesis. We then hear the voice of a
girl, Gail (Rachel McIntryre), who says 'Nothing', before a cut to the word
'nothing' in a close-up on a page as she speaks again: 'Nothing, she
supposed'. As she continues to speak ('This was real life and real life was
difficult, at best'), three shots from varying angles establish Gail reading in
her bedroom. She is still speaking (in voiceover) as Hopkins cuts to an
empty field, before returning to Gail looking out of her window. As her
voiceover continues we are presented with another arresting panorama: this
time a field just before sunset with the clouds visibly moving, followed by
a shot of a row of houses with a field in the foreground, a closer shot of a

house, an image of a garden, and – in the final shot of the sequence – the inside of a living room. Similarly, after the title sequence of *Dead Man's Shoes* we see Richard (Paddy Considine) and Anthony (Tony Kebbel) leaving a barn together and, as Meadows cuts to a static shot of a house, this is followed by another five static shots of a house or houses shot from varying perspectives, with each shot lasting between three and five seconds. The film then returns to handheld camerawork and a more fluid perspective with its shot of Richard and Anthony walking towards the camera and surveying their surroundings, before another two static frames featuring a pair of garages and part of a housing estate.

In both cases, we can identify *some* narrative function in the lingering treatments of space. In *Better Things*, Gail's stasis is juxtaposed with the open but barren spaces of the external environment – we later learn that she is agoraphobic. In *Dead Man's Shoes*, the sequence is part of the establishment of the narrative spaces in which Richard will seek his revenge and where Anthony's trauma will be revisited. However, as in *This is England*, the deployment of these shots – both their frequency and their duration – transcends narrative necessity. Where some themes in *Better Things* (drug abuse and mental illness, for example) and *Dead Man's Shoes* (petty crime, and abuse in small working-class communities) can be understood in line with the conventions of 'gritty' social realist cinema, their communication is not central. As these sequences show, to understand the films in purely thematic terms would be to miss the rich aesthetic treatment of realist *environments* as well as *subject matter*.

By so emphatically asserting the importance of the image as an independent signifier of meaning, the films exhibit the movement away from a doggedly thematic emphasis – where style is subordinated to the delivery of a message – towards a mode of expression which encourages readings based on its formal and stylistic constitution alone and where the 'issue' is not conspicuous, but woven into the aesthetic fabric of the films' textual systems. This heightened focus on aesthetics also has the effect of universalising the thematic potential of the new realist cinema. In renavigating the mode away from specific, didactic emphases and developing a less functional visual lexicon, the film text is opened up to broader potentials. For example, *This is England* is not simply concerned with the effects of the Falklands War on working-class communities; it is about family, loss and disconnection – broader concepts that are more universally communicated in poetic terms, as we have discussed. Moreover, *Better Things* transcends its primary social problem – drug-taking in rural communities – by framing its sparse narrative in a self-consciously poetic manner in which themes of miscommunication and lost love are rendered in bold, lyrical terms. Similarly, Samantha Morton's *The Unloved* may tread thematic ground which is familiar to traditional realism in its focus on the care system, but the film's treatment on an isolated young girl in a children's home does not make it a '*Cathy Come Home* part II'. Like in the aforementioned films, an image-led address is deployed which opens up the subject matter to broader interpretations. Narrative in the film is repeatedly broken up by sustained sequences which show its protagonist Lucy (Molly Windsor) walking alone across empty streets, in parks, or along hillsides which overlook the city beneath her.

This move outwards – from thematic specificity to universality – is achieved through recourse to a narrative strategy that is reliant on imagery and therefore negates the potential for prescriptive interpretations which may be derived from a primary focus on defined social issues and subject matter. Once again, broader concepts like solitude, the city and alienation abound through conspicuously figurative aesthetic patterns. In the absence of the imperative to accommodate a specific sociopolitical message, the realist location becomes open to more symbolic conveyers of meaning.

Andrea Arnold's *Fish Tank* can also be understood in these terms through its focus on Mia (Kate Jarvis), a troubled and aggressive teenage girl. The lack of diegetic music in the film in conjunction with a fluid and naturalistic shooting style may suggest a more traditional realist address. Indeed, the film's focus on an Essex council estate and dysfunctional, fatherless family may be read, reductively, as a meditation on contemporary discourses of 'Broken Britain'. However, by eschewing the explicit pursuit of these themes in favour of a minimal narrative system, the film achieves a more general and figuratively profound engagement with its protagonist and her environment. In *Fish Tank* the landscape is used repeatedly as a means of rendering graphically Mia's stasis and inability to move beyond her psychological and social containment. Mia is regularly framed alone, looking out of windows and observing the space beneath or around her. Even potentially joyous transgressive moments, such as when Mia dances in an abandoned flat, are countered by stark images of restriction and immovability (in this case, the window of the high- rise room). Unlike Loach in *Kes*, Arnold circulates these symbolic compositions alongside a narrative structure in which the sociopolitical significance of Mia's situation is not rendered didactically. Instead, as in the films of Meadows, the image is emancipated from a finite sociological position by the reluctance of the narrative to draw conclusions about the characters and locations it conveys.

Indeed, in films such as *Last Resort* the image or images can come to supersede traditional means of narrative presentation (dialogical exchange, plot structure, etc.). The sense of alienation and marginalisation which pervades the film's treatment of asylum seekers Artyom (Artyom Strelnikov) and Tanya (Dina Korzun) is articulated not through speeches or debates, but through arresting images of the Margate skyline, sustained point-of-view shots from tower blocks, and stark and static treatments of foreboding disused buildings. Alice Bardan notes the way in which the proliferation of these images represents a 'fragmentation of narrative' constituting 'a visual refrain, reiterating the constant feeling of entrapment of the asylum seekers' (Bardan 2008: 58). Thus, as in the repetition of wasteland and disused space used to characterise Shaun's portrayal in *This is England*, and the symbols of enclosure which pervade *Fish Tank*, new realist films use the associative qualities of recurring figurative tropes to offer an alternative means of narrative communication, moving beyond the conventions of the established realist mode.

A new chapter for British realism?

I hope to have suggested that contemporary British realism, of which Meadows is by far the most significant and prolific exponent, can be seen to have developed the mode significantly, insulating it from reductive assumptions about its aesthetic limits and contributing to a more diverse and artistically vibrant national cinema. However, by connecting the work of Ken Loach, specifically, to more recent realist films, I am also reasserting a sense of the historical lineage of realist cinema, an understanding of which illuminates numerous points of interest about our national filmmaking culture. For example, an aestheticisation of realist space is nothing new; it is simply reflective of a motif that has re-emerged and has been reimagined by contemporary filmmakers. For example, the more innovative moments within the documentary tradition of the 1920s and 1930s undoubtedly bear comparison with recent realist films. The films of Humphrey Jennings and Alberto Cavalcanti in particular are characterised by the use of bold formal strategies to break up and redeploy narrative information. Specifically, the treatment of landscape and space in the more expansive films of the documentary movement can be seen to inform the accented use of external environment and location in contemporary realist films.

Most significantly, the British New Wave of the late 1950s and early 1960s can and should be a reference point for recent realist film. When Samantha Lay talks of the British New Wave's directors' pursuit of an aesthetic which did not 'merely reflect the surface truths of everyday life' but penetrated the 'surface to reveal human truths' (Lay 2002: 52), she could have easily been referring to Meadows and his contemporaries. The notion of location as a poetic vessel and the deployment of young, alienated and aimless protagonists within ambiguously constructed textual and narrative environments are undoubtedly characteristics which have been reformulated in the work of Meadows and his contemporaries. Moreover, just as the films of Meadows, Hopkins, Morton et al. eschew an agenda-driven emphasis in their filmmaking, so too do the formal and stylistic elements of the New Wave resist simplistic sociopolitical approaches. The critical debates about the poetic treatment of working-class environments in the New Wave films are well known: to summarise, it has been suggested that the dominant aesthetic motifs in the New Wave, particularly its propensity for long takes and long shots of towns and cities often involving isolated protagonists, have the effect of exploiting or fetishising the working-class subject; Andrew Higson described the New Wave's approach to the formal representation of the Northern city as taking 'a place of poverty and squalor' and making it 'photogenic and dramatic' (Higson 1996: 148). Such assessments are partly derived from an awareness that the likes of Tony Richardson, Lindsay Anderson and Karel Reisz were Oxbridge-educated members of the middle classes who had little first-hand experience of the subjects that they were surveying. The same criticism would be far more difficult to level at the likes of Meadows, accurately described by Sheldon Hall as a 'native insider rather than a sympathetic visitor' (Hall 2006). Likewise, Hopkins, Arnold, Ramsay, Morton and Hogg are all directors who originate from areas close or demographically similar to the locations in which they have filmed. Crucially, they all make films which continue the practice of figurative treatments of space and character, pursuing image-led narrative and aesthetic patterns. Indeed, the films of Joanna Hogg – a middle-class filmmaker from the South of England whose work to date has focused entirely on the lives of privileged characters of similar class formation – can be comfortably understood within the contemporary realist paradigm on the basis of their use of space, naturalistic dialogue and performances, and open-ended, episodic narration. Thus, a rich vein of Britain's realist tradition, the poetic and artistically inclined approach to the everyday, can be liberated from a limiting sociological emphasis as it begins to flourish in a climate in which predictable and limiting questions of class and authenticity are no longer central.

For example, it is possible to view the aforementioned iconic shots and sequences of the New Wave entirely in line with similar features in the work of Meadows and his contemporaries, as offering a more nuanced thematic *and* aesthetic bridge across realist film moments, rather than as perpetuating and privileging specific and explicit thematic content of a sociopolitical nature. In this sense, the moments when Colin (Tom Courtenay), Mike (James Bolam), Audrey (Topsy Jane) and Gladys (Julia Foster) sit on top of a hill, contemplating their directionless lives in *The Loneliness of the Long Distance Runner* (Tony Richardson, 1962), or when Arthur Seaton (Albert Finney) in *Saturday Night and Sunday Morning* (Karel Reisz, 1960) stands angrily over a Nottingham cityscape with a newly built council estate in the distance, can be viewed alongside sequences such as that in *My Summer of Love* in which Mona (Natalie Press) and Tamsin (Emily Blunt) look down from a hill over Todmorden, or in *The Unloved* when Lucy and Lauren (Lauren Socha) share a moment out of their traumatic experiences of the care home on top of a grassy mound in their local park, or when Smell finds a depressed and isolated Lol looking down on the city in episode two of *This is England '86*. In understanding the similarities in these compositions on a primarily visual basis, and in so doing underlining their centrality to a less prescriptive realist paradigm, similar images of isolated protagonists in the aforementioned work of Joanna Hogg, which see Anna in *Unrelated* and Edward in *Archipelago* cast adrift in their landscape, could be linked as much to other British realist films as to the bourgeois alienation of Antonioni's protagonists. The New Wave's 'Long Shot of Our Town from That Hill' (John Krish quoted in Higson 1996: 133) is reiterated and repurposed, unmoored from its origins in queasy 'cultural tourism' (Higson 1996: 149).

Locating Meadows and his contemporaries within the context of a 'realist lineage' is crucial if we are to make useful judgements on the continued significance of the realist mode in British cinema. The manner in which varying realist cycles connect and depart on the basis of their formal and/or structural complexion can be seen to reflect the specific cultural requirements of their day, as John Hill argues:

> Realist innovations thus take place in a kind of dialectic with what has gone before, underwriting their own appeal to be uncovering reality by exposing the artificiality and conventionality of what has passed for reality previously. (Hill 1986: 127)

Hill's observation is very useful in that it offers a means of viewing contemporary realist filmmakers mounting a critique of their forebears. The tradition of realism as an overtly politicised mode in both aesthetics and narrative is actively interrogated in the films of Meadows and his contemporaries. As Hill implies, this kind of deviation is motivated by the requirement to develop a new mode of 'authenticity' in response to a hitherto dominant realist address which may no longer be prescient. Thus, in the post-war period – where sociopolitical dividing lines are visible and embedded within cultural practice – the pursuit of an authentic cinematic address with which to engage clearly with specific social issues is logically justifiable. For example, the divisive demise of political consensus gives realist practitioners working in the 1980s and early 1990s a necessary platform from which to interrogate issues of public sociopolitical significance. Thereafter, it is possible to begin to understand contemporary British realism as responding to an absence of such thematic material. As the stark ideological divisions that shaped much oppositional culture in post-war Britain blur and dissemble, a realist cinema that rejects overt political and/or social sentiment begins to emerge. Arguably, the move towards thematic and aesthetic ambiguity, and a resultant emphasis on psychological and emotional realism, reflects both the boldness of a new tradition aiming to critique established cinematic approaches and, more broadly, an acknowledgement of the absence of easily conveyed sociopolitical narratives from our daily lives.

In keeping with this cyclical understanding of British realism and as the political climate begins to alter, it is highly likely that the distanced and poetic approach of Shane Meadows and his contemporaries will, in turn, inspire a return to issue-driven realist realism. In acknowledging this eventuality, we can more substantively advance the case that Meadows has led the formation of a new realist tradition that reflects accurately the influences of his period while progressively reshaping the conventions of the mode. Indeed, by accommodating bold aesthetic practices, British realist cinema now comfortably occupies a position in which its virtues as art, rather than document, are proudly on display.

References

Bardan, A. (2008), 'Welcome to dreamland: the realist impulse in Paweł Pawlikowski's *Last Resort*', *New Cinemas: Journal of Contemporary Film*, 6: 1, 47–63.

Bazin, A. (1971), 'An aesthetic of reality: cinematic realism and the Italian School of Liberation', in André Bazin (ed.) and Hugh Gray (trans.), *What is Cinema? Vol. II*, Berkeley: University of California Press.

Brandon, G. and R. Stafford (1996), *The Media Student's Handbook*, London and New York: Routledge.

Foley, J. (2004), 'Paweł Pawlikowski: *My Summer of Love*': http://www.bbc.co.uk/films/2004/10/11/pawel_pawlikowski_my_summer_of_love_interview.shtml (accessed 2 February 2009).

Fradley, M. (2010), 'Shane Meadows', in Yvonne Tasker (ed.), *Fifty Contemporary Film Directors*, London: Routledge.

Hall, S. (2006), 'Shane Meadows': http://www.screenonline.org.uk/people/id/461763/index.html (accessed 6 July 2012).

Higson, A. (1996), 'Space, place, spectacle: landscape and townscape in the "kitchen sink"', in Andrew Higson (ed.), *Dissolving Views: Key Writings on British Cinema*, London: Continuum.

Hill, J. (1986), *Sex, Class and Realism: British Cinema 1956–1963*, London: BFI.

Lay, S. (2002), *British Social Realism: From Documentary to Brit Grit*, London and New York: Wallflower.

Leggott, J. (2008), *Contemporary British Cinema: From Heritage to Horror*, London and New York: Wallflower.

Raphael, A. (2010), 'Shane Meadows's This is England gang will give Channel 4 a kick up the 80s': http://www.guardian.co.uk/film/2010/sep/04/this-is-england-86-shane-meadows (accessed 9 September 2010).

Williams, R. (1977), 'A lecture on realism', *Screen*, 18: 1, 61–74.

CHAPTER 4

'Al fresco? That's up yer anus, innit?' Shane Meadows and the Politics of Abjection

Martin Fradley

The body that figures in all the expressions of the unofficial speech of the people is the body that fecundates and is fecundated, that gives birth and is born, devours and is devoured, drinks [and] defecates … Whenever men laugh and curse, particularly in a familiar environment, their speech is filled with bodily images. The body copulates, defecates, overeats, and men's speech is flooded with genitals, bellies, defecations, urine, disease, noses, mouths, and dismembered parts.

Mikhail Bakhtin, *Rabelais and His World* (1965 [1984]: 319)

I'm full up with burgers! I've just eaten half a cow's crack, so I'm desperate for a big shit! And a nice piss-piss! I'm gonna have to sneak off in a minute and drop one! I'm gonna walk the wire cable! I'm gonna release a chocolate hostage!

Paddy Considine, *A Room for Romeo Brass* (1999) DVD commentary

As usual, it begins innocuously enough. Prompted by his friend Shane Meadows politely enquiring whether the actor has enjoyed his lunch, Paddy Considine's extrapolated digressions quoted above typify the enjoyably lewd and irreverent tone of Meadows' DVD commentary tracks. Casually expressing their mutual boredom at the laborious process of narrating on earlier work, the conversation soon descends into tangential disarray: a series of raucous exchanges including anecdotes about youthful encounters with pornography, being caught masturbating and Considine's cheerful description of Meadows' dog emptying his bowels. However, absent from this transcription of the actor's scatological stream-of-consciousness is Meadows' own contribution: an explosively reciprocal cackle which spurs the actor to further exaggerate his euphemistic non sequiturs. Meadows' spontaneous laughter foregrounds the affectionate rapport between the two men, close friends since they met as teenagers. Joyfully superseding the contractual obligations of paid labour, the two friends reject professional decorum in favour of gleefully 'talking shit'. It is typically irreverent moments like this, I argue, which imbue Meadows' output with a powerful critique of the strictures of neoliberal culture, the earthy romanticism of the Meadowsian worldview serving as an affective riposte to the deadened logics of capitalist realism.

Considine's lavatorial outburst will come as no great surprise to aficionados of the director's films. Moreover, Meadows' body of work has itself been consistently drawn to the comic potential of the body. Indeed, the corporeal lexicon of the provincial everyday and an enthusiastic pre-occupation with bodily functions are among the hallmarks of Meadows' *oeuvre* to date. This bodily terrain is exemplified by bawdy trailers for the acclaimed *This is England '86* (2010). First broadcast on Channel Four in May 2010, the promotional teasers featured authentically low-grade analogue video footage of a raucous party celebrating England's appearance in the 1986 World Cup quarter-finals. Although ultimately excised from the series proper, the scenes of lavatorial horseplay, carnal banter and arse-baring japery were in no way misleading in their preview of coming attractions. By the end of the second episode of *This is England '86*, for example, viewers had been treated to a veritable cornucopia of earthy delights: celebratory toasts made with piss-filled catheter bags; gloriously corpulent couplings; lurid tales of root vegetables inserted in rectal passages; a heart attack triggered by violent bowel movements; allusions to vinegar strokes and leaking ejaculate; sportswear-clad '80s casuals with bum-fluff 'taches and grotesquely tumescent crotches; and a sexually *outré* 'arsehole Bloody Mary'. From as early as *Small Time* (1996), grotesque realism has played a pivotal role in Meadows' distinctively indecorous sensibility.

'You fuckin' thought of this fuckin' shit-arse plan!' Dirty protest and embodied politics

Raised in the small Staffordshire town of Uttoxeter, Meadows' unambiguously working-class background has served to rhetorically structure his films' representation of the derogated British underclass (Fradley 2010; Dave 2011). These representations overlap with broader discourses relating to the United Kingdom's post-industrial working class in the twenty-first century, a demographic aggressively constructed as 'abject' within neoliberal hegemonic norms (Skeggs 2004; Dave 2004; Lawler 2005; Baker 2009; Nunn and Biressi 2010; Adams and Raisborough 2011; Skeggs and Wood 2011). Yet in terms of contemporary British cinema, one need only look to the reactionary class nightmare of *Eden Lake* (2009) – set, like so many of Meadows' films, somewhere indistinct in the East Midlands – to measure the distance between Meadows' output and broader working-class stereotypes. Owen Jones' acclaimed book *Chavs: The Demonization of the Working Class* (2011) offers a succinct snapshot of 'just how mainstream middle-class hatred of working-class people is in modern Britain' (5). Jones underscores this point by pointing to the predominance of key tropes associated with the so-called British underclass: lazy, violent, criminal, drunk, pregnant, unemployed, tasteless, bigoted and stupid. As Stephanie Lawler (2005) points out, this mainstream discourse pivots on an affective disgust for the proletarian body which functions to normalise middle-class identities. '[T]he poor have long been associated with the material and the embodied [and] … their appearance, their bearing and their adornment … are central in representations of white working-class people' (432). Within the neoliberal imaginary, then, the abject proletarian body serves as an insidious social metonym, discursively framing the twenty-first-century working class as excessive, wasteful and out of control (Adams and Raisborough 2011).

By way of contrast, I want to suggest that Meadows' films insistently reject the interpellations of neoliberal self-regulation and instead celebrate the democratic 'leakage' of the working-class body. It is hardly coincidental that Considine's enthusiastic celebration of the affective pleasures of defecation echoes key moments of excretory abandon in *TwentyFourSeven* (1997), *Once Upon a Time in the Midlands* (2002) and *Somers Town* (2008). Moreover, long before *This is England '86* foregrounded a sustained engagement with serious sexual themes, Meadows' films were notable for their bawdy depiction of lascivious activities: Ruby's enthusiastic use of a vibrator in *Small Time*; lurid porn-inspired conversations in *Dead Man's Shoes* (2004); and Smell's lustful demand that Shaun 'suck me tits' and 'please wank me!' in *This is England* (2006) and *This is England '88* (2011). Elsewhere, the physiological proximity of anal and genital regions links the excremental and the sexual in Meadows' grotesque imagination. Bathrooms and latrines subsequently become sites of comic and ontological significance. In *TwentyFourSeven* closeted gay duo Daz and Benny bond while sharing a row of urinals, the simple act of simultaneous urination tentatively liberating the friends from the strictures of heteronormalcy. In *Dead Man's Shoes*, Soz's unselfconsciously stoned evacuation of his bowels in an overcrowded bathroom typifies the homoerotic dynamic of Meadows' films, a lavatorial continuum further illustrated by Shaun and Smell's belated consummation of their relationship in a pub toilet at the conclusion of *This is England '86*.

Rather than dismiss these grotesque interludes as licentious comic relief from Meadows' more serious concerns, I suggest that the director's preoccupation with the corporeal is invested with political resonance. Although seemingly throwaway or inconsequential, it is in such moments that Meadows affirms resistance to the self-regulatory norms of neoliberal culture. While Meadows' emphasis on the economically marginal communities of provincial England renders his characters abject in the national imaginary, this abjection is embraced as affectively vital and politically efficacious. As Paul Dave suggests, the pernicious ideological construction of an emergent British 'underclass' serves to conceal 'the systematically destructive effects of capitalism on particular sections of the working class' (2006: 83). Looking across Meadows' career to date, I argue that in wilfully foregrounding the alterity and eruptive vitality of the body, the director's work thematically valorises mutuality and working-class commonality through recourse to corporeal terrain. Politics, then, are significantly embodied in Meadows' films. By emphasising their excessive bodily habitus, Meadows' characters expose the performative contrivances of middle-class social normalcy (Skeggs and Wood 2011). In rejecting the regulatory fictions of atomised individualism and the primacy of the self-regulating consumer-citizen, Meadows' work functions as a form of 'dirty protest'. In endorsing the grotesque body as a corporeal metonym, Meadows ideologically repudiates – to appropriate Bakhtin's terminology – the dominant neoliberal fiction of 'a closed individuality that does not merge with other bodies and with the world' (1968: 320). In doing so, I wish to suggest that Meadows' devotion to the abject significantly underscores his commitment to an inclusive pro-social agenda.

'Yer just a fuckin' minge!' Abjection, class and the grotesque imagination

It almost goes without saying that Meadows' employment of grotesque humour and low comedy places his films within one of Western culture's most enduring comedic traditions, traceable back to the folk narratives and profane demotic of Chaucer and Rabelais. Moreover, the unrefined provincial vernacular which characterises Meadows' output is arguably one of the most distinctive features of his authorship. Capturing the brittle rhythms and coarse verbal textures of everyday working-class Midlands life, this expressive idiom uses the corporeal as its primary referent. In turn, this brash lexicon should itself be understood as a metonym for Meadows' thematic emphasis on demotic incivility (Turner 2010). A short scene at the start of *Somers Town* is illustrative in this respect. Attempting to improve his broken English, Polish migrant Marek practises conversation with his father, Mariusz. Impressed with Marek's precise use of the word 'shit', Mariusz ruminates on how he is regularly taught 'bad words' by colleagues at work. Responding to his father's enquiry about what unruly language he has learned during his short time in England, Marek wagers that his crude vocabulary is already more expansive than his father's. After Mariusz agrees to this profane challenge, Marek demonstrates the linguistic rewards of working-class pedagogy in a hilariously utilitarian idiom: 'Shit. Bloody. Asshole. Boobs.'

Andrew Tolson (2011) argues that this excessive and 'unhygienic' verbosity is a distinctive marker of class. Within dominant discourses about language and social difference, Tolson argues, 'some uses of language are condemned as pathological':

> They are seen as manifestations of ignorance and inferior moral character. They are constantly and explicitly related to social class, if not the poverty of the 'abject' working class, then certainly the 'class envy' of the disadvantaged for their cultural superiors. According to this discourse, the right way to deal with these problems is to recognise their limitations … and to accept that there are more appropriate ways to speak. (55)

As the emblematic scene from *Somers Town* demonstrates, however, Meadows' films embrace this corporeal demotic as part of their everyday reality. In contradistinction to censorious middle-class norms, 'low' discourse actively functions to celebrate bodily eruptions and emissions. In doing so, it offers a transgressive riposte to an arbitrarily normative nexus which subjugates the self to the demands of middle-class neoliberal propriety.

Anuses, genital regions, shit, piss, saliva and semen: allusions to sexual fluids, excremental wastes and bodily orifices abound in Meadows' work. Julia Kristeva (1982) has influentially defined these orifices and excretions as the *abject*: corporeal substances and bodily openings which both disgust and fascinate us because they signify the illusory nature of bodily integrity. Culturally marked as disgusting and unclean, the abject is both physically and ontologically uncertain, blurring the boundary between the individual self and the external world. While cultural taboos surrounding bodily wastes and orifices regulate our relationship to the corporeal by insisting on a repudiation – indeed, a psychosocial 'flushing away' – of pleasure(s) associated with certain bodily functions, our collective fascination with the sexual and scatological is omnipresent in everyday discourse. Stephanie Lawler carefully dissects the way the constructions of an 'abject' working class are writ large in 'the affective and cathetic aspects' of contemporary social discourse:

[E]xpressions of disgust at white working-class existence remain rife among middle-class commentators [and] … such expression of disgust can tell us a great deal about the ways in which middle-classness relies upon the expulsion and exclusion of (what is held to be) white working-classness. (2005: 430)

As Lawler explains, the abject working class is a structuring fiction designed to affirm middle-class identities that rely on not being 'the repellent and disgusting [working-class] other' (431). Sustained by a disavowal of systemic inequality, this process serves to produce 'a normative and normalized middle-classness' (431) by virtue of the insistent symbolic violence of abjection.

By contrast, Meadows' celebration of social abjection and physical grotesquerie rejects the class bigotry identified by Lawler and functions instead to embrace socioeconomic alterity through corporeal metaphors. In ridiculing the repressive imperatives of social conditioning vis-à-vis bodily functions, Meadows reimagines the corporeal self as a site of efficacious social resistance. Through allusions to urination, defecation and sexual impulses, Meadows repeatedly eulogises the abject materiality of the body. In *This is England '86* the material emissions of the lower regions are reimagined as proof of the interconnectedness of the social body. Woody and Lol move into a fetid flat whose previous occupant – a borderline coprophile according to local legend – died in the building surrounded by his own faeces. 'Circle of life, that is!' remarks one of their friends on uncovering a horde of writhing maggots under a carpet in the derelict flat. The visual allusion to the pivotal 'rotten meat' sequences of *Battleship Potemkin* (1925) is striking, the image expounding Meadows' philosophical embrace of abjection and, by extension, working-class social fecundity.

In contrast to the coherent, self-disciplining individual of neoliberal mythos, the grotesque body in Meadows' worldview is – both literally and metaphorically – porous, open and inseparable from the larger world. In a social universe characterised by material lack, Meadows' expedient Midlanders embrace their abjection as a form of affective resistance to a world circumscribed by impoverishment and limited opportunities. As witnessed in Dek's adjustment of his engorged crotch following a fleeting canoodle with Shirley in *Once Upon a Time in the Midlands*, Flip's lurid ejaculatory fantasies about 'fingering' Gemma in *This is England '86* or Herbie's remark in *Dead Man's Shoes* that he can 'taste' Soz's pungent faeces in his beer, Meadows is preoccupied with the tactile materiality and unruly potency of the body. Rather than a closed unit, then, the Meadowsian body revels in its abject excesses. Following Bakhtin's celebration of the 'open' grotesque body, in Meadows' films the arbitrary separation between the individual body and the broader world is repeatedly overcome. Neither apolitical nor naively 'cosmic', Meadows' persistent rejection of middle-class disgust in relation to the body serves to philosophically underpin the singular political thrust of his output.

The transgressive politics of bodily excess and low humour have long been the subject of theoretical and philosophical debate (Foucault 1977; Bataille 1987; Jervis 1999; King 2002; Leverette 2008). Transgression is typically understood as a reflexive cultural mechanism, drawing attention to the rules, regulations and taboos that govern the socialised behaviour of the rational self. Yet the body always and inevitably exceeds the arbitrary limits of subjugation and sublimated individualism. Echoing the orifices and excretory excesses of Bakhtin's grotesque body, Georges Bataille (1987) argues that we are 'discontinuous beings' cruelly bound to a 'random and ephemeral individuality' which compels the neoliberal citizen ambivalently to renounce 'a primal continuity linking us with everything there is' (15). Although Bataille's work primarily relates to sexual communion, this longing for organic sociality and de-individualised *communitas* is at the epicentre of Meadows' earthy philosophy. Whereas the visual preoccupation with corporeal excess in genres such as hardcore pornography and horror cinema has been interpreted as transgressive and even 'radical' (Kryzwinska 1999; McRoy 2010), Meadows consistently challenges taboos relating to the abject body. In *This is England*, for example, Shaun returns to a crowded sitting room after his first amorous liaison with Smell. As the couple are warmly welcomed back into the fold, Smell returns to her friends to share her experience before a brief shot reveals an initially bashful Shaun offer his pungent fingers to willing comrades for nasal inspection. Rather than being predicated on prurient disgust or infantile humour, however, it is in moments such as these that Meadows offers an affirmative vision of commonality and continuity via the vaginal mucous that binds. As Dave (2011) suggests, Meadows uses space to express a common culture which 'supports individual and collective flourishing':

> One frequently repeated example of this is the squeezing of bodies into domestic settings, Meadows' often cramped interiors radiate an informal ease – these are spaces in which the comfortable intimacy of many individuals creates an image of 'equality of being' – which ... work[s] against an emergent culture of neoliberalism. (35–6)

The gaggle of adolescent bodies warmly collected together in 'comfortable intimacy' in *This is England* thus functions as a subcultural – and therefore abject – communal body, affirming commonality through physical proximity.

By normative standards, of course, a fixation on bodily functions is typically dismissed as puerile or infantile: a regressive pre-Oedipal fascination with excreta which spurns commitment to the social world (King 2002). To this end, the thematic homology between bodily abjection and the social was established in Meadows' earliest output. Ruby's covert use of an unseen vibrator in *Small Time*, for example, is depicted as both comically excessive and a defiant affirmation of self-willed sexual pleasure. Complete with rhapsodic gurning and extravagantly vocalised ardour, Ruby's orgasmic rapture serves to reclaim a body that is otherwise subjugated to persistent domestic violence. Elsewhere, through gloriously absurd scenes featuring the cast cavorting en masse, Meadows democratically champions dancing as a form of polymorphous *communitas* within Sneinton's otherwise spartan terraced environs. In *TwentyFourSeven* this trope becomes more directly bound within discourses of class identity and commonality. While 'hunting' in the local woods early in the film, Gadget is ridiculed by friends for his ungovernable bowel movements. Gadget is further associated with abjection when he disappears into the foliage to defecate only to return triumphantly clutching the decaying corpse of a rabbit. Taunted by his associates, Gadget's guileless pragmatism – he unselfconsciously admits to using his underwear as a substitute for toilet paper – marks him out as heroically grotesque. The broader thematic significance of this scene is underscored when Darcy takes his downtrodden collective on a camping trip to Wales. Temporarily removed from the restrictions of their everyday lives, the utopian spirit of commonality which underpins the excursion is affirmed when the lads unselfconsciously piss and shit en masse in the forest. This use of the excremental as an ideological barometer is reaffirmed in a related scene earlier in the film. Here, local businessman–cum–gangster Ronnie vocally registers his disgust at the odour emanating from the toilet cubicle Darcy has just used. Darcy's weary bewilderment at Ronnie's reaction serves once again to mobilise the abject as a way to symbolically underline the ethical polarity between the two men.

As Bakhtin notes, defecation and excrement are often linked to processes of reproduction, renewal and material interorientation. Excrement is conceived 'as something *intermediate between earth and body*, as something relating the one to the other':

> It is also an intermediate between the living body and dead disintegrating matter that is being transformed into earth, into manure. The living body returns to the earth its excrement, which fertilizes the earth as does the body of the dead … combin[ing] the grave and birth in their lightest, most comic, least terrifying form. (1968: 175; original emphasis)

The grotesque imagination thus privileges excremental fecundity and regeneration over cultural taboos relating to debasement and bodily disgust. This sense of the cyclical is ultimately affirmed and endorsed in *TwentyFourSeven*. While Darcy's nurturing paternalism helps resurrect his disaffected 'lads' from a state of social abjection, so too does Darcy's funeral in the film's narrative coda offer the ritualised promise of rebirth and communal renewal. Gently reincorporating the memory of Darcy's derelict 'forgotten man' into the community, the funeral foregrounds his corpse – the abject body *par excellence* – as the corporeal centrepiece for the film's vision of personal and social renewal.

'Donk seemed to have it all … but now his life is shit': social disgust and self-acceptance

From the dissolute survivalists of *Where's the Money Ronnie!* (1996) and *Small Time* onwards, Meadows' Midlanders are invariably abject in socio-economic terms: the inevitable human detritus of the 'new economy'. Through collective strategies of empathy, mutuality and self-acceptance, however, Meadows' favoured characters negotiate their place in the material world by rejecting neoliberal individualism and instead embracing their malignancy. As illustrated by Donk's overwhelming sense that his life is 'shit', perceiving one's own abjection is, for John Limon (2000), a form of psychic worrying over one's sense of alterity:

> When you feel abject, you feel as if there was something miring your life, some skin that cannot be sloughed, some role (because 'abject' always, in a way, describes how you act) that has become your only character. (Limon: 4)

Limon's emphasis on the performativity of abjection – 'how you act' – is apt. For sure, the key running gag in *Le Donk and Scor-zay-zee* is precisely the gulf between Donk's tenuous maintenance of a would-be freewheeling rock 'n' roll persona – how he wishes to be perceived by others – and the abject failure of that performance. Shot in 'mockumentary' style, *Le Donk and Scor-zay-zee* mobilises the formal trappings of documentary and reality TV to underscore and critique the genre's preoccupation with the hypervisible rendering of class and socioeconomic alterity. Echoing Dek's humiliation when his marriage proposal is rejected on a reality television show in *Once Upon a Time in the Midlands*, Donk's delusional belief in the transformative potency of on-screen performance functions as a rebuttal of the cultural impetus towards self-improvement and the commodification of self-performance.

As Skeggs and Wood (2011) point out, within the dominant reality TV format '[c]lass inequalities in access to resources are revealed by the TV producers' demand for people in need of transformation: the abject are required to perform their abjection and the excessive are asked to perform their excess in order to display their need for transformation and education in the normative' (17). Like many of Meadows' troubled male characters, Donk's neurosis and feelings of abjection lead him to perform a competitive and aggressive individualism which stands in a dichotomous relationship to Meadows' more heroic characters. Similarly, Ronnie's entrepreneurial ambition, phallic aggression and material aspirations in *Twenty-FourSeven* are thrown into sharp relief by the nurturing imperatives of Darcy's profit-free '101 Club'. Like the inclusive skinhead collective in *This is England*, Meadows emphasises the social bonds founded in shared alterity. In *This is England* in particular, the youthful dispossessed of the 1980s transform their abject social status into a form of collective empowerment. Through defiant habitation of public spaces (subway tunnels, public parks, municipal swimming baths) and use of DIY expressive forms, the adolescent gang announce their presence through the assertive semiotics of subcultural style. The film's often bleak *mise-en-scène* is tellingly decorated with the young skinheads' omnipresent graffiti, itself a potent form of symbolic smearing.

Moreover, despite their economic hardship Meadows' heroic characters arc largely disinterested in upward social mobility. Tomo's exodus from the Midlands in *Somers Town* is typical in this respect, mired as it is in desperation rather than the socioeconomic ambition which traditionally necessitates migration to London. When a downtrodden Uttoxeter farm labourer in *Shane's World* (2000) ponders relocation to the prosperous South-East he is angrily chastised for his naïve ambition. 'London's not paved with gold,' proclaims Tank Bullock (Meadows) – an affectionate caricature of the director's defiant provincialism – 'it's paved with shit!' Indeed, the affluent middle classes barely register in Meadows' social imaginary. Rare interlopers in Meadows' working-class universe, the yoga-practising couple befriended by Kate in *Small Time* have their domestic life thrown into disorder by Malc's casual inebriation and Jumbo's indecorous intrusions. In *This is England '88*, Shaun is bewildered by the aspirational habitus of his middle-class girlfriend's family. Wearing clothes expediently appropriated from a launderette, Tomo's plaintive remark in *Somers Town* that he 'look[s] like a female golfer' is grounded less in feelings of gendered abjection and more in a crushing sense of socioeconomic incongruity. Tomo's ironic makeover leaves him clad in garb which signifies a middle-class exclusivity utterly discomfiting to any self-respecting Meadowsian hero.

Despite this gleefully sustained inversion of class snobbery, life in Shane's world is not all shits and giggles. If indifference to middle-class social norms and rebuttal of bourgeois niceties serve to underpin the low-rent fortitude and solidarity of Meadows' characters, problematic figures such as Sonny in *Dead Man's Shoes*, Combo in *This is England* and Morell in *A Room for Romeo Brass* (1999) are crippled by low self-esteem, psycho-social abjection and neurotic performances of aggressive individualism. This thematic strain remains even in Meadows' most light-hearted work. In *Le Donk and Scor-zay-zee*, Donk's incredulous disgust on discovering that his ex-girlfriend continues to enjoy penetrative sex while heavily pregnant typifies the way Meadows' characters sublimate feelings of personal abjection into incoherent and self-defeating anger. While working class femininity is invariably an overdetermined site of abjection (Lawler 2005; Skeggs 2005; Tolson 2011; Adams and Raisborough 2011), it is significant that – in keeping with his sustained interrogation of working-class masculinity – Meadows' films more typically associate abjection with his troubled menfolk. Like his overwrought insistence that he 'can't shit with someone in me room', Donk's misogynist inability to accept maternal sexuality typifies his subjugation to the social super-ego. Unlike the unself-consciously 'public' generosity of spirit embodied by Meadows' more loose-bowelled characters, Donk's uptight proclamations about the impor-tance of defecating 'in private' underline the insistent conflation of the corporeal with the political in Meadows' work. Meadows' interest in the politics of defecation is further underscored elsewhere. In *This is England*, Meggy's aborted attempt to empty his bowels on an Asian shopkeeper's floor becomes perversely comical precisely because of his body's refusal to collude with the ideological barbarity of his desires.

A crippling insistence on illusory concepts of self-reliance and the rejection of supportive social networks serves as the root cause of pathology in both *Dead Man's Shoes* and *This is England*. Whereas Meadows' favoured characters embrace their malignancy, Richard and Combo are ultimately consumed by it. For Dave (2011), both characters are emblematic of the brutality and aggression which underpin neoliberal social policies. Combo's intolerance and viciously illusory rhetoric of exclusivity and ethnic purity, for example, mark him out as the Meadowsian character most consumed by the terror of abjection. As Clair Schwarz points out elsewhere in this book, Richard's vengeful psychosis in *Dead Man's Shoes* is ultimately a gothic mirror to the tyrannical reign of local drug lynchpin Sonny. While

Richard's violent revenge underscores a proto-fascist loathing of weakness, ambiguous flashbacks also reveal Sonny's long history of latent violence and sexual exploitation, particularly in scenes where he violently coerces Richard's younger brother to the point of oral rape. After being spiked with hallucinogens, however, Sonny's authoritarian tyranny dissipates and the intimate communal potential of this underclass collective comes intriguingly into view. Like the stoned camaraderie in *This is England*, the sequence featuring Soz, Herbie and Sonny intimately sharing a bathroom provides a glimpse of an egalitarian alternative to the otherwise aggressively regulated homosocial structure of Sonny's gang. In doing so, *Dead Man's Shoes* reiterates the abject paucity of social relations under the logic of free-market fundamentalism.

'I need a poo really badly!' Excremental heroism in *Somers Town*

In contradistinction to the debilitating neurosis of Donk or the phallic aggression of Morell, Sonny, Combo et al., Meadows' films valorise those figures who embrace their alterity in a form of non-sublimating heroism. Whether literally or figuratively wallowing in excrement and abjection, Meadows' favoured characters are disruptive and irreverent neo-tricksters who reject embarrassment and shame as the most absurd of social conventions. The bestial energies of Meadows' excremental heroes render them liminal child-men with uncontrollable appetites, convulsed by raucous laughter and compulsively driven by physical urges. Embodying profanity and absurdity, the trickster's impulsive transgressions reflexively draw attention to the arbitrary nature of social boundaries and cultural constructions (Waddell 2010; Bassil-Morozow 2012). The titular hero of *A Room for Romeo Brass* is one of Meadows' many on-screen doubles in this mode. Romeo's physical bulk, compulsive overeating and precocious enthusiasm for pornography make him a clear antecedent for Tomo in *Somers Town*, a character who is arguably the leading exponent of excremental heroism in Meadows' oeuvre to date.

Somers Town begins with Tomo expelled from the Midlands, left bereft and bloodied after being mugged shortly after arriving in London. This opening tableau of impoverishment and dislocation foregrounds the inevitable struggle of those left alienated by the self-seeking ethos of neoliberal capitalism. As Helena Bassil-Morozow (2012) points out, the trickster is inextricably bound up in the contradictions of the neoliberal economy, his unruly behaviour exposing class divisions and the symbolic

fictions of self-sufficient individualism. A liminal figure unable to contain
or sublimate the impulses of his unruly body, Tomo's impulsive
humanism is unveiled in his urgent need to defecate while hiding in
Marek's bedroom. Echoing Gadget's uncontainable bowel movements in
TwentyFourSeven, Tomo's irrepressible need to shit associates him with
an excessive anality, a symptomatic inability to retain anything in the
impoverished world of *Somers Town*. Similar impulses are evident in the
scene where Marek inadvertently intrudes on Tomo masturbating in the
bathroom. A private act brought incongruously to the attention of others,
the abject scenario of being caught masturbating is culturally defined as
humiliating and shameful. Tomo, however, is characteristically unbound
by such basic social etiquette. With his exposed backside perched
suggestively over the rim of the bathtub, Tomo tugs away using one of
Marek's cherished photographs of French waitress Maria (Elisa Lasowski)
as an onanistic aide-memoire. Echoing the earlier scene in Marek's
bedroom, Tomo again renounces the normative use of domestic space.
Not content with using the bathtub as a venue for inappropriately 'dirty'
sexual acts, Tomo's posture also resembles someone squatting in order to
defecate. Unfazed by Marek's untimely intrusion, Tomo's lackadaisical
reaction underscores his role as trickster. Rather than apologising or
attempting to conceal his furtive sojourn, Tomo simply offers a
shamelessly perfunctory excuse – 'I'm lonely' – before bursting into manic
laughter.

Like Meadows' own infectious cackle, then, Tomo's giggling flaunts
his refusal to be associated with normative feelings of shame or disgust vis-
à-vis bodily functions. Even as Marek's anger rises – lapsing back into
native Polish to morally disparage his deviant accomplice as a 'dirty pig' –
Tomo's base laughter simply increases, continuing as a sound bridge into
the subsequent shot of the young men leaving the flat. To this end, the
contrasting sensibilities of the two friends are telling. Whereas Marek is
sensitive and introverted, Tomo is brash and unrefined. While Marek's
photographs ultimately fetishise Maria, Tomo rejects romantic idealism
and instead uses her image for more efficacious and utilitarian purposes.
Happily degrading the lofty aspirations of Marek's work, Tomo's
animalistic impulses merrily trump artistic sublimation. In true Bakhtinian
fashion, the lower stratum turns traditional cultural topography on its
head: the genitals and the levelling impulses of laughter triumph over the
intellect and the bourgeois aestheticisation of beauty. With Marek's
monochrome photography an obvious synecdoche for the understated
visual poetry of *Somers Town*'s cinematography, Tomo's dissolute

appearance – penis in one hand, photograph in the other – is in many ways a metonym for the core dialectic of Meadows' oeuvre.

Tellingly, the subsequent scene features *Somers Town*'s most celebrated moment. Opening his front door to the two boys, would-be wheeler-dealer Graham appears dressed in dishevelled dressing gown, threadbare Y-fronts and gloriously exposed pot belly. Like Tomo's lavatorial urges and unapologetic onanism, the corporeal excess of Graham's semi-naked body is unself-consciously brought into public view. Like Tomo, then, Graham embodies the democratic and life-affirming abundance of the grotesque. Casually plucking banknotes from the crotch of his grubby underwear, Graham nonchalantly blows pubic residue from the crumpled readies before handing his tender to the giggling adolescents in exchange for their appropriated loot. Directly associating money and commercial exchange with the 'lower regions', the scene again exemplifies the topographical reversals of the grotesque mode. Mirroring earlier scenes in which bootlegged replica football strips were handed over in exchange for the young men's temporary labour, the non-exploitative reciprocity of the transaction is quietly eulogised. A far cry from the casual brutality underpinning the business dealings of Ronnie in *TwentyFourSeven* or Sonny in *Dead Man's Shoes*, entrepreneurship here is removed from associations with phallic power and material exploitation. Indeed, Graham's misspelt Arsenal shirts and shoddy deckchairs serve primarily as a jocular parody of neoliberal entrepreneurial zeal. The image of Graham rummaging around his crotch in turn echoes Tomo's masturbation and reaffirms the gently abdominal exigency of *Somers Town*'s unruly heroes. Meadows depicts these folk exchanges and reappropriation of cultural artefacts as reciprocal and mutually sustaining. Where Sonny in *Dead Man's Shoes* sexually exploits those weaker than him, Graham's appalled reaction when Tomo assumes that he is negotiating sexual favours in exchange for money points to the corroding logic of a neoliberal culture in which human beings are viewed primarily as 'resources'. Conversely, in *Somers Town* stolen clothes and poorly bootlegged knock-offs of globally branded football shirts – the commodified 'shit' of a market-led social universe – are reappropriated as objects for exchanges grounded in understated protectionism and correlative social bonding.

The celebratory scene towards the end of the film in which Tomo and Marek work through their mutual heartbreak is pivotal in terms of heroic abjection. After drinking away their sorrows in a local park, Marek's home is subsequently transformed into an expressive liminal space strewn with the detritus of a frugal banquet. A Dionysian orgy by the standards of

Somers Town's otherwise spartan social world, the flat is filled with the sound of pounding techno. The primacy of affective pleasure is further underscored by Tomo and Marek's exuberantly drunken dancing, itself echoing the low-rent Bacchanalia of *Small Time*. Introjecting Graham's idiosyncratic cosmopolitanism, the boys prance like demented sprites while stripped to their underpants. Renouncing heterosexual mourning, the image of Tomo flaunting his backside at Marek while tugging suggestively at his underwear is as deliriously homoerotic as anything in Meadows' oeuvre. The return of Marek's father abruptly curtails the orgiastic delirium. Repeating Marek's porcine descriptor earlier in the film, a disgusted Mariusz brands the chaotic flat 'a pigsty'. Reining in the excesses of the adolescent id, Mariusz's paternal super-ego asserts mature authority ('I'm a grown up') and rejects their appropriation of the flat through recourse to the language of capital and ownership ('this is my home!'). The boys' unrestrained giggling underscores their affective delight ('don't laugh!' Mariusz angrily reprimands them), the carnivalesque impulses of the trickster temporarily reinscribing functional domestic space with a democratic and near-utopian physicality. Mirroring the scenes in *This is England* where the skinhead gang dress up as absurd savages and joyfully vandalise disused council homes, the debauched scenes in *Somers Town* are emblematic of the Meadowsian worldview. While the agency of his characters is always circumscribed by harsh socioeconomic realities – the film's sudden shift to colour in the final reel a transparent nod to the compensatory wish-fulfilment of *The Wizard of Oz* (1939) – excremental heroism temporarily suggests a form of micro-political resistance to hegemonic neoliberal constraints.

Conclusion: 'I'm gonna go with the man boobs'

Following the announcement that *This is England* had won the award for Best Film at the 2008 BAFTAs ceremony, Shane Meadows' acceptance speech was a somewhat surreal affair. Leaving long-time friend and collaborator Paddy Considine beaming gleefully in his seat, Meadows and Warp Films supremo Mark Herbert were presented with the BAFTA by none other than muscle-bound 1980s icon Sylvester Stallone. Characteristically irreverent, the opening to Meadows' brief acceptance speech was telling in its immediate reference to his own embodiment of class:

> Cor, this is the third time I've been nominated and the previous two times I took a regime on after Christmas – press-ups, sit-ups and that sort of thing to get myself into shape in case I won. And this year I gave up on that idea and, er, just

thought I'm gonna go with the man boobs … and it's turned my luck around which is fantastic!

Couched in his distinctive Staffordshire burr, Meadows' speech drew attention to the obvious disparity between his rotund figure and the gym-honed bulk of Stallone. Yet the director's allusion to the physically inscribed realities of social difference also marked him out from the audience of privileged middle-class film industry professionals he addressed.

In highlighting the way social difference is powerfully inscribed on the corporeal – the way the body 'speaks' the realities of class – Meadows underscored the centrality of the abject and unruly body within his distinctive worldview. Like Tuff and Soz's hilarious misrecognition of 'al fresco' as a pornographic euphemism in *Dead Man's Shoes*, the porous boundary between the 'inside' of the mythic individual self and the 'outside' of the social engage in a Bakhtinian dialectic of interchange and interorientation. Rejecting the neoliberal fictions of economic self-reliance and self-regulating individualism, Meadows' characters are inextricably of their world. In normalising the abject and profane, Meadows' lavatorial romanticism invokes a caustic politics of the body. Grounded in folk wisdom and centuries-old conceptions of renewal and worldly materiality, the Meadowsian worldview is scarcely revolutionary. His work, however, resonates powerfully within the systemic reifications of the neoliberal present. At the same time that one should be wary of romanticising Meadows' philosophy of abjection, it would also be a mistake to sidestep the insistent longing for commonality foregrounded in his output. Ultimately, Meadows' films rebut the atomisation of the individual under the conditions of neoliberal capitalism. Just as ordure endures in Shane's world, so too does Meadows' insistence on the primacy of the social.

References

Adams, M. and J. Raisborough (2011), 'The self-control ethos and the "chav": unpacking cultural representations of the white working class', *Culture & Psychology*, 17: 1, 81–97.

Baker, S. (2009), '*Shameless* and the question of England: genre, class and nation', *Journal of British Cinema and Television*, 6, 452–67.

Bakhtin, M. (1968), *Rabelais and His World*, trans. Helene Iswoksky, Cambridge, MA: MIT Press.

Bassil-Morozow, H. (2012), *The Trickster in Contemporary Film*, Hove: Routledge.

Bataille, G. (1987), *Eroticism*, London: Marion Boyars.

Biressi, A. (2011), '"The virtuous circle": social entrepreneurship and welfare programming in the UK', in B. Skeggs and H. Wood (eds), *Reality Television and Class*, London: Palgrave Macmillan–BFI, pp. 144–55.

Biressi, A. and H. Nunn (2005), *Reality TV: Realism and Revelation*, London: Wallflower.

Bonila, P. C. (1995), 'Is there more to Hollywood lowbrow than meets the eye?', *Quarterly Review of Film and Video*, 22, 17–24.

Dave, P. (2006), *Visions of England: Class and Culture in Contemporary Cinema*, Oxford: Berg.

Dave, P. (2011), 'Tragedy, ethics and history in contemporary British social realist film', in D. Tucker (ed.), *British Social Realism in the Arts since 1940*, Edinburgh: Edinburgh University Press, pp. 17–56.

Douglas, M. (1966), *Purity and Danger: An Analysis of the Concepts of Pollution and Taboo*, New York and London: Routledge.

Foucault, M. (1977), 'A preface to transgression', in D. Bouchard and S. Simon (trans. and eds), *Language, Counter-Memory, Practice: Selected Essays and Interviews*, Ithaca: Cornell University Press, pp. 29–52.

Fradley, M. (2010), 'Shane Meadows', in Y. Tasker (ed.), *Fifty Contemporary Film Directors*, London: Routledge, pp. 280–8.

Jervis, J. (1999), *Transgressing the Modern: Explorations in the Western Experience of Otherness*, Oxford: Blackwell.

Jones, O. (2011), *Chavs: The Demonization of the Working Class*, London: Verso.

King, G. (2002), *Film Comedy*, London: Wallflower.

Kristeva, J. (1982), *Powers of Horror*, New York: Columbia University Press.

Kryzwinska, T. (1999), 'Ciccolina and the dynamics of transgression and abjection in explicit sex films', in M. Aaron (ed.), *The Body's Perilous Pleasures: Dangerous Desires and Contemporary Culture*, Edinburgh: Edinburgh University Press, pp. 188–209.

Lawler, S. (2005), 'Disgusted subjects: the making of middle-class identities', *Sociological Review*, 53: 3, 429–96.

Leverette, M. (2008), 'Cocksucker, motherfucker, tits', in M. Leverette, B. L. Ott and C. L. Buckley (eds), *It's Not TV: Watching HBO in the Post-Television Era*, New York and London: Routledge, pp. 123–51.

Limon, J. (2002), *Stand-Up Comedy in Theory, or, Abjection in America*, Durham, NC: Duke University Press.

McRoy, J. (2010), '"Parts is parts": pornography, splatter films and the politics of corporeal disintegration', in I. Conrich (ed.), *Horror Zone: The Cultural Experience of Contemporary Horror Cinema*, London: I. B. Tauris, pp. 191–204.

Nunn, H. and Biressi, A. (2010), 'Shameless? Picturing the "underclass" after Thatcherism', in L. Hadley and E. Ho (eds), *Thatcher and After: Margaret Thatcher and Her Afterlife in Contemporary Culture*, London: Palgrave Macmillan, pp. 137–57.

Skeggs, B. (2004), *Class, Self, Culture*, London: Routledge.

Skeggs, B. and H. Wood (2011), 'Introduction: real class', in H. Wood and B.

Skeggs (eds), *Reality Television and Class*, London: Palgrave Macmillan-BFI, pp. 1–29.

Tolson, A. (2011), '"I'm common and my talking is quite abrupt" (Jade Goody): language and class in *Celebrity Big Brother*', in H. Wood and B. Skeggs (eds), *Reality Television and Class*, London: Palgrave Macmillan-BFI, pp. 45–59.

Turner, G. (2010), *Ordinary People and the Media: The Demotic Turn*, London: Sage.

CHAPTER 5

No More Heroes: The Politics of Marginality and Disenchantment in *TwentyFourSeven* and *This is England*

Jill Steans

In an interview in *Indie London* (2006), Shane Meadows referred to *This is England* as 'probably the closest thing I'll ever make to a political film'. In this chapter I argue that both *This is England* (2006) and his late-'90s debut feature *TwentyFourSeven* (1997) speak to the political zeitgeist of time and place. *TwentyFourSeven* does not engage with political themes in an overt way, and, indeed, the youths who occupy the world of the film are entirely disengaged from mainstream politics. However, it does not follow that it is a non-political film. As Martin Fradley observes: 'although never directly mentioned, the spectre of Thatcherism haunts every frame of *Twenty-FourSeven*' (Fradley 2013). In *This is England* the story centres on the main protagonist's brush with the extremist fringe of British politics. This pre-occupation with the margins of British political life has everything to do with the marginality of the social group who are the main focus of Meadows' work: young, working-class men/youths in the forgotten towns of England's former industrial heartlands (Fradley 2010).

I further argue that in both films, political themes are also explored in a more subtle way. Both films are infused with a deep sense of disenchant-ment with politics. Instead, the protagonists look to charismatic local heroes to infuse their lives with a sense of meaning – something to believe in – and invest a collective sense of pride in their communities at a time when 'everybody thought the working class was fucked' (Meadows quoted in *Indie London* 2006). But ultimately, those heroes disappoint.

Never had anything to believe in: lives in the shadow of Thatcherism in *TwentyFourSeven*

Shane Meadows embeds his stories in landscapes and the lives he knows well. The world of *TwentyFourSeven* is no post-modern, post-Thatcher dystopia, in marked contrast with Mike Leigh's *Naked* (1993), for example. However, the social and political legacy of Thatcherism is evident from the film's opening scene. Tim walks his dog along a disused railway line, his body swamped by the surrounding landscape of urban decay. He arrives at an old freight carriage. It is burnt out: a poignant symbol of industrial decline and an appropriate refuge for the burnt-out refugee within, Alan Darcy (Bob Hoskins). Darcy will later describe himself as a 'forgotten thirty-something in the '80s'. In a monologue that plays over images of Darcy restoring the same freight car, he reflects on the divisive politics and aggressive neoliberal economics of that decade:

> Everything was a boon, a transaction, or a big take-over. Money was God. Money is God. When our town died, we with our young in hand were just beginning, but we weren't living. I feel as though I'm a casualty, but that's cool, because most of us feel that way.

The opening scenes and the accompanying voiceovers set up the storyline and also signpost the themes that will underpin the unfolding drama. *TwentyFourSeven* tells of a place as much as it tells a story; the social conditions of the characters – young working-class British men – are inseparable from the landscape they inhabit. As the camera pans from Darcy's attempt to re-establish his relevance, significantly through his labour (on the freight car), to the housing estate where Tim lives, the polarised geographical/spatial and social divisions of the town are revealed. Darcy's commentary turns to the conditions of life in the small world of the film's protagonists:

> Housing development or what? Two thousand people in an area that should be two hundred max. Development's a cagey word. It's like fresh frozen. Twelve square feet of turf, a different colour door to the neighbour, maybe a tiled front if you know somebody in the trade. Other than that, four walls of bricks, furniture that cries out second hand and poor and the demoralised inhabitants who've lost touch with their origins.

The story in *TwentyFourSeven* recounts a personal tragedy that befalls Darcy. The narrative of the film follows his particular downfall, but it is more than a tale of individual tragedy. The tragedy is shared by the lads in a town that had 'died' in the beginning. The world of *TwentyFourSeven* is one in which young men are not so much apathetic as disempowered. As Darcy's monologue turns from the big picture, the legacy of Thatcherism, to the small picture of Tim's life behind 'four walls of brick', he says, 'The guy's getting shit twenty-four-seven. The problem is he thinks there's nothing he can do about it.' While Darcy might appear, at first sight, to be alluding only to Tim's difficult relationship with his bullying father, in the next scene it becomes evident that the whole town is 'getting shit twenty-four-seven', enveloped in a cloud of hopelessness:

> The lads and people in this town have been living in the same day all their lives, none are singularly strong enough to break away and say wait a minute there must be more than this ... That's why nothing ever changes.

This is a world that appears to be wholly disconnected from the political process. The absence of politics is evident in this imagery of stasis: nothing changes. Working-class collectivism and solidarity is dead to these youths, and the possibility of singular action as a path to individual betterment – the promise of neoliberalism – is seemingly a chimera. Unlike *This is England*, there is no sideswipe at the Tories akin to that later film's 'Maggie is a Twat' graffiti. Indeed, this disengagement from politics reflects the actual disengagement from the political process in Britain in the 1990s, with young people among the most disaffected constituencies (Butler 1995; Stoker 2006; Dillow 2007; Hay 2007).

Political disenchantment

While understated, *TwentyFourSeven* speaks to the theme of political disenchantment. Loosely defined, disenchanted means disillusioned: an apt term to describe the 'demoralised inhabitants' of the world of *TwentyFourSeven*. A more precise usage of the term was employed by Max Weber over one hundred years ago in reference to the decline of religion and other mystical belief systems that followed in the wake of secularisation, capitalism, bureaucratisation and the rationalisation of all spheres of life, including the political sphere. In an essay on 'Science as vocation', Weber wrote:

> [Precisely] the ultimate and most sublime values have retreated from public life either into the transcendental realm of mystic life or into the brotherliness of direct and personal human relations. (Weber 1998 [1948]: 155)

Weber's musings on modernity and disenchantment might seem a world away from a Shane Meadows film produced in the 1990s, and yet there is much in the story and in its telling that resonates with this idea. Weber mourned the likely passing of charismatic heroes: those men (Weber likely thought only of men) able to inspire the population into a virtuous re-engagement with and active participation in public life, hence his – highly problematic – championing of nationalism and imperialist expansion in the glorification of the state. Weber proved to be both wrong and right insofar as nationalism, as the dominant form of political identification, and war dominated the politics of the twentieth century. It was a new vision of British nation in the aftermath of the Second World War that inspired the socialist dream of 'building Jerusalem' and embedding a new class settlement in British society. Ironically, it was Thatcher who arguably served as the last charismatic hero of British politics in the twentieth century, who dismantled much of that dream/settlement and also, with the Falklands conflict, led the country into its final (post-)imperial war.

The setting for *TwentyFourSeven* is post-Thatcherism Britain as it was – and is – lived in working-class communities in the post-industrial towns of the Midlands and the North. Solid industrialised, working-class jobs have vanished and working-class masculine identities are under sustained sociopsychological pressure. And it is here that the narrow economic rationality of the market and political managerialism has finally triumphed over political projects of big ideas, grand ambitions and communal values. Now social problems attendant on industrial decline and the expansion of neoliberal economic and social relations can be – at best – only ameliorated. As far as the geographical and social margins are concerned – Britain's post-industrial black spots and sink estates – there seems to be political consensus that decline is pretty much inevitable and irreversible.

The release of *TwentyFourSeven* shared the same moment as the landslide election victory of New Labour – a movement Margaret Thatcher would claim to be her 'greatest achievement'.[1] A culturally 'Cool Britannia' would be run by a new elite who promised that 'things could only get better', but who artfully de-politicised social problems and managed conflicting values. Many have contended that New Labour marked the end of politics (Dillow 2007; Hay 2007) and with it the death of political heroes or heroic political projects; there was nothing to believe in.

Into this world steps Darcy. Most of the film documents the period between his existence as that 'forgotten thirty-something' and his absolute nadir as disgraced hero, driven into self-imposed exile. In between, Darcy has a dream, something to believe in. If the world and lives of the central protagonists in the drama are marked by a retreat from engagement in political life, they might yet forge something of that 'brotherliness' in building the 101 Boxing Club. For a short while at least, Darcy inspires the (male) youth of the town to believe in his dream.

The characteristic that most perfectly defines the charismatic hero is his/her utopian imagination and demand that others follow him/her by virtue of his/her mission. For Darcy, the purpose of human life is not material advancement – the privatised consumerism of neoliberalism having been implicitly rejected in his earlier monologue – but the realisation of more noble aims. His voiceover tells the audience: 'If you've never had anything to believe in, you're always going to be poor.' There is something of the mystic in Darcy. For him, life is full of wonder: magical. Life is also pregnant with possibilities. In the face of despondency all around him and an evident lack of concrete opportunities for self-advancement, he can still believe that

> This morning is a gift. Every morning you have another chance. How often do you wake and seize that day with your own hands? This morning, my friends, is the morning I remove my life from the hands and strings of fools and try to build a dream.

Like all charismatic heroes, Darcy must first prove himself. Drinking raw eggs and beating the lads at their own game – football – hardly evidences superhuman qualities, but, as Weber understood, charismatic authority is bestowed by disciples: Gods might grace football pitches. Darcy's feats between the goalposts win him kudos among lads in a town where 'librarians don't hold a lot of sway'. Once he has won the lads over, his power rests on his ability to inspire others to believe in and embrace his values, his ability to secure their membership in an extraordinary organisation, characterised by symbols and rituals, discipline and disciplinary training, and through this to achieve a transformation from within. 'This is the space, lads,' Darcy tells the youths: 'As soon as you go through these ropes you must master control.' Boxing does not, however, provide the discipline and training required to succeed in a mere *sport*. In a beautifully choreographed scene in which the youths train in the gym, the action is slowed down to emphasise the creativity and beauty of bodies in action; as in *Raging Bull*, this is boxing as *art*.

As the drama unfolds, the rise and fall of the hero is charted to his charismatic death. As Gerth and Mills (1991: 249–50) state in their reflections on Weber: 'The mission must prove itself in that those who faithfully surrender to him must fare well. If they do not fare well, he is obviously not the master sent by the gods.'

But it is not the crushing defeats in the boxing ring at the hands of their opponents that cause the disciples to lose faith in Darcy – victory was never promised – but the loss of control, of discipline, in the ring that evidences that their transformation was only ever skin deep. The death of the dream is followed immediately by the symbolic death of Darcy as hero as he confronts Tim's father. In a moment of unbridled aggression, Darcy 'loses it': he is lost and all is lost. In betraying the values of discipline and self-control he sought to instil in the lads, his own fate is sealed. This comes at a point in the narrative when the dream of the 101 Boxing Club is effectively over. Significantly, it is here that the use of religious symbolism in the film is evident, in the musical accompaniment to the moment of Darcy's 'fall': the mystical (and funereal) *Parce mihi Domine*. After the symbolic death of the hero and the dream, there follows the symbolic funeral, as the youths torch the 101 Spot rather than see it repurposed as storage space.

It is fitting that in the final scene in the film – Darcy's actual funeral – his long-term legacy is represented not just in the remembrance of him, but in the enduring bonds between the lads who were once part of different warring factions and in lives that have actually been transformed. For the youths – now men – meaning, *something to believe in*, has been found within the private sphere of personal relationships, in family and, for some, children. However, even as the film ends on a note of retreat into the private, the personal/political nexus is evident throughout the film. Darcy's personal tragedy is also a wider tragedy of people, places and times in which dreams are seemingly predestined to end in disappointment or even disaster, in which heroic visions will likely turn to ash. It is as if the dream of the 101 Boxing Club was destined to die 'in the beginning' and be put to the torch.

'This is England. And this is England, and this is England': the shadow of Thatcherism reprised

In contrast to *TwentyFourSeven*, *This is England* explicitly confronts the politics of the era in which it is set. While the drama takes place in the shadow of Thatcherism, the focus is not the mainstream of British political life, but its fringes. By Meadows' own account, it is a semi-autobiographical film. The central protagonist, Shaun Fields, a pseudonym occasionally used by Meadows, plays out the director's childhood experiences. The storyline mirrors Meadows' youthful encounter with and initial admiration for skinheads and skinhead culture. In an interview for *The Guardian*, Meadows recalls:

> A great deal of it is based on my own childhood and I tried to recreate my memoirs of being an 11-year-old kid trying to fit in ... Like most 11-year-old kids who wore jumpers with animals on, I got bullied by the older kids at school. So I looked for my own tribe to join. It was the skinhead movement that enamoured me the most ...

Skins appealed to me because they were like soldiers: they wore their outfits like
suits of armour and demanded respect.

Just as Shaun's initiation into the skinhead gang occurs at a time when
attempts are afoot to appropriate the skinhead movement, and specifically
the predominantly white, male, working-class membership, to the cause of
right-wing political extremism, Meadows has recounted his brushes with
violent and racist factions in the movement. Undoubtedly, part of his intention in making the film was to rescue the reputation of skinhead culture
that had been tarred with the brush of racism and association with the
extreme right in the wider public perception. This association/perception
wholly neglects the varied cultural influences on the movement and the
political diversity of its membership. As Meadows relates in an interview
for *Indie London*:

> My older sister was going out with a skinhead who took me under his wing and
> taught me about the roots of the whole culture. He was a nice bloke who bore no
> relation to the stereotypical racist yob that people now associate with that time. It was
> him that I based the character of Woody on in the film. I learned from him that
> skinheads had grown out of working class English lads working side by side with
> West Indians in factories and shipyards in the late-60s. The black lads would take the
> whites to blues parties where they were exposed to Ska music for the first time. This
> was where the whole skinhead thing came from – it was inherently multicultural. But
> nowadays when I tell people that I used to be a skinhead, they think I'm saying I
> used to be racist. My film shows how right-wing politics started to creep into
> skinhead culture in the 1980s and change people's perception of it.

This is England also affords Meadows the opportunity to put some clear
water between his mature self, a man whose films explore and problematise
the intimate and troubling connections between constructions of (working-
class) masculinities and violence, and Meadows as a boy/youth who had
his own close encounter with the dark side of skinhead culture. For
Meadows' skinheads were defined not by race, but by class. In the same
Indie London interview, Meadows says:

> The Eighties was still a time when the skinheads I hung around with understood
> where they were from. They knew they were second wave skinheads and they knew
> they weren't original 1969 skinheads but they wanted to be true to that. It was always
> a working class thing. There were no middle class skinheads where I came from.
> Everyone thought the working classes were fucked, but we were really proud of
> being working class and were going to wear the equivalent of work-boots, jeans, a
> white shirt and some braces, which we can all afford, and are going to create an image
> of something so powerful. So as a kid I was very drawn to that idea and was made
> to feel very proud of being working class. It was political but it was never extreme,
> one way or the other. Some would be left or right wing – as in terms of Labour or
> Conservative rather than militant or fascist – and the bands were much the same.

The opening montage of *This is England* sets up Shaun's story against the backdrop of the polarisation and confrontational politics that characterised Thatcher's Britain, and so reiterates that 'the Meadows *oeuvre* has from the outset insistently registered the long-term social costs of Thatcherite policies upon peripheral working-class communities' (Fradley 2010: 281). Footage of the violent confrontation between miners (in the 1984–5 strike) and the police graphically signals the crushing of organised labour and the death of consensus politics and foreshadows the unabated destruction of solidarist working-class communities throughout the 1980s. However, rather than setting out to critique Thatcherism per se, Meadows is more interested in the 'fucked' condition of the working class and the effort to restore pride and meaning in a Midlands town very much like the one he grew up in.

The dismantling of the old class-based politics of post-war Britain also marked the emergence of significant new political cleavages, reflecting the diversity of British society, but also exposing deeply rooted divisions. The confrontations between the state and miners were anticipated in the confrontations between the police and marginalised ethnic groups on the streets of Brixton, Toxteth and elsewhere at the beginning of the decade. Skinhead nationalism was not only rooted in a perceived marginality rooted in class, but was also a politically reactionary response to social and cultural change. Nick Knight's *Skinhead* (1982), an exploration of skinhead nationalism that is partly sociological and partly journalistic, describes this sense of marginality and the reaction it fostered:

> They are denied any useful role in the present. So instead they turn to the past, to an idea of what an unspoiled working class community might have looked like. ... The irony is that skins in trying to be 'authentic' have ended up reviving the idea of working class culture which is frozen at precisely the point when a 'real' 'authentic' working class identity was being eaten away from outside. (Knight 1982: 30)

In his review of *This is England*, Jon Savage (2007) notes that Meadows stages the film in 1983, 'the year that *Time* magazine ran a major feature on the country's warring youth, called "The Tribes of Britain."' Meadows has spoken about the same period in similar terms: '[W]e were part of this mental time. It was the most enormous amount of tribes that could have ever existed in one place' (*Indie London* 2006).

Amid the emerging intellectual climate of post-modernism and in an era when, in the words of Pet Shop Boys' Neil Tennant, everything had become a 'phenomenon' (quoted in Bracewell 1998: 212) and more or less anything could be commodified, the appropriation of national symbols in youth culture could be interpreted as merely ironic. Yet, 1980s Britain was not a playful place at ease with an emerging identity as a diverse and multi-cultural society. Beneath this cultural 'land of a thousand stances' (Savage 2007) milieu, the reality was a deeply factionalised society.

Moreover, in Thatcherism, the full-throttle drive to market liberalisation, privatisation and the opening up of the UK economy was combined with an oddly schizoid attitude to questions of nationhood and identity. The Thatcherite wing of the Conservative Party was almost as hostile to one-nation Tories as it was to leftist communitarians. Simultaneously, however, Thatcherite ideology defended British sovereignty at every turn and was articulated in the exclusionary language of 'enemies within' (Milne 1994) and 'one of us' (Young 1993). It was a politics that excluded gays (see section 28 of the 1988 Local Government Act, prohibiting the 'promotion' of homosexuality) and, later, ethnic minorities who failed Norman Tebbit's 'cricket test'. The divisiveness inherent in this curious mixed bag of economic liberalism and political parochialism provided a near-perfect political stage on which charismatic figures might make their entrance in the skinhead movement.

Political disenchantment revisited

Disenchantment is a theme in *This is England*, as it is in *TwentyFourSeven*. The extremist nationalist rhetoric of Combo (Stephen Graham) finds a receptive audience with an assorted bunch of youths and men, all of whom seem to be drifting aimlessly, with no real sense of purpose: nothing to believe in. The appeal of charismatic heroes is similarly evident. In the figures of Woody and Combo, Meadows creates two diametrically opposed heroes who vie for Shaun's affection and allegiance, to the accompaniment of occasional voiceover snippets from Thatcher's most memorable and rhetorical speeches.

Woody represents the open face of skinhead culture: a movement that embraces all regardless of colour, creed and, initially, the width of your flares. However, Combo offers more than comradeship. He provides the vulnerable and impressionable Shaun with a *cause*, and, in the short term at least, this enables him to make sense of his father's death. If Shaun's father has been sacrificed in a 'phoney war' (killed in the Falklands conflict), Shaun can salvage something from his sacrifice in fighting the 'real war' on the streets: the battle for the *England* of *Englishmen* espoused in Combo's firebrand oratory:

> That's what this nation has been built on, proud men. Proud fucking warriors! Two
> thousand years this little tiny fucking island has been raped and pillaged, by people

– two fucking world wars! Men have laid down their lives for this. For this ... and for what? So people can stick their fucking flag in the ground and say, yeah! This is England. And this is England, and this is England.

While very different characters, in the narrative structure of the film, the rise and fall of Combo in *This is England* mirrors that of Darcy in *TwentyFourSeven*. First he wins over his 'troops' in the public admonishment of Woody as a traitor. There then follow the tropes of symbolism, ritual and discipline as his 'band of brothers' are forged into a cohesive entity united by their cause. As with Darcy, it is Combo's loss of control and the eruption of violence that brings about his fall and exile.[2] Unlike Darcy, Combo's departure is not entirely self-imposed, but Combo suffers the same psychological disintegration that preceded Darcy's exile. Shaun alone marks the symbolic death of his erstwhile hero and – along with him – the death of the dream: a mythological vision of England and Englishness. At the boundary of the national body, a desolate seashore, he hurls the St George's Cross (with its associated nationalist connotations) into the sea.

This is England probes the nature and consequences of disenchantment more deeply than *TwentyFourSeven*, not least because it confronts head-on the politics of nationalism and identity as well as the politics of marginality. While ostensibly a secular ideology, nationalism is infused with mysticism and mythology, and while not all forms of nationalism appeal directly to religious belief, ultimately all forms of nationalism arc rooted in beliefs and rituals surrounding sacrifice and, especially, death (Anderson 1983). The religious connotations of Combo's brand of nationalism run deeper than his 'serpent from the Bible' denunciation of Woody or a flag that bears the cross of a medieval saint. Nick Knight saw in skinhead nationalism a close relationship between 'Englishness', nostalgia and hopelessness, which, significantly, he expressed in religious imagery:

> [T]he skinheads often see themselves as victims of almost Biblical proportions – as a stricken race of Jobs, as modern wanderers cast out into a cheerless world. ... As with all myths, there's a kernel of truth in the skinheads' perception of themselves as outcasts. (Knight 1982: 30)

Nationalisms depend on the telling of stories about past, present and future that are as much about forgetting as remembrance. In exploring ambiguities and divisions in skinhead culture, Meadows also probes the ambivalence in constructions of 'Englishness' or, specifically, the tension between social class and constructions of Englishness. Dominant conceptions of Englishness typically evoke an imaginary of a pre-industrial, rural idyll, an arcadia which has been blighted by the brute forces of modernisation and industrialisation. Such constructions evoke an inherently elitist imaginary. *This is England* immortalised in Philip Larkin's mourning for the England of shadows, meadows, lanes, guildhalls and carved choirs, disfigured by the ugly scars of 'concrete and tyres' (cited in Bracewell 1998: 46). *This is England* as 'a province and privilege of the rich', most often 'translated by way of a classical education' (Bracewell 1998: 54). *This is England* in which the working class, the progeny of industrialisation, have no place. Perhaps this is why Meadows can scarcely shoot his subjects in rural settings without including some industrial vestige within the frame: an ugly – or beautiful? – blot on the landscape.

It is telling that as the troops rally to hear Lenny deliver the St Crispin's Day speech, Meadows' visuals paint the environs in decidedly uninspiring colours: a run-down pub, its crumbling facade adorned with ragged flags, skirted by a car park-cum-garden. The tatty corrugated-iron static caravans on the periphery make this English rural idyll look a bit like the office hub of a building site. The incongruity between nationalist rhetoric delivered in the language of Shakespeare and the reality of the lives of those who listen is astutely observed by Pukey, who asks Combo, 'Do you really believe in all that shit?'

Even as war has served as a force for national consolidation in some contexts, war might also be divisive, laying bare existing divisions, belying the notion that sacrifice and death serve to unite the 'national family' through common experiences of mortality, bereavement and sorrow. If social class is an actual or potential thorn in the side of the nationalist ideologue, the linkages between nation and subject can be forged through a particular construction of masculinity and a particular construction of nation.

In *This is England* another central motif of Meadows' films is evident: a preoccupation with violent masculinities and how these identities play out in everyday practices. In this film he takes this preoccupation a stage further in linking masculinity and violence to a nationalist project and state practice: specifically war. Perhaps the most arresting and significant images in the opening montage in *This is England* are those gleaned from news footage of the Falklands war. They are significant not only because these images anticipate Shaun's personal tragedy and loss, but also because Meadows has identified the Falklands conflict as a crucial moment in his own political awakening. In an interview in *Future Movies* (2006), Meadows said:

[I]t was a war handled in the media as if it were a World Cup summer. Like when England go into the World Cup, there are Union Jacks on the papers, and you can look at headlines from the time and it sounded just like that. Ultimately, I was privy to footage from ITN archives – that wasn't shown on television – of the people we were fighting, and it was shameful. It was bullying. It was really horrible. How could we have been proud of winning that? It was the equivalent of putting Mike Tyson in the ring with a 7-year-old kid from an infant school. So that was always running in the back of this film – *the root level of that horrible racism, that bullying and violence that exists in someone can also be inherent in a nation without us knowing it*. (My emphasis)

Meadows invests these same interconnected qualities – racism, bullying, violence and nationalism – in the person of Combo. Unlike Darcy, Combo's authority is ultimately founded not in his vision or his capacity to inspire, but in the underlying sense of menace that pervades his presence. Despite his emotive appeals to the poetry of nation, there is always something visceral about him. It is no accident that Combo's first appearance in the film is foreshadowed by the intimidating entrance of his henchman Banjo.

In documenting Shane's/Shaun's flirtation with nationalist skinhead culture, Meadows is able also to interrogate the confluence of violence, homoerotic male bonding and constructions of masculine identities. The boundaries of Combo's band of brothers are determined as much by gender as by class and race: when Combo marshals his troops, the girls in the gang are left behind. In the relationship between Combo and Shaun, Meadows is further able to dramatise the connections between the personal and political that he observed in the jingoism surrounding the Falklands conflict. In Combo, the bereaved Shaun finds a surrogate father, in Combo's rag-tag band of NF skins, the lonely Shaun finds a family, and in defending the feminised body of a 'raped and pillaged' England, he finds a cause and thereby discovers what it means to be a man: a 'proud fucking warrior'. Skinhead nationalism further consolidates this trilogy by providing a backing track of *Oi* music: music that *Crass* magazine once disparagingly described as 'nasty Nazi music for real men' (cited in Bracewell 1998: 95).

Yet, for all of the effort that goes into the making of nations, states and men, the foundations of these constructions are, if not quite built on sand, always somewhat shaky. The contradictions with which both Combo and Shaun must contend are alone powerful enough to pull apart the edifice. In Savage's review of the film, he ranks it among other 'state-of-the-nation broadsides such as Alan Clarke's *Made in Britain* and Derek Jarman's *The Last of England* referring to the disenchantment of 1980s working class youth in an England that is a "damaged place"' (Savage 2007). Certainly it was a place in which the divisiveness of unchecked market forces, cultural and racial tensions, social fragmentation and political factionalism all hacked away at the wobbly foundations of the national project – so too the national psyche.

As the drama builds in the penultimate scene of *This is England*,

Combo's world – solid and sure on the surface, but frighteningly unstable beneath – gradually unravels and eventually falls apart. Combo lashes out in a fury of brutal aggression. In his discussion of the work of Meadows as a whole, Fradley argues:

> Masculinity in Meadows' films is invariably unsettled and often psychotic. Veering incoherently between paternal *gravitas*, dope-fuelled homoeroticism, violent rage and childlike tears, Combo's (Stephen Graham) behaviour in *This is England* (2006) exemplifies the troubled state of contemporary British manhood in Meadows' output. (Fradley 2012: 64)

This vacillation between paternal concern, violent rage and childlike tears also describes the dark hero Morell (*A Room for Romeo Brass*, 1999) and the equally dark Richard (*Dead Man's Shoes*, 2004), insofar as he acts as both guardian and avenging angel to his brother Anthony. There is more going on in *This is England* than the documentation of troubled or damaged manhood. Immediately after Combo has viciously beaten Milky, Meadows cuts from Combo's disturbingly vacillating sobs of 'I'm sorry, I'm sorry' and 'stop it now, real men don't cry' to footage of both trauma and triumphalism evidenced in the Falklands conflict, the pain and ecstasy in the last gasp of British imperialism. The film concludes appositely with Shaun's solitary sojourn through a rural landscape, again scarred with a few rusty relics of national past industrial glory, as he wanders down to the beach and jettisons the final remnant of the dream – symbolised by the English flag – that is now nothing but dust (Savage 2007).

Conclusion

This is England was an important film in changing critical perceptions of Meadows, bringing him recognition as a director who tackled political themes. However, Meadows' earlier films centre on personal lives and tragedies played out within a broader social context. In *TwentyFourSeven* and *This is England* the personal and the social are, in turn, contextualised within the political conditions of the period. Both films speak to the politics of marginality; both films speak to the politics of disenchantment. Meadows offers close-up observations on lives, people and locales he understands and cares about, while also painting on a larger canvas, linking the personal and political, tapping into the zeitgeist and situating local environs and particular stories within national – and global – contexts.

Notes

1. At a dinner party in 2002, Thatcher was reportedly asked what she believed was her greatest achievement while in political office. Her reply was 'New Labour'. See http://conservativehome.blogs.com/centreright/2008/04/making-history.html (accessed July 2012).
2 The fate of both characters is echoed by that of Morell and Richard, the dark heroes of *A Room for Romeo Brass* (1999) and *Dead Man's Shoes* (2004), both of whom are ultimately undone by psychic trauma that manifests in violence.

References

Anderson, B. (1983), *Imagined Communities*, London: Verso.

Bracewell, M. (1998), *England is Mine: Pop Life in Albion from Wilde to Goldie*, London: Flamingo.

Butler, D. (1995), *British General Elections since 1945*, London: Wiley-Blackwell.

Dillow, C. (2007), *The End of Politics: New Labour and the Folly of Managerialism*, Petersfield: Harriman House Publishing.

Fradley, M. (2010), 'Shane Meadows', in Y. Tasker (ed.), *Fifty Contemporary Film Directors*, London: Routledge.

Fradley, M. (2012), 'Directors: Shane Meadows', in E. Bell and N. Mitchell (eds), *Directory of World Cinema: Britain*, Bristol: Intellect.

Fradley, M. (2013), '*Twenty Four Seven*', in E. Bell and N. Mitchell (eds), *Directory of World Cinema: Britain*, 2nd edn, Bristol: Intellect.

Future Movies (2006), 'This is England': http://www.futuremovies.co.uk/filmmaking.asp?ID=203 (accessed July 2012).

Gerth, H. H. and C. Wright Mills (1991) (eds), *From Max Weber: Essays in Sociology*, Oxford: Oxford University Press.

Godfrey, S. (2013), '"I'm a casualty, but it's cool": 1990s British masculinities and *TwentyFourSeven*', *Journal of British Cinema and Television* (forthcoming).

The Guardian (2007), 'Under my skin': http://www.guardian.co.uk/film/2007/apr/21/culture.features (accessed July 2012).

Hay, C. (2007), *Why We Hate Politics*, Cambridge: Polity Press.

Indie London (2006), 'This Is England – Shane Meadows interview': http://www.indielondon.co.uk/Film-Review/this-is-england-shane-meadows-interview (accessed July 2012).

Knight, N. (1982), *Skinhead*, London: Omnibus Press.

Milne, S. (1994), *The Enemy Within: The Secret War Against the Miners*, London: Verso.

Savage, J. (2007), 'New boots and rants', *Sight & Sound*, 17: 5, 38–42.

Stoker, G. (2006), *Why Politics Matters: Making Democracy Work*, Basingstoke: Palgrave.

Weber, M. (1998 [1948]), 'Science as vocation', in *Essays in Sociology*, London: Routledge.

Young, H. (1993), *One of Us: Life of Margaret Thatcher*, London: Pan.

My thanks to Martin Fradley and Shane Meadows forum (http://shane-meadows.co.uk) members Bill Edwards, Ria Krause and Richard Proctor for their comments on the first draft of this chapter and to Sarah Godfrey and Melanie Williams for further helpful suggestions for revisions.

CHAPTER 6

'Now I'm the monster': Remembering, Repeating and Working Through in *Dead Man's Shoes* and *TwentyFourSeven*

Paul Elliott

We must be prepared to find, therefore, that the patient, yields to the compulsion to repeat, which now replaces the impulsion to remember ...

Sigmund Freud (1914 [2000]: 151)

Freud's essay 'Remembering, repeating and working through' appears remarkably early on in his conception of the compulsion to repeat, an idea that would come to obsess him for the rest of his life and that would find ultimate expression in the latter chapters of *Beyond the Pleasure Principle*. 'Remembering, repeating and working through', as M. Guy Thompson tells us, is arguably the most dense of all his technical papers; in a few short pages it manages to dismiss the technique of hypnosis, assert the importance of transference, explore the relationship between memory and repression *and* suggest ways that encysted trauma can be worked through in analysis – a concept that was to pave the way for the psychoanalytic talking cure itself (Thompson 1995: 192). In some ways, this small paper represents the point of rupture between the hypnotherapy of the late nineteenth century and the psychotherapy of the Freudian era.

At its heart, Freud's paper concerns itself with the relationship between memory and psychological pain, and so too, I would assert, do films like *Dead Man's Shoes* and *TwentyFourSeven*.

For Freud, impossible memory manifests itself in the compulsion to repeat. Unable to recall painful and thus repressed experiences, the patient is doomed to repeat some original trauma in a variety of ways until either it is worked through in analysis or it ceases in death. The Death Drive, the mortido, is nothing more than a simple longing for the stillness beyond this repetition, the place at which our constant need to replay pain stops – the organic turning into the inorganic, as Freud himself stated in one of his last expository works in 1938 (Freud 1938 [1993]: 371–444).

By 1914, Freud had all but abandoned the hypnotic and cathartic methods of his teachers and was concentrating on how transference and psychoanalysis could enable patients to work through their trauma, breaking the cycle of repetition that manifested itself in psychopathological symptoms. 'Remembering, repeating and working through' was a first attempt at articulating this position, but all the elements of his later, more robust technique are present.

Rather than encouraging the patient to remember painful experiences (an act that by now Freud considered unfruitful if not impossible), his new conception of analysis, outlined in this essay, examined the nature of patients' repeated behaviour and exposed their resistance. When this was done, memories were free to flood back, and, as Freud remarks, patients were often surprised at the degree to which they had forgotten their own past. In other words, memory returns of its own accord, when its resistive barriers have been breached by a cessation of the compulsion to repeat. As Freud states:

> We have learnt that the patient repeats instead of remembering, and repeats under the conditions of resistance. We may now ask what it is that he in fact repeats or acts out. The answer is that he repeats everything that has already made its way from the sources of the repressed into his manifest personality – his inhibitions and unserviceable attitudes and his pathological character traits. (Freud 1914 [2000]: 151)

It is here that we find the first inklings of this essay's value as a heuristic tool for films such as *Dead Man's Shoes* and *TwentyFourSeven* – are they not concerned, at their heart, with 'pathological character traits' born out of some forgotten trauma? In both films, do we not find lost centres that continuously escape remembrance? Are they not concerned with the struggle to overcome repetition, obsession? Often centred around fathers, around violence or around abandonment, are these films not about loss, and has that loss not itself been forgotten?

Freud's essay can be seen in terms of its temporal flow, which also makes it ideal for a study of cinematic narrative. Remembering, repeating and working through are steps along the path to, and through, trauma, illness and recovery. They are also developmental stages in psychoanalytic technique from hypnosis, through early Freudian theory to his later practice. This triadic temporal framework also finds a correlative in *Dead Man's Shoes* and *TwentyFourSeven*: both films span three distinct time frames: a distant past, which is symbolised by childhood memory and a longed-for innocence, a more recent past that is often violent and shocking, and a meaningful present that attempts to come to terms with the pain and the anguish of encysted trauma. This structural arrangement, I would contend, is nothing less than remembering, repeating and working through, and the narrative closure of both films closely resembles the stillness after death that Freud suggests is characteristic of the mortido.

However, let us look more closely at this idea in the films themselves. Meadows' work is steeped in a British social realist tradition and therefore not immediately commensurate with a psychoanalytic reading; realist criticism often privileges considerations of form and/or ideology over psychology, especially as it is theorised through the lens of psychoanalysis.[1] However, unlike the classical realist text, neither *Dead Man's Shoes* nor *TwentyFourSeven* strives for representational objectivity or documentary naturalism; both invite viewers into the psychologies of the main characters – *Dead Man's Shoes* through the shared viewing space of Richard's fantasy and *TwentyFourSeven* through Darcy's diary and the film's monochromatic palette. It seems reasonable then that we might extend Meadows' journey into the minds of his two protagonists by employing Freud as a guide for their analysis.

Dead Man's Shoes has been viewed by many as being primarily a revenge film.[2] The fact that it was produced immediately after *Once Upon a Time in the Midlands* (2002) invites comparisons to works such as *Shane* (1953), *The Good, the Bad and the Ugly* (1966) and *The Searchers* (1956); and we can also see reflections of, or references to, *Taxi Driver* (1976), *Death Wish* (1974) and *Dirty Harry* (1971). Such comparisons are borne out by both the director and the text itself: in one scene, for example, set in Sonny's house, we briefly glimpse a poster of *Taxi Driver* on the wall, and some of the menacing sense of Scorsese's classic permeates Meadows' film and his own comments on it.[3]

The generic trope of the avenging angel that haunts cinematic texts from the Western to the Japanese Samurai film seems to fit easily with both the narrative and the visual style of *Dead Man's Shoes*, and the prevalence of blood and violence has often obscured its more poetic intents. The narrative is shot through with absurd humour, and yet, underneath this there is the constant threat of rapid and bloody violence. In *Dead Man's Shoes*, as with many of Meadows' films, the violence is swift, brutal and ugly; he does not glamorise death, and people die alone, scared and in pain. The *Empire* magazine review of *Dead Man's Shoes* that claimed it could 'do for slasher movies what *28 Days Later* did for zombie flicks' further concretised it as being concerned primarily with killing and with murder, rather than with the pain of loss, guilt and mourning.

I would like to suggest here, however, that *Dead Man's Shoes* is more than a revenge flick centred on the figure of some dark avenging angel.

Meadows' narrative choices and shot selection, his twinning of scenes of intense horror and violence with contemplative and sensitive images of mourning and loss, elevates *Dead Man's Shoes* above the average slasher movie to a more universal and psychologically aware text and furthermore one that can stand a more rigorous theoretical exegesis. As I shall demonstrate, this film, along with others in Meadows' catalogue, can be seen to be concerned more with memory and encysted trauma than with killing and revenge; more with remembering, repeating and working through in the Freudian sense than with the simple payment of some masculine debt; more with coming to terms with one's own guilt than with punishing the guilt of others. It is this mixture of violent social realism with a deep sense of psychological insight and mythopoesis that, I would contend, is *the* primary characteristic of Meadows' cinema as a whole.

Remembering …

The opening montage of *Dead Man's Shoes* provides us with the first inkling that the film will deal with the fragile and brittle nature of memory. Comprising around twelve different shots and lasting 4 minutes and 3 seconds of screen time, it contains several key motifs that will be used throughout the rest of the film: the use of different film stocks to signify different timeframes and perspectives, the twinning of music with visuals and the creation of an Edenic visual trope that ties the two brothers together in a kind of revelry of remembrance, as they are surrounded by the green countryside of Derbyshire. Only once in the film will those outside the central relationship between Richard and Anthony invade their private world, an invasion that will inevitably end in bloodshed and death.

These opening scenes between Richard and Anthony are intercut with grainy snatches of Super 8 film, today an accepted signifier for memory, that depict what we assume is the childhood of the two brothers. We see smiling faces, parties, Christmases and a familial closeness depicted through the medium of amateur film. In other words, *Dead Man's Shoes* begins with an act of remembrance; in fact, this will be the first and last time in the film that memory is linked to a happy rather than a traumatic event.

It is significant, I think, that memory here is represented by moving images, albeit amateur and 8mm. As André Bazin suggests in 'The ontology of the photographic image', film is often seen as a form of embalmed time; its indexical nature elides the subjectivity of human intervention and reassures the viewer of an event's inherent truth (Bazin 1967: 9). Even if the veracity of the later black-and-white segments can be challenged (are they memories? Are they projections? Are they imaginings?), the audience is surely asked to accept as fact these grainy images of the brothers' past, being as they are films within a film. These images of Richard and Anthony's childhood only occur against the backdrop of their shared paradise; they are, at once, signifiers for their relationship and traces of some lost innocence. The dialogue between Richard and Anthony throughout the film mirrors the air of nostalgia as they talk of their school days and their childhood:

> Anthony: Do you remember when you came to our school and did that run Richard?
> Richard: I do yeah.
> Anthony: Good day that was, wasn't it?
> Richard: Hmmm.
> Anthony: You was the best … you earned the most money didn't you?
> Richard: 'Bout three hundred quid I think.

Freud termed these 'screen memories', consoling and ameliorating images that shield us from pain and loss. Like Richard, we draw on them to get us through. It is surely no coincidence that such memories fade into the distance as the true horror of Anthony's death is revealed.

Repeating …

The colour film representing happier times is contrasted, of course, with the black and white of the more recent traumatic past. Unlike the opening montage, these scenes cannot be thought of as remembrance, and they are not attached to any discernible diegetic subjectivity; instead they are free-floating, existing not as memory but as an imagined replaying, a repeating if you will, of what is an unfaceable truth for Richard – the torture and death of his brother.

These scenes are not so much flashbacks as glimpses of the Real, an encounter with a psychological wound that refuses to scar over. The black-and-white sections have their own narrative flow, exterior to that of the film itself; they progress gradually towards what can only be thought of as Anthony's sacrifice at the Devil's House. It is noticeable that the figure of Anthony becomes less and less tied to Richard's psychological present (that is, the colour sections of the film) as the repetition becomes more and more intense. This is totally commensurate with Freud's schema, as memory gets replaced and obscured with repeated action and behaviour.

The sacrifice of Anthony is at the heart of the film. It is arguably *the* event that sets the narrative in motion, and we must not forget that in diegetic time Anthony is already dead before the film begins; however, neither Richard nor the audience can fully confront this until its end. Like all trauma, it leaves its trace; like all painful events it resonates powerfully and distinctly in the compulsion to repeat.

So, the memory of the opening montage is translated into the repeated action of murder, as Richard wreaks his revenge on Sonny and his gang. Time after time blood is spilt: first Gypsy John, then Tough, then Sonny, then Soz, then Herbie and finally Richard himself. Six deaths which can be read as one, six deaths which repeat the first, six deaths that would have been more, as Richard himself says, if he were not killed. Rather than revenge, Richard is merely repeating the encysted trauma of what he knows, or what he imagines he knows, has happened to his brother. *Dead Man's Shoes* is structured around this repetition, as we are made witness to Richard's attempt at overcoming the encysted trauma of Anthony's murder. Periods of intense violence are intercut with melodic and poetic passages that can be read as failed attempts to come to terms with a central loss, a failure to mourn.

And working through

However, this is not the end of the film or of the commensurability of Freud's essay. If *Dead Man's Shoes* were a typical revenge movie we might stop here, but it isn't. In the final scene we witness what can only be thought of as Richard working through his own guilt and his own complicity in the murder of his brother. Faced with the last of the killers, Richard articulates what has been kept hidden throughout the narrative – his own embarrassment about, even hatred of, Anthony's disability.

Slavoj Zizek declared that Chaplin's *City Lights* was a film that 'stakes everything on its final scene' (Zizek 2001: 3), and I think we can see some of this in *Dead Man's Shoes*. Richard finds the last of the killers of his brother and takes him to the Devil's House, where, rather than killing him and exacting revenge (à la *Death Wish*), he begs to be killed himself. The dialogue is both simple and powerful:

> Richard: They're all fucking dead. I executed them. And you are the last one ... Now I'm the monster. Was he calling for me? When you were torturing him, was he calling for me?
> Mark: Yeah.
> Richard: Was he screaming my name?
> Mark: Yeah he was.
> (Long pause)
> Richard: He still is.

This statement, 'Now I'm the monster', has of course two meanings: one that points to Richard's position as the killer of Sonny's gang, and one that points to his guilt at the abandonment of his brother. Here he acts as his own psychoanalyst, working through his repressed feelings, abreacting his pain and allowing the memory of his own guilt to come flooding back. Richard *is* the monster but, we understand, has been all along. He is as guilty as the others, as much a part of Sonny's gang as any of them, but this has been lost to him, repressed, only to emerge at the moment of working through. It is this that allows *Dead Man's Shoes* to transcend its generic constraints, this complicity that makes it a film about real human emotions rather than simple revenge.[4] As John Fitzgerald suggests, *Dead Man's Shoes* also tapped into the moral and ethical zeitgeist regarding contemporary British society's guilt over the treatment of vulnerable young people, high-profile cases such as the death of Adam Morrell in 2002 sparking debates not only on retribution and punishment but also on social and collective responsibility.

We have here, then, the three stages of Freud's essay: the failure to remember, the repeating of some painful psychological trauma and, finally, the working through that brings back a flood of images. As Freud says:

> We must be prepared to find, therefore, that the patient, yields to the compulsion to repeat, which now replaces the impulsion to remember ... he repeats all his symptoms in the course of his treatment ... We have only made it clear to ourselves that the patient's state of ill being cannot cease with the beginning of his analysis, and that we must treat his illness not as an event of the past, but as a present-day force. (Freud 1914 [2000]: 151)

This concept would manifest itself in Freud's work over six years later with the notion of the Death Drive: the idea that we all long for a place beyond the repetition that characterises human existence, that death symbolises a return to the sanctity of some lost organic stasis. Richard articulates this in the last scene when he asks Mark to kill him: 'I just want to lie with my brother,' he says. Could we ask for any clearer statement of the desire for inorganic silence?

In the small documentary that accompanies *Dead Man's Shoes*, Shane Meadows talks of his experiences on witnessing needless violence in his adolescence. He talks of his own complicity as he stood back and watched the boyfriend of a Down's syndrome neighbour being beaten by a friend: 'The whole basis of *Dead Man's Shoes*', he says, 'is evicting all that fucking guilt.'

Meadows here articulates, in a few short words, the processes highlighted by Freud. What is remembering, repeating and working through but the eviction of guilt? This insight comes close to Freud's conceptions in his 1914 paper and illuminates the director's personal stake in the psychopathology of his films' characters. Although we must be wary not to reduce a text like *Dead Man's Shoes* to this structural triadic framework, Meadows' statements do suggest that he himself sees his cinema as not so much a master plot as his own attempt to remember, his own compulsion to repeat and, sometimes, his own inability to work through.

'A quilt to hide my loneliness'

I want to suggest, however, that the image of remembering, repeating and working through can illuminate more than this one film. We see it most particularly in an embryonic form in *TwentyFourSeven*, Meadows' first full length feature, released in 1997. It has been suggested that the character of Darcy is a form of prototype for the father figure in Meadows' work, and in this he also serves as a kind of early draft for the triadic pattern of remembering, repeating and working through.[5]

As I have already stated, *TwentyFourSeven* is based around the same temporal structure as *Dead Man's Shoes*: when the film opens we are in the diegetic present, and Darcy, even more than Richard perhaps, is depicted as a man broken by time and circumstance, caught by some trauma or turmoil that keeps him apart from the rest of society. If Richard and Anthony had their Edenic countryside, then Darcy has his abandoned railway carriage; each psychogeographical space is a literal rendering of the otherness that trauma engenders. As the narrative develops we again realise that we are being presented with two more temporal series: a recent traumatic past that is characterised by violence and a distant past that is enshrined in memory.

The 1 on 1 boxing club repeats the triumphs and disasters of the past as we are constantly made aware of the screen memories attached to it. It is an image that suggests both mutual support and confrontation and ironically provides the spatial organisation for both psychotherapy and boxing match – restitution and destruction in equal measure.[6]

That the refounding of the 1 on 1 club is a repetition of some former trauma can be attested to in Darcy's poetic narration:

> When fishing, we sit and watch our floats in still water, bobbing up and down like Rocky. On the surface things seem fine, whilst below the winded maggot folds and dies. Dancing with my Aunty Iris gives me the quilt to hide my loneliness.

These lines, which are at once telling and beautiful, are linked to Darcy's past: the scenes in which he prepares himself to dance with his aunty (shaving, dressing, etc.) are intercut with images from what we can assume is his own childhood. Again Meadows uses the cinematic signifier of grainy amateur film stock to suggest a concrete memory, and again this is resonant of happier times, before the symbolic fall into trauma. This also provides the most distant layer of the triadic temporal span. Like the patient on the psychoanalyst's couch, Darcy recalls his childhood memories, but they are separated from the present by a traumatic scar that refuses to heal.

Of course, what distinguishes *TwentyFourSeven* from *Dead Man's Shoes* is that, in the former, the trauma is never faced, never completely worked through: neither Darcy nor the audience fully realises what its nature is. Whereas Richard is able to understand and articulate his own experience, thus bringing about abreaction, Darcy is left literally dumb to his, not able to speak, offering only his previous thoughts through his diary; his catatonic muteness in the diegetic present is a testament to his failure to undergo the talking cure. It is suggested that Darcy's attack on Tim's father is the repeated action of some forgotten violence, but it is never overtly stated, never completely articulated. The audience is left to draw its own conclusions.

As Freud suggests, the analysand often displays an 'ostrich-like policy' towards their illness, sheltering in screen memories for safety and comfort. As Freud continues:

> Thus it can happen that he does not properly know under what conditions his phobia breaks out or does not listen to the precise working of his obsessional ideas or does not grasp the actual purpose of his obsessional impulse. (Freud 1914 [2000]: 152)

Could this be the quilt that hides Darcy's loneliness, the resistance to break through the screen memories that hides the trauma around which his obsessions are built? As the previous quotation from *Dead Man's Shoes* testifies to, the nostalgic reverie that Richard and Anthony share (the one that is built on the foundation stones of happy memories) is only broken when the former realises his brother is screaming his name. In a kind of textual rendering of Freud, Richard listens to 'the precise working of his obsessional ideas', where Darcy is smothered by a warming quilt that baffles both feeling and sound.

We could view *TwentyFourSeven* then as a form of abortive attempt to work through some of the narrative issues that Meadows would return to in his later work. Coming seven years before *Dead Man's Shoes*, *TwentyFourSeven* (and to a lesser extent *A Room for Romeo Brass*, 1999) possesses some of the same tropes and structures of the later film but displays them in an unformed fashion, as if the director himself were trying to work through the concept of encysted trauma but failing. It is also interesting to note that after *Dead Man's Shoes* Meadows' work becomes concerned with cultural, rather than personal, trauma and transformation: *This is England* (2006) and *Somers Town* (2008) are as much about the difficulty of social trauma (war, migration, economic instability) as personal, and both films display a much lighter, brighter take on reality.[7]

We must be careful here not to make the mistake of reducing the complexity of Meadows' films (much less his career) to the simple equation of a theoretical structure. The commensurability of remembering, repeating and working through to Meadows' work is complicated by a whole raft of different factors, not least the collaborative, anti-auteur nature of his working methods. Of all his films so far only *This is England* was written solely by Meadows, and his working methods constantly make use of improvised and part-improvised dialogue, so any attempt at establishing a masterplot or even a distinct autobiographical thread is made instantly difficult. However, I have attempted in this chapter to suggest ways that Freudian psychoanalysis can be used to uncover some of the discursive patterns in Meadows' cinema in the hope that this redresses some of the balance of earlier opinions of his films, mainly, it has to be said, proliferated in the popular press. Films like *TwentyFourSeven* and *Dead Man's Shoes* are richer, deeper texts than many reviewers have suggested, not simply adhering to the Western, revenge or boxing genre but to a wider cultural tradition of poetic realism where psychosocial tropes and issues are reified on screen.

Both *TwentyFourSeven* and *Dead Man's Shoes* conclude with the stillness of death; Richard's, however, is more of a liberation, as the camera symbolically performs his final ascension over the town that has both created and killed him. Darcy's death is a slow, silent one. It is an old man's death, a demise rather than an ascension. There is nothing of the transcendence of *Dead Man's Shoes*; the final scenes are claustrophobic, close and uncomfortable. Darcy's failure to work through the trauma that leads to his repeated violence (both legitimate and illegitimate) results in a death that is ignominious and drawn out. Although he achieves resolution of sorts, there is no sense of redemption.

For Laura Mulvey, in her essay 'The Death Drive: narrative movement stilled', cinema itself is a form of compulsion to repeat – caught between the two stillnesses of the opening and closing credits, a cinematic narrative works through its own traumas and its own desires, caught on the pulsive force of repetition. Taking her cue from Peter Brooks, for example, she states that

> For cinema, the movement and momentum that carry narrative desire into the space of the story's journey and the elongation of its delay echo its own movement. The

representation of the end as death and quiescence can suggest a return of the repressed stillness on which cinema's illusion depends. (Mulvey 2006: 79)

The stillness at the end of a film like *Dead Man's Shoes* is more, thinks Mulvey, than a diegetic death; it is the death of the repeated narrative that we, as viewers, long for all along. The stopped images at the conclusion of films such as Truffaut's *Les quatre cents coups* (1959) or Mohsen Makhmalbaf's *Nun va Goldoon* (1996) are a form of literal rendering of the desire for diegetic quietude and a halt to what is an otherwise repeated experience for the viewer.

Remembering, repeating and working through then not only occurs in the narrative; it *is* the narrative, as repetition forces the audience onwards, eagerly seeking the point at which it is worked through and thus stilled. Of course, such theory does not lend itself well to films such as *A Room for Romeo Brass* or *This is England*, which do not feature a death at their conclusion. Instead we are left to wonder about the nature of future repetition: will the characters overcome their experiences? How will the story continue? How will they deal with the respective trauma that has been set up in the narrative?[8] The process of viewing a film then can also be seen to be based on the interconnected processes of remembering, repeating and working through. Ultimately some cinema allows us to remember, some to repeat and some to work through, but truly great cinema, like the cinema of Shane Meadows, allows us to do all three.

Notes

1. See, for example, Christopher Williams (1980).
2. See, for example, Fitzgerald (2010: 127), Leggott (2008: 74), Shail (2007: 149).
3. We can compare, for example, Travis Bickle's opening monologue with statements made by Meadows when discussing the motivation behind the story of *Dead Man's Shoes*: 'They're all animals. All animals come out at night: whores, skunk pussies, buggers, queens, fairies, dopers, junkies, sick, venal ... Someday a real rain will come and wash this scum off the streets' (Schrader, 1976). Meadows states: 'I saw these things first hand ... as you get older and you start, you know, to investigate your life because that's the sort of person I am, you start to think, "That person was a scumbag", that guy has done this and this and he's maybe slept with really young girls, you know, like got them off their head, you know like really awful things.'
4. For a discussion of the intersection between mourning and Meadows' visual style, see Fradley (2010).
5. See, for example, the discussion of Darcy as a 'nurturing paternal figure' in Fradley (2010: 282).

6. It is interesting to note that the title of the second chapter of the DVD release of *TwentyFourSeven* ('Past, Present and Future') acknowledges the tripartite nature of the narrative.
7. See, for example, the review of *This is England* by Roxy Wilding (2004: 353–6).
8. The desire to witness the repetitions inherent in the futures of surviving characters is exemplified in the proliferation of the cinematic sequel, *This is England '86* being a case in point.

References

Bazin, A. (1967), *What is Cinema?*, London: University of California Press.

Fitzgerald, J. (2010), *Studying British Cinema: 1999–2009*, Leighton Buzzard: Auteur.

Fradley, M. (2010), 'Shane Meadows', in Yvonne Tasker (ed.), *Fifty Contemporary Film Directors*, London: Routledge.

Freud, S. (1914/2001), 'Remembering, repeating and working through', in *The Standard Edition of the Complete Psychological Works*, trans. James Strachey, London: Penguin.

Leggott, J. (2008), *Contemporary British Cinema: From Heritage to Horror*, London: Wallflower.

Mulvey, L. (2006), *Death 24x a Second: Stillness and the Moving Image*, London: Reaktion Books.

Shail, R. (2007), *British Directors: A Critical Guide*, Carbondale: Southern Illinois University Press.

Wilding, R. (2004), 'This is England', *Attachment: New Directions in Psychotherapy and Relational Psychoanalysis*, 1: 3, 353–6.

Williams, C. (1980), *Realism and the Cinema*, London: Routledge and Kegan Paul.

Žižek, S. (2001), *Enjoy Your Symptom! Jacques Lacan in Hollywood and Out*, London: Routledge.

CHAPTER 7

'An object of indecipherable bastardry – a true monster': Homosociality, Homoeroticism and Generic Hybridity in *Dead Man's Shoes*

Clair Schwarz

Desire [is] … the affective or social force, the glue, even when its manifestation is hostility or hatred or something less emotionally charged that shapes an important relationship.

Eve Kosofsky Sedgwick (1985: 2)

The problems with gangs of men is that thing of leading and egging and creating your own laws as you go along. In its worst form it's like the most disturbing form of abuse. Some of it's homoerotic as well.

Shane Meadows, *The South Bank Show*[1]

Misery has come home, and men appear to me as monsters thirsting for each other's blood.

Mary Shelley, *Frankenstein* (1818: 89)

Birth of a monster: the gestation of *Dead Man's Shoes*

Following his creative disappointment with the Film 4-funded Western pastiche *Once Upon a Time in the Midlands*, Shane Meadows' subsequent film, *Dead Man's Shoes*, saw a return to a smaller budget, complete directorial control over the final edit and a positive director–producer relationship with Mark Herbert of Warp Films. Co-written with lead actor Paddy Considine, *Dead Man's Shoes* can be seen as a creative reaction against the filmmaker's negative experience with *Midlands*, an attempt to creatively 'erase' the aberrant film. Meadows clearly alludes to this motivation during his talk at the Brief Encounters Film Festival held in Bristol in November 2004:

> I think *Dead Man's Shoes* is what *Once Upon a Time in the Midlands* was meant to be. If you look at the very, very barebones of the story, it's the story of a stranger that comes back to town to confront a situation … I almost push that film (*Midlands*) out of what I think of the films I've made and put *Dead Man's Shoes* in its place as a kind of my first feature.[2]

However, while both films share a keen acuity to the codes and conventions of genre (*Midlands* adopting the conceit of a Western and *Dead Man's Shoes* that of a revenge-thriller), the above quote suggests that – for the director – the latter film is the superior twin of the earlier 'disappointing child', and thus meets the expectations of what Meadows meant the 'elder sibling' to be. This contextual notion of expectation, disappointment and the quest for atonement resonates within the very narrative of *Dead Man's Shoes*, which explores troubled fraternal and quasi-paternal relationships. Moreover, Meadows' concise explanation of the film's plot given above hints that its simple premise is drawn from a long-standing cultural tradition: that of the returning avenger.

The cinematic binary of sex and violence is channelled through this figure of vengeance, both by precipitating the vengeful quest and, more importantly for the purposes of this essay, as a continuous thematic twin. In this essay, I argue that the eroticised violence of the vengeance narrative in *Dead Man's Shoes* is shaped by the homosocial, creating a particular homoeroticism that allows fantasies of physical contact between men to be played out. Meadows knowingly employs the generic codes and themes of the vengeance narrative, underscoring them with other recognisable generic indicators (such as the Western or the horror film), creating a hybrid which supports such eroticised homosociality. This range of generic heredity, aligned with the monstrousness expressed through the violent subject and the problematic excesses of male violence, is perfectly captured in the phrase which forms the title of this essay.[3] Looming over the small town which makes up the primary diegesis of *Dead Man's Shoes*, Riber Castle is a visual metaphor for a range of male follies: the actual folly of Riber Castle, the folly of its architect, and metaphorically the follies of the characters in the film. The looming presence of the castle accents the gothic ambience of the film, portentously heralding a future tragedy. Indeed, *Dead Man's Shoes* itself – with its amalgam of generic conventions – can be read as a monstrous hybrid of cannibalised material gathered from textual 'corpses'. This chapter will explore how such generic hybridity is presented in a distinctly Meadowsian way, and how it furthers the key thematic preoccupation of Meadows' work: the homosocial relationships between men.

The pink(ish) triangle: the geometry of homosocial desire

The vengeance tradition engages with the notion of *lex talionis*: the desire to rewrite wrongs, to regain power. However, desire here is not limited to a single form. The psychological drive for justice and for physical and social supremacy in this tradition is often accompanied by a distinct strain of erotic desire. This is most readily presented through the form of the erotic triangle, wherein a fraught network of triangulated desire is formed by two male characters and one female. In *Between Men: English Literature and Male Homosocial Desire*, Eve Kosofsky Sedgwick identifies such a dynamic in a range of literary texts, with greatest attention given to the mid-eighteenth- to mid-nineteenth-century novel. Here, Sedgwick describes the erotic triangle as a mode formulated as an economy of exchange where 'the ultimate function of women is to be conduits of homosocial desire between men' (1985: 99). While the female character may seemingly be the one over which the two male rivals compete, it is the struggle between the men which is most erotically charged, creating and sustaining a conduit of homosocial desire. Utilising this trigonal model, this essay examines the representation of homosocial desire in *Dead Man's Shoes* with broader reference to Meadows' oeuvre.

Shane Meadows' feature films are primarily concerned with homosocial relationships. Women are generally marginalised, their stories largely serving as supporting functionaries to the central male figures and the development of male-to-male relationships.[4] This is made clear in the episode of *The South Bank Show* dedicated to Meadows and quoted at the outset of this essay. Here, the filmmaker states his understanding of the likely trajectory of an all-male milieu, where an absent or marginal female presence often results in a competitive escalation of masculine traits which border on the homoerotic. Visually accompanying Meadows' oratory is a scene from *Dead Man's Shoes*, indicated as a flashback through its monochrome cinematography and book-ended with close-ups of Sonny indicating him as originator of the memory. Here, Sonny orders Anthony to fellate him, punching the boy when he refuses. Meadows poses the question of whether Sonny actually wishes the act to be consummated, but this question is revealed as redundant as the remainder of the scene illustrates Anthony's 'rape' by proxy, where Patti is used as a vessel for Anthony's sexual initiation. Patti does not desire Anthony, nor Anthony her; it is Sonny's desire for Anthony, both sexually *and* sadistically motivated, which orchestrates and controls the action. Patti thus forms the apex of the triangulated desire described by Sedgwick, becoming a conduit through which Sonny expresses his sublimated desire for Anthony. Indeed, the positioning of Patti as a transferable commodity within Sonny's gang is underscored in shots of her sitting on Big Al's lap before being reluctantly coerced by Sonny into 'servicing' Anthony. Anthony's sexual initiation is subsequently witnessed by the other men in the gang, who voyeuristically celebrate his

attainment of manhood – an achievement an initially reluctant Anthony
eventually shares in rejoicing. Patti flees the bed humiliated, but uncom-
plaining and silent. Her quiet acquiescence to Sonny's commands is shown
to continue into the present day, when she is warned by Sonny and Big Al
not to speak to Richard about the physical violation of Anthony. Thus,
despite being the physical means through which Anthony is first
humiliated, then raised up by the men of the group, Patti is denied any
voice, remaining mute within the controlling male agencies.

Moreover, there are numerous examples of women being exchanged as
commodities in Meadows' work. In *A Room for Romeo Brass*, pornography
is circulated in a homosocial continuum from father to son and, eventually,
to fraternal accomplice. Indeed, Romeo explicitly professes ownership by
declaring the crumpled pages '*my* girls'. Similarly, the relationship between
Romeo and Morell is predicated on the latter's possessive sexual desire for
Romeo's older sister, Ladine. McClure again plays the object of (unwanted)
desire in *This is England*, where pornography forms part of Combo's
interior decoration, alongside Nazi insignia. *Somers Town* revisits this idea,
mapping Marek and Tomo's incipient sexual desire through mediated –
and thus easily controlled – images of Maria in Marek's fetishistically
cherished photographs. In the virtually all-male world of *Dead Man's Shoes*
women can be so absent as to not even warrant an image. In one telling
scene, Herbie refers to a commonly known local girl, '*that Jane*',
enthusiastically describing what he would like to do to her sexually. This
description is less about an articulation of heterosexual desire per se than
it is a means to initiate a conversation with the other men, cementing the
bonds of homosociality through a common object of knowledge with whom
they can all share. Later, the visual is added to the oral/aural description
of a female sexual object when a pornographic magazine serves as a locus
of comic exchanges between Soz and Tuff. This 'dirty mag' later joins Soz,
Sonny and Herbie in the bathroom during their drug-spiked triptych of
defecation, ablution and contemplation. Here then women – or rather,
images of women – do not represent a site of erotic contemplation as much
as they serve as a means of masculine *communitas* and as a means to camou-
flage any disavowed homoeroticism.

Mano-a-mano: male rape and the feminised subject

The ideological positioning of Patti as the third corner of the erotic
triangle, suspended between Sonny and Anthony, is, however, a minor one:
the major dynamic of the film is the triangulated relationship between

Sonny, Anthony and Richard. Anthony is the ostensible object of desire, as indicated through Sonny's sexualised desire for control and Richard's thirst to avenge Anthony's death. Here, the desires are generically mated, as the vengeance narrative is often explored through a plot line which includes the subject of rape, often acting as the precipitating event which triggers a vengeful quest. Commonly represented as male-on-female rape, the traumatic event may be avenged by a paternal figure – as in *Death Wish* (1974) – or by the rape victims themselves, most clearly exhibited in the rape-revenge cycle of the 1970s and '80s (Read 2000).

Male-on-male rape, while relatively rare, is most often found in texts which concern exclusively male spaces/places, as in prison dramas such as *Scum* (1977; 1979) and *The Shawshank Redemption* (1994) or male-bonding adventures in the vein of *Deliverance* (1972). Here the rape victim is often marked as a culturally feminised 'other', physically or emotionally depicted as 'less masculine' than their companions. While the Alpha Males may be desired, within the gendered economy of these films it is a structural necessity that they remain (sexually) untouched. Both physically and metaphorically, no one 'fucks or fucks with' Lewis (Burt Reynolds) in *Deliverance* or Frank Morris (Clint Eastwood) in *Escape from Alcatraz* (1979). Conversely, the delicate sensitivity of Andy Dufresne (Tim Robbins) or the obesity of Bobby (Ned Beatty) is transmuted into an 'acceptable' penetrability cemented by their Beta male status.[5] Similarly then Anthony's learning difficulties and concomitant naivety in *Dead Man's Shoes* all serve to place the victim in a decidedly disadvantaged place.

One noticeable exception to this is Quentin Tarantino's *Pulp Fiction* (1994), which features the rape (and potential rape) of hyper-masculine crime boss Marsellus Wallace (Ving Rhames) and grizzled boxer Butch Coolidge (Bruce Willis). Meadows' own intertextual nods to *Pulp Fiction* and *Reservoir Dogs* (1992) – from the bungled heist of *Where's the Money Ronnie!* through to the sartorial cool of *This is England* – reiterate a shared concern with male-to-male relationships and the competitive homoerotic tensions involved. As Sharon Willis (1997) has argued, the aggressive homoeroticism of the Tarantinian worldview is predicated on a thematic preoccupation with *anality*. Tarantino's gleeful rendering of Marsellus' sexually sadistic vengeance ('I'll get a couple of hard pipe-fitting niggers to go to work on Mr Rapist here with a blow torch and pliers') continues in the homoerotic tenor of *Dead Man's Shoes*, not least in the murder of Gypsy John, who – like *Pulp Fiction*'s Vincent Vega (John Travolta) – meets a bloody end on the toilet, his trousers crumpled suggestively around his ankles.[6]

The maze and the Minotaur: monstrosity and spatial invasion

The physical and emotional invasion of the body through the act of rape is echoed in *Dead Man's Shoes* through the entrance of Richard into the hierarchical arrangement of 'Sonny's world', where the long-standing economic, physical and emotional relationships of the men are disturbed by the activities of an intrusive male force. Action is split in the film between the realist/material and the supernatural/metaphorical, yet it is consistently embodied through the character of Richard, who controls and drives the narrative. However, the precipitating events which led to Richard's return are controlled by his doppelganger, Sonny. The film can thus be understood as a contemporary rendering of Sedgwick's 'paranoid gothic' where the 'male hero is in a close, usually murderous relationship with another male figure' (2002: 172). The adoption of parts of the avengee's personality by the avenger is central to understanding the gender dynamic of *Dead Man's Shoes*. Indeed, the film develops a clear dialectic between Richard and Sonny, with aspects of each character mirroring or oscillating with areas of contrast between the two men. John Kerrigan (1996) recognises this marriage between triangulated desire and structures of mirroring and opposition as key to revenge tragedy, wherein fraternal rivalry manifests itself as 'a psychodrama of likeness and difference' (250).

Thus, the likenesses and differences between Richard and Sonny are predicated on a mobile oedipal positioning. As Martin Fradley and Sean Kingston argue elsewhere in this volume, fraught father–son relationships are thematically central to Meadows' oeuvre. In *Dead Man's Shoes*, Sonny is positioned as the paternal head of a highly dysfunctional family, yet Richard is the original father who returns to reassert his supremacy over the upstart Son(ny). In turn, Anthony is the fraternal/son spectre enthralled by the myth of the phallus as embodied by his brother/father. It is only at the end of *Dead Man's Shoes* that Richard's largely unspoken introspection seems to suggest a moral awakening akin to a Shakespearean soliloquy. The alignment of *Dead Man's Shoes* with traditions of vengeance theatre is extended to the theatrical effects of the *Grand Guignol*. However, rather than an acceleration of gore, there is a decrease in the amount of blood on show, from the blood-saturated framing of Gypsy John's murder to the almost hygienic bloodlessness of the plastic bag utilised to dispatch Sonny.

Dead Man's Shoes continues in the fertile cinematic tradition of the revenge narrative, often based within the Western or the crime/gangster thriller, referencing such films as *The Searchers* (1956), *Point Blank* (1967),

Death Wish, Eastwood's *High Plains Drifter* (1973) and *Pale Rider* (1985) and, most closely, Mike Hodges' *Get Carter* (1971). In his extensive 2003 study of *Get Carter*, Steve Chibnall discusses the film's generic cross-fertilisation. 'In this "north-eastern"', he argues, 'the familiar iconography of the western genre is knowingly adapted to give Newcastle a frontier quality.' Chibnall warns against a monotheist identification with its generic roots, arguing that 'to think of the terraces and back alleys of Tyneside as merely substitutes for the mean streets of Los Angeles or Dodge city, however, is to ignore the fact that the generic roots of *Get Carter* run deep into European soil', whether the tragedies of ancient Greece or Jacobean revenge theatre (7). Similarly, James J. Clauss (1999) deconstructs the mythic elements of *The Searchers*, detailing the alignment to Greek tragedy and, in particular, the structuring form of *katabasis*, or 'descent' (into hell). Not only does *Dead Man's Shoes* share this revenge theme, but the descent motif is continued in Meadows' film with Sonny as a figurative Hades, a god of the underworld. Sonny rules the 'underworld' realm of the small-time criminal, his club substituting for the subterranean environs of hell, and indeed, the underworld analogy can be extended to the under*class*. Moving among the depths of the lower (social and moral) strata, Richard's travels into this arena thus mark a moral descent, a downwards movement from his elevated position as a decorated soldier into that of a vengeful murderer. However, as the end of the film suggests, this journey is less about the *creation* of a monster than it is about the *unveiling* of one: the revelation of Richard's monstrous desire to be rid of his brother's dependency.

This suturing of the vengeance narrative with the horror film is facilitated through the figuring of Richard as a monster. This is manifested physically through his adoption of a military-issue gas mask, a residual signifier of his previous existence as a SAS soldier made strange in the civilian world. Its peculiarity outside a legitimate military situation symbolically underscores that, for Richard, this *is* a combat situation. The function of the mask here is not protective but *uncanny*. Indeed, the mask makes Richard strange and frightening; it unsettles those he seeks and manipulates their responses to him. It is more than a mere covering of his face to avoid recognition; it is an evocation of the Freudian uncanny through its very particular form and altered function. Indeed, Freud's classification of the uncanny as a *return* is constituted through Richard's physical and emotional return to his home town, the place of his brother's death. But, of course, the mask does not function as a disguise at all, inasmuch as Richard is known to his victims. Rather the mask can be read as a physical representation of that which Richard seeks to keep hidden. In her 2002 discussion of Henry James' short story 'The Beast in the Jungle' (1899), Sedgwick discusses the trope of the 'closeted person', wherein the closet does not function as the hiding place of the man, but of a secret – in this case, the homosexuality of James' character John Marcher. James' evocation of the metaphorical mask resonates with Meadows' use of a physical one:

> What it had come to was that he wore a mask painted with the social simper, out of the eye holes of which there looked eyes of an expression not in the least matching the other features. (Quoted in Sedgwick 2002: 167)

In this sense, Richard is a closeted man. Whether that closeting refers to his sexuality or other parts of his personality is equivocal. We do not know Richard in any real sense, just as his brother did not know him, and until his *anagnorisis* and the belated recognition of his own monstrousness, Richard barely seems to know himself.

Thematic distillation is achieved through *Dead Man's Shoes*' fusion of a number of classical narrative tropes and mythic allusions. Stephen Daniels and Simon Ryecroft (1993) have examined the way in which Alan Sillitoe describes the East Midlands city of Nottingham as *labyrinthine*.[7] While *Dead Man's Shoes* is not set in Nottingham, but in the smaller Derbyshire town of Matlock, the common link to labyrinthine worlds cannot be missed. These meandering country lanes, estate streets, stairwells and outbuildings create a labyrinthine world through which Richard moves easily and swiftly. His seemingly easy transition from one space to another through physical means – Richard, unlike Sonny, walks everywhere – and his ability to be in the right place at the right time, unseen and unheard by those he is chasing, indicates abilities which border on the supernatural.[8]

In addition to the resonant trope of the mask, *Dead Man's Shoes* utilises less materialist devices to represent unstable identities. While Anthony's presence can be explained in psychological terms as the projection of Richard's melancholy imagination (a reading which would adhere to the dictates of realism), nothing in the text prevents him being understood as a supernatural figure. Moreover, *Dead Man's Shoes* very carefully keeps Anthony 'hidden' from anyone other than Richard, in turn becoming the memento mori of Jacobean theatre, the ghost who reminds Richard of the wrongs he needs to set right. However, we never know Anthony's true experience, or indeed Anthony himself; he is only presented through others, via their projective imaginings or subjective remembrances. Anthony is a spectral presence who stalks the text as a mere simulacra, created by and mediated through others. He becomes the perfect victim: a phantom both weak and trusting, eager to please and in awe of those who would exploit those traits. Thus, Anthony is feminised and made as marginal as the other female figures of the text, including the almost invisible spectre of his own mother, viewed as a distant figure at Anthony's graveside during a flashback to his funeral.

This theme of escape and concomitant guilt over the flight from one's origins is common to the revenge narrative. Chibnall writes, 'when the prodigal sons return, their drive to avenge the damage done to their families may be read as an attempt to assuage the guilt they suffer as deserters of the communities that nurtured them' (2003: 9–10). Aligned to these feelings of guilt is the *thanatos* drive, the psychic desire for one's own demise. To this end, Richard and Sonny are both twinned and opposed in the film. Richard had 'escaped' the claustrophobia of Anthony's cloying devotion and, concomitantly, his small-town existence for a life beyond. His army life would have been one of discipline and hierarchy, seemingly different to Sonny, who stayed behind to control his underclass 'soldiers'. However, while Sonny only commands, whether ordering Patty to have sex with Anthony or telling Big Al to persuade Richard to leave, Richard *does*; he is the man of action. However, there is a reversal in the action dynamic where Sonny achieves that which Richard secretly desires, namely the punishment and death of Anthony. One flashback sequence, portrayed from Sonny's perspective, shows him taunting Anthony with the statement 'my brother Anthony's a fucking retard and that's why I'm leaving for the army'. This imagined taunt is supported at the film's denouement when Richard utters an almost identical statement to Mark. Sonny then is unwittingly the agent of Richard's hidden desire, the removal of the embarrassment of a disabled brother, a desire which Richard has to address through the annihilation of his double and, ultimately, himself.

A dagger of the mind: phallic blades and redemptive fallacy

The tendency for vengeance texts to be resolved via the motif of redemption is rendered problematic in *Dead Man's Shoes*. The beginning of the film introduces a teleological framework through the pre-title voiceover from Richard: 'God will forgive them. He'll forgive them and allow them into heaven. I can't live with that', a proclamation which boldly displays the film's place within the revenge narrative tradition. Religious rhetoric overlays the human drive for *lex talionis*, overriding the 'rule' of the symbolic father. From the very beginning then, Richard is shown as appropriating the word of law, pointing the moral compass and creating the axis

of action. However, such a pronouncement suggests hubris, thus fore-
shadowing his eventual punishment for his mortal transgressions.
Moreover, this bleakly impassioned voiceover complicates the secularist
position of social realist cinema, aligning both the narrator and *Dead Man's
Shoes* with the metaphysical, allowing space for an allegorical or mythic
reading of narrative events.

Despite Richard's righteous moral intent, *Dead Man's Shoes'* denouement
is profoundly ambiguous. In the film's final scene we have the final trigonal
arrangement, formed between Richard, Mark and the knife. If the final
exchange between the men is considered mindful of Richard's will to
power, his adoption of the voice and power of God, then a non-redemptive
reading can be ascertained:

> Richard: Take this from me.
> Mark: No, I don't want to.
> Richard: You. You were supposed to be a monster. Now I'm a fucking beast. Now
>   there's blood on my hands. Look what you made me do.
> Mark: I've got kids. I've got children.
> Richard: I just want to lie with my brother. I want you to help me. Stick it in me
>   [Mark shakes head]. It's OK, yes, *yes.*

Richard's speech recognises his own monstrosity, but it does not release
Mark from his culpability in Anthony's death. Indeed, his imploring Mark
to 'help him' sutures Mark into the cycle of violence, leaving him – literally
– with blood on his hands.

This becomes clearer when the scene is compared to the alternative
ending included on the *Dead Man's Shoes* DVD release. Here, Richard
taunts, rather than cajoles, Mark into killing him, threatening to kill Mark's
wife and children if he does not. In this scene, the struggle is between the
avenging man (Richard) and another (Mark) who precipitates the need for
vengeance by preventing the offence from occurring by committing another
one: the murder of Richard. However, this murder may be justified as a
defensive one, where a father acts to protect his family. Here, Mark's participation is active, with the blood on his hands a visible sign of his protective
paternalism. The theatrical cut does not allow Mark an active role, even
though he holds the knife. Richard speaks to him in soft, imploring tones,
urging him to '*stick it in*' while they embrace in a confused intimacy.
Richard does not 'release' Mark, a man whose crime was that he *passively*
failed to intervene in Anthony's demise; rather, he turns his inaction into
a continuation of guilt, infecting him with his own. Richard's emotional
release comes at the cost of Mark's taking up of the burden, his name
knowingly signalling his fate. The superficial veneer of redemption is thus

revealed as yet another myth in a text saturated with allegory. The 'flight of the soul' which the camera takes in the film's sustained final shot is merely a fantastical wish, an empty promise of release from the horrors of a continuing cycle of violence and guilt in the material world below.

All the world's a stage: *Dead Man's Shoes* and social realism

The revenge narrative usually concerns the assertion of a personal retributive justice in response to the failure of legal means, either through incompetence, complacency or corruption. However, a striking element of *Dead Man's Shoes* is the very absence of any regulatory authority – or, indeed, of any real community – outside the limited milieu of Sonny and his gang. Indeed, much of the film's sparsely populated *mise-en-scène* resembles the post-social desolation and economic impoverishment of the Western 'ghost town'.[9] The absence of any tangible social framework is palpable, whether Anthony and Richard's extended family or simply the intervention of the welfare state. These omissions are lamented in a review by Geoffrey Macnab (2004):

> Though *Dead Man's Shoes* purports to explore 'the underbelly of contemporary rural Britain,' Meadows isn't really interested in exploring the reality of life in a provincial town. He portrays a world in which half-a-dozen people in a small-knit community can be killed without the neighbours raising the alarm or the police intervening.

However, this critique imposes a rigid framework of social realism which the film does not support; its kinship with Jacobean theatre and myth allow such an economic use of social context. Indeed, Meadows' employment of the gothic mode underlines the brutal truism that despite the full social construct of contemporary civilised society, people are in reality murdered, raped or abused on a daily basis, despite the presence of neighbours and a range of civil authorities. *Dead Man's Shoes* thus employs myth and allegory rather than a straightforwardly materialist exploration of the sociopolitical realities of contemporary Britain. The logic of the film deviates from the project of social realism, working instead on the basis of individual agency with an overlay of mystical allegory.[10]

Where *Dead Man's Shoes* does engage more directly with social factors is in its attentive depiction of the trade in illicit drugs and their commodity value, a cultural phenomenon illustrative of the neoliberal logics of a free-market economy. However, Sonny is still a relative success by the standards of the area, exercising power and authority. There is a hierarchical arrangement of 'staff', a capitalist preoccupation with the loss of profit when the 'gear' is stolen by Richard, and a demonstration of the means of distribution to their customers. Here Meadows makes a statement about the milieu of a small working-class town, isolated by topography and governed by local 'ways' based on word-of-mouth reputation. However, the economy with which the film is cast, the seeming lack of extended social context, combined with the hierarchical structure of Sonny's gang, can be explained more plausibly if it is considered as a contemporary example of the main site of revenge theatre: the Jacobean court. The sociopolitical mores of the mid-seventeenth century are shrewdly transposed to a twenty-first-century East Midlands town, with Meadows employing an historical conceit within a contemporary context by suturing together the old and new around the revenge motif.

This motif is most often predicated on retribution for wrongs against family members, and for the majority of its screen time *Dead Man's Shoes* focuses on Sonny's dysfunctional 'family'. The only other family unit we see in the film – Mark's domestic life with his wife and two young sons – functions as a mirror to Sonny's licentious collective. The doubling is thus thematically underscored: both units depend on the repression of history – and concomitant guilt – in order to sustain themselves. *Dead Man's Shoes* is thus illustrative of Meadows' attention to the day-to-day interaction of homosocial groupings in order to question the validity of their phallocentricity. Through their representation of groups of menfolk, Meadows' films repeatedly question the positive aspects of homosociality beyond a certain life stage. Moreover, the position of the nuclear family is shown to be the prime model for positive social ordering. However, families are rarely seen as uncomplicatedly 'happy' or as functioning effectively.

For example, the relationship between Jumbo and Ruby in *Small Time* is shown to be fractured, stagnant and abusive. In true Meadowsian fashion, Jumbo enjoys an extended youth, preferring to spend his time in a juvenile homosocial limbo, while Ruby finds the reliability of her vibrator a more than adequate substitute for her partner. Inevitably, Jumbo ends the film in prison with his dissolute compadres. This overtly dysfunctional couple are contrasted with the more developed familial relationship between Malc and Kate, who, with their young child, attain a renewed togetherness by fleeing the social and personal confines of Sneinton. However, the suggestion of the inescapable homosocial triangle is continued through the character of 'Mad Terry', who accompanies them. Elsewhere, *A Room for Romeo Brass* eschews the solution of 'escape', utilising instead the device of the eternal threat (Morell) to reunite the Brass and Woolley families, although the childhood fantasy of magical performance/resolution at the film's end alludes to the possible temporariness of domestic harmony (Godfrey 2010: 290). A denouement of familial reconciliation also marks *TwentyFourSeven*, but the violence which precipitated it arguably marks this too as a fragile truce rather than a thing of permanence.

Dead Man's Shoes appears to promise the traditional family unit as a means of escape from the negative effects of the 'bachelor bands' which breed violence and misogyny.[11] In this sense, Meadows' work appears conservative, critiquing the very object of its fascination, working-class masculinity, proffering a return to family as the only route to a (compromised) escape from the destructiveness of male-only groups. However, the presentation of the family as a positive alternative is complicated through the trope of cyclical behaviour being passed on and through the family dynamic. Richard's method of self-destruction morally implicates Mark, continuing the themes of violence and guilt. Moreover, the meeting between Richard and Mark's sons imbricates the new generation of young males into the destructive force of vengeful masculinity, literally handing over the tools of murder through the gifting of the knife and mask. The family then is posed paradoxically as solution *and* problem, both a route of escape and a closed loop of continued violence.[12] It is clear that homoerotic desire is the unspoken spectre which haunts Meadows' homosocial milieu. Moreover, the persistent homophobia endemic in all areas of social interaction is especially concentrated within the particular insularities of some working-class male cultures. Like a crucible, the poverty of experiences available causes a concentration, a boiling down of the competitive essences of masculinity into explosive violence. Within this hothouse atmosphere, Meadows' work suggests that not only is this form of homosociality destructive for the women who circle the periphery, but ultimately through its degeneration into homoerotophobic violence, it destroys the very bonds of male friendship it professes to form.

'When you die it ain't the end, it ain't the end when you die ...'

Meadows' use of the equivocal, the deliberate precariousness of the endings which resist easy resolution, are the key way in which his use of genre is ultimately abandoned or problematised. Endings are not resolved happily or cleanly, as my reading of *Dead Man's Shoes* demonstrates. Indeed, for a director whose *oeuvre* is marked by a playful approach to genre, this film excels as an example of a generically hybrid text. Meadows describes his approach as a 'bastardization of different genres' and explains that his difficulty with *Once Upon a Time in the Midlands* stemmed from adhering too much to a specific genre, of 'setting out to make a western', whereas *Dead Man's Shoes* 'has kind of got horror in it, and it's got super-natural things in it, it's got western and there's also the social comedy that's in my [his] other films'.[13] For Meadows, partial appropriation rather than holistic adoption of generic codes and conventions allows for a creative space, room to move in terms of improvisation of the film's narrative, whether through script changes, input from actors or reshaping in the editing suite. His magpie-like approach in *Dead Man's Shoes* can thus be likened to the eclectic architectural style of Riber Castle itself, which prompted one contemporary commentator to profess it 'an object of indecipherable bastardry, *a true monster*'.

Dead Man's Shoes may not necessarily be 'indecipherable', but there are certainly many curious ambiguities and omissions in the film which render it haunting and inscrutable. The deliberate lack of narrative transparency and refusal to subscribe to strict realist conventions raise endless questions which linger long after the credit sequence. Assuredly, however, it is Meadows' bastardised mix of genres, his powerful employment of generic hybridity and suturing together of intertextual references – resembling the monstrous stitches of Mary Shelley's surgeon – which have ultimately produced such a resonant contemporary slice of British rural horror. Like the fictive doctor who sought to make redundant the female presence in order to unitarily produce a progeny, only to reject it once materially realised, Meadows similarly marginalises the feminine in his creation. Here, as in Shelley's gothic ur-text, the progeny born from male desire brings only devastation and death. That such destruction is shown to be perpetually renewed is, in the end, the true monster.

Notes

1. *The South Bank Show: Shane Meadows* (ITV1, first broadcast 29 April 2007).
2. Brief Encounters Film Festival; event transcript (2004) available at www.shanemeadows.co.uk (accessed 1 August 2009).
3. Quotation about Riber Castle (constructed in 1862) attributed to the poet Sir John Summerson, who stated: 'Had Smedley [who commissioned the building] employed a professional he would have got a house unmistakably, however crudely, shaped with style – Italian Gothic or baronial. As it was, he produced an object of indecipherable bastardry – a true monster.' See King (2005).
4. As several contributors to this collection also note, Vicky McClure's award-

winning performance in *This is England '86* arguably signals a deliberate shift in Meadows' formerly homosocial worldview.

5. My thanks here to Martin Fradley for his suggestion of *The Shawshank Redemption* and his assessment of Robbins' character.

6. While there is not space here to discuss the auteurist credentials of Meadows, it is important to note the similarities (and dissimilarities, such as Meadows' 'anti-cool' stance, which stands in contrast to Tarantino's hyper-cool) between the two filmmakers and, by extension, key examples of homosociality, such as the absent female sexual object, with the subjects of the smutty joke (Madonna, Pam Grier and Elois in *Pulp Fiction*) functioning in the same way as 'that Jane', and the sharing of pornographic material between groups of men.

7. Sillitoe's representation of Nottingham was informed by the work of writers such as Victor Hugo and Daniel Defoe, whose stories of vengeance utilised the spaces and places of their locations to create maze-like topographies, which supported and informed the spiralling plotlines.

8. This particular dynamic evokes the dream logic of John Boorman's *Point Blank*, whose protagonist, the knowingly named 'Walker', moves among the locations in a similarly uncanny way.

9. My thanks to Martin Fradley for this point.

10. In this respect *Dead Man's Shoes* differs from the traditional Loachian model of social realism – consistent from *Cathy Come Home* (1966) to *It's a Free World* (2007) – which grants sustained attention to the local sociopolitical context of the narrative in order to raise questions about the overarching structures which encourage such conditions.

11. 'Bachelor band' is a zoological term for young male animals that, having been turned out of herding groups on reaching puberty, form all-male subgroups and often display violent and destructive behaviour.

12. This impasse is most fully realised in the closing freeze-frame of *This is England*, which refuses the partial resolution offered through the family unit portrayed in Meadows' previous films.

13. Brief Encounters Film Festival event transcript (2004).

References

Chibnall, S. (2003), *Get Carter*, London: I. B. Tauris.

Clauss, J. J. (1999), 'Descent into Hell: mythic paradigms in *The Searchers*', *Journal of Popular Film and Television*, 27: 3, 2–17.

Daniels, S. and S. Ryecroft (1993), 'Mapping the modern city: Alan Sillitoe's Nottingham novels', *Transactions of the Institute of British Geographers, New Series*, 18: 4, 460–80.

Godfrey, S. (2010), 'Nowhere Men: Representations of Masculinity in '90s British Cinema' (unpublished PhD thesis).

Kerrigan, J. (1996), *Revenge Tragedy: Aeschylus to Armageddon*, Oxford: Clarendon Press.

King, R. (2005), 'In need of modernization?', *The Daily Telegraph*, 14 March: www.telegraph.co.uk/property/ (accessed 13 September 2009).

Macnab, G. (2004), 'Dead Man's Shoes', *Screen Daily*, 20 August 2004: http://www.screendaily.com/reviews/uk-ireland/features/dead-mans-shoes/4019820.article.

Read, J. (2000), *The New Avengers: Feminism, Femininity and the Rape-Revenge Cycle*, Manchester: Manchester University Press.

Sedgwick, E. K. (1985), *Between Men: English Literature and Male Homosocial Desire*, New York: Columbia University Press.

Sedgwick, E. K. (2002), 'The beast in the closet: James and the writing of homosexual panic', in R. Adams and D. Savran (eds), *The Masculinities Studies Reader*, Oxford: Blackwell, 157–74.

Shelley, M. ([1818] 1992), *Frankenstein*, London: Penguin.

Willis, S. (1997), *High Contrast: Race and Gender in Contemporary Hollywood Film*, Durham, DC and London: Duke University Press.

CHAPTER 8

A Message to You, Maggie: 1980s Skinhead Subculture and Music in *This is England*

Tim Snelson and Emma Sutton

> In the early eighties there was little to keep the disenchanted youth anesthetised indoors, so as unemployment figures rose and YTS Schemes fell, the kids refused to toe the factory line and spilled out onto the streets. The stage was set for a revolution.
>
> *Oi! This is England* pressbook (2005: 3)

As the above quotation suggests, Shane Meadows' *This is England* (2006) mediates the 1980s through a nostalgic rendering of subcultural resistance via key iconographic and musical cues. In so doing, the film engenders an idealised image of skinhead subculture – or more accurately subcultures – that recalls the romanticised sociological accounts of Birmingham University's Centre for Contemporary Cultural Studies from the 1970s and early 1980s. Reproducing these early subcultural scholars' focus on the 'magical realms' of ritual and style (Cohen 1972), Meadows juxtaposes the lush colours, dreamlike slow motion and joyful non-diegetic soundtrack of the skinhead gang – at least before its ideological infiltration by far-right extremism – with the 'colourless walls of routine' (Chambers 1985: 15) of Thatcher's Britain. However, this chapter will provide neither a purely textual nor an auteurist approach to the film. Instead it will situate the textual strategies and authorial signature of *This is England* within their wider historical contexts of production, mediation and consumption, through analysis of its key intertexts – chiefly the music and sociological literature it draws on – and a range of pre- and post-production reception materials such as interviews with the director, publicity material, and reviews from mainstream and niche presses.

The intention of this chapter is not so much to question the historical accuracy of the film, but rather to analyse how it synthesises diverse inter-textual frameworks in constructing a collective memory of the early 1980s period that appeals both to contemporary youth's 'overwhelming nostalgia for the days when youth culture was genuinely transgressive' (McRobbie and Thornton 1989: 565) and to Meadows' generation, who, as the reception material suggests, saw the film as reflecting their own personal experiences of youth. It is interesting to note here that many of the critics who praised the film were from exactly the same era as Meadows/Shaun and saw the film as authentically reflecting their memories of youth – whether as twelve-year-old skinhead in Margate (Aitch 2007) or as twelve-year-old Asian boy who lost his best friend to skinhead culture (Manzoor 2007). As the pre-production pressbook for the originally titled *Oi! This is England* suggests, the film is intended to simultaneously transcend and appeal to the 'current couch potato culture' and its desire for a simplified and stylised restaging of *authentic* youth 'revolution' (2005: 3).

Much of the promotional literature for *This is England* centres on how the narrative and characterisation is grounded in Meadows' experiences of being a young skinhead in 1980s Uttoxeter. This biographical influence is venerated not only as authorial signature but also as a stamp of historical authenticity. The film is celebrated for capturing the political, social and economic climate of Thatcher's Britain, as well as the government's effects on working-class culture and the resultant resistance of youth subcultures – the 'shit on the heel of Thatcher's jackboot' (Bochenski 2007: 26). As discussed elsewhere in this book, Thatcher and the legacy she left behind are symbolic presences running through much of Meadows' films, particularly in *TwentyFourSeven* (1997). However, these thematic concerns are not unique to Meadows; his work can be situated within a wider tradition of post-Thatcherite British cinema, in which 'an edge of bitterness against a political system which had devastated traditional working-class culture' (Murphy 2002: 396) has been retained in films that paint a much harsher portrait of Britain. Furthermore, 'the erosion of the traditional working-class which 1960s realism began to map reached a logical conclusion in films of the 1980s, where there is virtually no representation of community as such and very few images of collective action' (Hill 1999: 275). As this chapter will go on to discuss, subculture can be viewed as an attempt to recreate this sense of community and collective action within a wider community that is in the process of degeneration.

This is England and its television sequels are set during and centred around the Thatcher administration, presenting her as an all-pervading force dominating 1980s youth cultural identity. In *This is England* Thatcher is an omnipresent figure; in a fine Orwellian touch, Thatcher's voice on the clock radio is the first piece of diegetic sound to greet Shaun, and resultantly the audience, as it wakes him from his slumber. Her image recurs throughout the film, particularly through news footage and montage sequences. The revulsion towards Thatcher is not just expressed through a juxtaposition of nostalgic 1980s iconography and images of riots, speeches and the Falklands war, but is also explicitly inscribed through *mise-en-scène* such as the 'Maggie is a TWAT' graffiti on the side of a church. Additionally, the effects of unemployment, welfare cuts and housing redevelopment are presented throughout the film in the form of establishing shots of local authority housing, boarded-up homes and a derelict school. Socialist filmmaker Ken Loach highlights:

> The Thatcherite programme was a three-pronged attack on working people and their representatives. The Tories allowed factories to close to create mass unemployment; unemployment created poverty and alienation, which we're still living with today. (2009)

As suggested here, one of the most enervating factors of the government was its role in creating mass unemployment and breaking up working-class families through the decimation of local industries and construction of new housing estates that splintered kinship networks. While Conservative Party rhetoric foregrounded the centrality of family, its model of family structure and values was based on inappropriate middle-class ideals. As such, traditional families are absent from the film; Shaun's single-parent family is the only one presented on-screen, but it is made clear at the outset that this is the direct result of a Thatcherite decision, with Shaun having lost his father in the Falklands war.

In Meadows' film, subcultural youth collectivity is a strategy for filling the voids that Conservative policies had created while countering the Thatcherite ideology of individualism. Teenagers Woody and Lol become surrogate parents to Shaun, and the rest of the gang fill the roles of brothers and sisters. Shaun's mother, Cynthia, cannot alone fill the void that has been left by her husband; Shaun feels the need to break away from his mother, foster a sense of independent identity and sociability within a peer group, and, later, as this group fragments, succumb to and ultimately reject the hyper-patriarchal authority of Combo and the National Front. In this sense, Shaun moves through the fairly traditional oedipal journey staged in many youth films (Driscoll 2011), but outside a traditional familial structure. Shaun's dramatic rites of passage within these improvised subcultural structures is an embellishment of the director's memories of the summer of 1983 – a period of palpable personal transition and identity formation staged against a narrowly, perhaps naively, experienced backdrop of wider social and political change.

In addition to these biographical and sociopolitical influences on *This is*

England, Meadows' perspective on youth and subculture appears to have been influenced by Birmingham University's Centre for Contemporary Cultural Studies (CCCS) and its seminal sociologies of youth. These approaches saw post-war subcultures as simultaneously symptoms of and temporary solutions to the decline of working-class community and traditions. Drawing on Antonio Gramsci's theory of hegemony, they suggested that while problems of class division and economic opportunity remained at a material level, subcultures like the skinheads, mods and teddy boys challenged or at least negotiated dominant ideology by winning back 'space' in the cultural realm of ritual and style (Cohen 1972; Clarke 1973; Hebdige 1979). Analysis of *This is England* and its intertexts suggests that Meadows, like the CCCS, saw what 1970s and 1980s youth were doing as political, resultant of historically specific socioeconomic change, and symbolising class divisions.

In a 2007 interview for *The Guardian*, Meadows highlights his nostalgia for the working-class youth cultures of the past. He explains that despite the lack of employment opportunities, early 1980s skinheads:

> had this arrogance about them that was like 'We don't give a flying fuck that we haven't got a job. We're going to cause you so much bother and we're going to let our voices be known.' And that kind of energy has disappeared from youth. You look around the streets now and you can spot a chav and a skate kid but apart from that there doesn't seem to be any separation with kids anymore. (Solomons 2007)

Therefore, like the CCCS subcultural scholars, Meadows sees early 1980s skinhead culture as a collective and historically specific response to political and economic upheavals with their resultant effects on the break-up of traditional working-class communities. He sees subcultures as exclusively working class, but also potentially counter-hegemonic through their ritualistic and stylistic challenges to dominant culture. Drawing on his own experiences as a skinhead in Uttoxeter in the early 1980s, he explains:

> the thing that was put across to me was that I could be a skinhead because I was working class. It wasn't a rich boy's game. A pair of Docs, a pair of work jeans, white shirt, braces if you'd got 'em, shaved head and that was the job done. (Solomons 2007)

Summarily, in the semi-biographical *This is England*, the skinhead gang provides a structure that allows Shaun and his friends to address the contradictions born of the social, economic and political upheavals that Meadows raises, but only within the 'symbolic' realms of style, symbolism, territoriality and ritual.

This challenge to authority was largely evinced not within the realm of work, but that of leisure. As Phil Cohen states in his seminal essay 'Sub-cultural conflict and working class community', 'it seems to me that the latent function of subculture is this: to express and resolve, albeit "magically", the contradictions which remain hidden or unresolved in the parent culture' (Cohen 1972: 71). Here the parent culture refers to the authentic, working-class culture of the youth subculture's previous gener-ation – with its sense of community, solidarity, shared culture and kinship networks – that was being lost through modernisation and the shift towards a consumer economy. Cohen suggests that through urban redevelopment, and particularly the shift to new housing estates and tower blocks rather than traditional terraced streets, communal spaces were lost and traditional family structures and kinship networks were broken up.

In addition, changes in economic infrastructure – particularly the loss of unskilled and semi-skilled labour and the shift towards a consumer economy – meant that community was no longer tied to workplace solidarity and traditional ideologies of production. Again this can be seen in *This is England* in the mass unemployment and debris of a now defunct industry that litters its landscape. Moreover, Meadows subverts mass unemployment under Thatcher's regime through the character of Combo. There is an underlying contradiction that runs through Combo's ideology: he rants about the lack of employment and immigrants taking 'English' jobs, but we hear nothing of any of the racist gang working or attempting to find work. The two factions of the skinhead culture collide in terms of unemployment, the original skinheads having a more work-orientated life which is carried through to *This is England '86*, where Woody's embrace of a Thatcherite work ethic leads to the breakdown of communication in his relationship with Lol. Therefore, Cohen suggests that working-class youth were summarily pulled one way by family and neighbourhood – the values and traditions of parent culture – and the other by the new consumer society: hence the hidden or unresolved contradictions. Thatcher's creed was the creed of the individual: belonging to a subculture was a way of countering that by filling the void that Conservative policies had created. Summarily, youth's solution was social, forming new social groups such as the skinhead gang that recreate working-class community and workplace solidarity, but predominantly within the symbolic or 'magical' realm of style, ritual and consumption, rather than in their working lives.

This can be seen in *This is England* in Cynthia's (Shaun's mum) lack of family support, as well as Combo's explosive jealousy when Milky reveals the extended kinship network in his life. Woody's gang are intensely familial and protective, both respecting and retaining elements of the parent

culture; they are apologetic to Cynthia after they shave her twelve-year-old
son's head and, more importantly, Cynthia, as a mother, entrusts this group
with the responsibility of looking after her son. Nick Knight emphasises
this idea that 'attitudes to parents, school and the police were not specifically skinhead, but like that of other working class youths. Being a skin did
not normally imply a break with your family' (Knight 1982: 53). Rather
than setting itself in opposition to parental and mainstream culture, the
'original' skinhead gang led by Woody bridges the gap between the parent
culture and its youth opposition – in this sense, it is a progressive
representation of youth cultural solutions.

So how does this resolution of societal contradictions manifest in the
skinhead subculture? In terms of style, skinheads adopt the work wear of
their parent culture – Doctor Martin boots and donkey jackets – which
represent the production economy but within the leisure realm. Even the
shaving of the head represents a commitment to the work ethic in
remaining vigilant in being neat and tidy. This symbolism manifests in
other, more nefarious ways, through symbols of national identity grounded
in more stable times, particularly through iconography and argot or slang
that relates to World War II – the bulldog, Union Jack, 'warrior spirit'. In
regard to ritual and values, the right-wing skinheads adopt the imagined
'patriotism' of their parent culture (if at all, more attributable to their
grandparents', even great-grandparents', generation) as well as a very traditional conception of masculinity. Furthermore, they attempt to retrieve
class solidarity and community in the form of the gang. Central to their
mob mentality is the idea of 'territoriality' or protecting your patch. As
Clarke suggests, in the absence of power (job) or ownership (home) in the
economic realm, skinheads claim ownership of public spaces. This 'magical
way of expressing ownership' can be seen in Woody's gang's territorial use
of the underpass and later, more nefariously, in Combo's gang's reclaiming
of the playground and taking of the newsagents (Clarke 1975).

In addition to the biographical influence on Meadows' film, it is possible
to feel the influence of two key intertexts. The first is Gavin Watson's photo
essay *Skins* (1994), which features pictures of very similar 'hunting' rituals
that are present in the film; Woody's gang uses the term 'hunting' to refer
to the smashing up of abandoned houses and schools that previously served
the industrial community that has now been lost. In the press notes for *This
is England* Meadows states: 'I hold that book really dear to my heart, they
feel like my friends, and feel like the people I grew up with […] some
images of a young kid in a crombie and he's stood with a bigger lad, that
really became the ideal of Woody and Shaun' (Warp Films 2006). The

model for Shaun was Watson's little brother Nev, who, like Meadows and Shaun, was the 'mascot' for older skins and central protagonist in his brother's photo essay. The book's influence on *This is England*'s iconography and narrative is clear in terms not only of Shaun, but also the look and dynamic of the gang and in key moments such as Nev/Shaun's first kiss and the rituals they participate in, such as 'hunting'.

Another key text that Meadows draws on – and used extensively to illustrate his 2005 pre-production marketing for *Oi! This is England* – is Nick Knight's *Skinhead*, published in 1982. Significantly, the book features an essay based on ethnographic research by key CCCS subculture scholar Dick Hebdige called 'This is England! And They don't live here'. The title is a quotation Hebdige has taken from an interview with an older skinhead, Mickey (in his thirties like Combo); Mickey's racist rant is very similar to Combo's 'This is England' speech delivered in an attempt to unite the politically divergent skinhead groups in the film. Mickey's speech, like Combo's, harks back to war against the Nazis as representing the defining moment of stable British national identity at the same time as it constructs a 'them and us' dichotomy, with Asian immigrants seen to be stealing housing and jobs from white working classes in 1982. Here we see the key inspiration for Combo's speech and the title of the film. Mickey rants:

> We fought the Germans, the London people … They [the skinheads] are just wearing the flag because they're patriotic. What's wrong with being patriotic? … This is England. And They don't live here. They [the Pakistanis] know nothing about it … living in detached houses. Driving around in a Rolls. Be honest. What the fuck are They going to know about Us …? (Knight 1982: 31)

And in *This is England*, Combo reiterates:

> Two fucking world wars! Men have laid down their lives for this. For this … and for what? So people can stick their fucking flag in the ground and say, Yeah! This is England. And this is England, and this is England. For what now? Eh, what for? So we can just open the fucking floodgates and let them all come in? And say, Yeah, come on, come in. Get off your ship. Did you have a safe journey? Was it hard? Here y'are, here's a corner, why don't you build a shop? Better still, why don't you build a shop and then build a church? Follow your own fucking religions. Do what you want.

However, there are also key convergences between Hebdige's overarching argument in the essay, largely a restating and updating of the CCCS approach to subculture, and Meadows' approach to skinhead culture in the film. Like Meadows, Hebdige's intention is to explore contradictions within skinhead culture: the racist politics and traditionalism of some factions *and*, sometimes simultaneously, the positive embrace of the diasporic influence on music, style, ritual and drug use. Hebdige suggests that 'real skins are much less coherent than the stereotype. Subcultures, after all, don't offer solutions to material problems. They play back the problems symbolically in style' (1982: 33). Therefore, skinheads signify the loss of *and* nostalgia for the parent culture through style; however, this is not about rejection of consumerism, but rather about having the right Fred Perry shirt and DM boots that symbolically *represent* a rejection of consumer culture. Hebdige continues, 'the skinhead style, for all its apparent knuckle-headedness, is a consciously held pose, a deliberate turning back to earlier, more certain times when men were men [...] When an observer could tell an individual's social status by merely glancing down at the footwear' (27). This nostalgic search for stability and authenticity in skinhead culture can not only be detected in *their* behaviour and style, but is also recreated in the sociology of the CCCS and in Meadows' film.

Like Meadows, the CCCS attempted to understand and perhaps even rationalise their subjects' often problematic values and behaviour. This is perhaps why, like the CCCS, there has been some criticism of Meadows' nostalgia and attempt to redeem skinhead culture. The film was mostly praised, with some critics seeing the film as serious sociology in the CCCS tradition that looked to a distinct and more authentic period of youth culture. For example, *The Independent* deemed it 'uncompromising in its exploration of British tribal youth culture. An authoritative and deeply serious piece of cinema sociology' (Romney 2007). The *Evening Standard* went further, hailing it as 'a portrayal of a certain time and place that has lessons for us about the twisted loyalties of today's gang culture'; beyond a serious sociology it might even provide solutions to the myth of 'Broken Britain' (Malcolm 2007). However, some reviewers saw the film as nostalgic and sentimental. The *Telegraph* review titled 'Nostalgia Boot Boy' deemed the film a 'rose tinted account of skinhead culture [...] Meadows may be a realist but he is also a die-hard sentimentalist' (McTear). Meadows is in fact openly and unapologetically nostalgic about his own period of sub-culture participation – one he sees as marked by genuine commitment, political resistance, working-class solidarity, strong beliefs and values, and anti-media sentiments. Like Hebdige and others in the CCCS tradition, with this era's passing, Meadows mourns contemporary youth's loss, not just of class consciousness but self-consciousness.

Summarily, perhaps some of the same criticisms of the CCCS's approach could be levelled at Meadows' film. Post-subculturalists have accused the CCCS's 'lumbering modernist paradigm' (St John 2004: 67) or 'Heroic Phase' in subcultural studies of 'over-politicising' subcultures, over-emphasising resistance, commitment and oppositional politics (Marchant 2004: 85) as well as coherence and authenticity. As we have seen, Meadows has also been accused of romanticising skinhead culture, portraying it as more coherent, authentic and political than perhaps in reality it is. In addition to its 'rose tinted' view of skinheads, the *Telegraph* reviewer went on to criticise the film for 'trying to squeeze too much socio-political significance from the material' (McTear 2007). Meadows also reduces the diversity of experiences and historical complexity of skinhead subcultures. In Shaun's shift from the inclusivity and diasporic influence of rude boy culture in Woody's gang to the racist politics and defensive traditionalism of Combo's 'foot soldiers', Meadows transposes the 'waves' of skinhead culture that emerged, fused and clashed from the 1960s to the 1980s to a single summer in the north Midlands in 1983. Again this criticism of reductively constructing subcultures as 'coherent and homogenous formations that can be clearly demarcated' has also been levelled at the CCCS's approach (Muggleton and Weinzier 2004: 7).

However, perhaps the main challenge to the CCCS's subcultural studies, and arguably to Meadows, is in regard to the undue sociological focus on men by men. Even *within* the CCCS's seminal *Resistance Through Rituals* (1975), feminist critics highlight the gender bias of these studies in regard to the exclusion of discussion of female involvement and female 'subcultures' (McRobbie and Garber 1975); they highlighted that female subculturalists such as the 'mod girl' were often defined in relational roles or as an extension of more visible male counterparts. Meadows' has certainly been seen to be male-centred cinema, and in *This is England* we mostly see females in more peripheral and relational roles as girlfriends. However, in the figure of Smell we see something new in terms of *visible* female subcultures, with regard to the New Romantics of the early to mid-1980s. This is a far more female-centred subculture, where gender performance is played with; certainly female participants do not merely adopt a watered-down version of the masculine style as with skinhead girls or mod girls. Meadows addresses this lack of exploration of female subculturalists and female perspectives in *This is England '86*, where it is not just Smell who takes on a more significant role, but Lol, who becomes both centre of the narrative and linchpin of the group's, albeit waning, subcultural identity. This centrality of the female subculturalist is hinted at in *This is England*; although peripheral to the gang, Lol is one of the strongest and most interesting characters in the film, and plays a central symbolic role in shoring up – or not – the masculinity of Woody and Combo. As Stallybrass and White suggest, 'what is *socially* peripheral is so frequently *symbolically* central' (1986: 7); it is a crisis in masculinity and *not* class that seems central to skinhead culture in the film.

The CCCS's emphasis on class – and the downplaying of the importance of ethnicity and gender, for example – has been subject to criticism by subsequent sociologists of subculture (Redhead 1990; Thornton 1996; Huq 2006). If the CCCS does address ethnicity, its focus is on the diasporic influence on 'white ethnicity', not on how black youth creatively appropriate and subvert white culture (Hebdige 1979). This criticism could be levelled at *This is England*, even though there is some exploration of Milky's cultural hybridity and diasporic identity in the film. However, Meadows does hint at a more complex understanding of class in the film. Chambers criticises the CCCS's approach by suggesting that, in fact, some use subcultural style to escape class-based identities rather than recreate them. In the film's slow-mo 'Louie Louie' (Toots and the Maytals) scene, Meadows here, like Chambers, does highlight subcultural style and consumer culture as liberations from working-class life. It is through such use of music that Meadows is able most evocatively to represent the sub-culture's simultaneous entrenchment within *and* escape from the 'realities' of Thatcher's Britain.

Although frequently central to the construction of both cinematic *and* subcultural style, the role of music has been historically overlooked in both auteur studies and sociologies of youth. As David Hesmondhalgh suggests, 'the CCCS work on youth subcultures was never really about music, it was about youth collectivities that used music, amongst other means, to construct their identities' (2005: 31). The same might be said of Meadows' discriminating use of music in *This is England* and, in a different way, *This is England '86*. Echoing his 'hero' Martin Scorsese's practices, narrative momentum and emotional effect take precedence over notions of realism and authenticity in his work (Meadows 2002). Music in *This is England* is used to elicit emotion, conjure nostalgia and produce unsettling juxta-positions while providing a shorthand for the era as shaped by Meadows' 'memories' of his youth. As with Scorsese's selection of music to sound-track many of his films, it hinges on the director's own musical recollec-tions. As frequent Meadows collaborator Vicky McClure suggests:

> The actual era was different for many people. Shane saw it from that point of view, whereas there might be people who watch the film and say 'It was nothing like that when I was a skinhead or when I was growing up in 1983'. We had to take it from Shane's experience because it was his story he was telling. (McClure 2007)

Meadows' choice of music is filtered through his recollection of the early 1980s, but the director's 'nostalgia' is shaped more through politically motivated processes of editing and reconstruction than it is through wistful misremembering.

While the Oi! subgenre of punk was central to 1980s skinhead culture – and, at least initially, was acknowledged as such in the film's original title, *Oi! This is England* – Oi! bands are excluded from the film's soundtrack. Oi! was the label ascribed to a number of late-1970s bands who rejected the artistic pretensions and experimentalism of the emergent post-punk scene, sticking with a 'real punk' sound and ethos addressed to the shared interests of punk, skinhead and other working-class youth (Reynolds 2011: 259). A key influence of the 'real punk' sound was the seminal punk band the Clash, whose final single, 'This is England' (1985), provides another key reference point for the film – though perhaps more for critics than for Meadows himself (Savage 2007). The Clash's swansong mourns a downtrodden British working-class culture, breaking from their earlier syncretic sound that, like *This is England*, embraced the vibrant rhythms and protest spirit of reggae and Rasta culture. While, like the Clash, some of the late-1970s and early-1980s Oi! bands had explicitly left-wing and anti-racist agendas – most notably the Angelic Upstarts – Oi! increasingly became associated with far-right politics. In the film's audio commentary, Meadows discusses how he considered including Oi! music in the film, but he was concerned at its links to the National Front and did not want to contribute financially through publishing royalties; here therefore personal ethics, understandably, overrides authenticity.

Meadows does make the concession of including contemporary street punk band the UK Subs' 'Warhead' (1980) at a key moment within the film's narrative. While the UK Subs never associated themselves with the Oi! movement, because of its associations with violence and far-right extremism, their music is stylistically similar to some of the more proficient Oi! bands. The UK Subs' inclusion is used, however, to indicate Shaun's departure from the affable Woody's 'rude boy' gang into the menacing Combo's neo-Nazi mob, who are united through far-right ideology rather than the shared interests of youth, music or style. The song demarcates the two parts of the film in which the skinhead culture begins to evolve into something more nefarious – though in fact the UK Subs are fervently left-wing. However, the far-right manifestations of Oi! do make their presence felt through *mise-en-scène*: the neo-Nazi band Skrewdriver (though misspelt 'Screwdriver') is represented early in the film through graffiti in the tunnel – a hint of the lurking influence of the imprisoned Combo that will soon reinfiltrate the gang. So, *This is England* uses different musical genres to demarcate the divergent and overlaying factions within skinhead culture, but privileges the diasporic music favoured, initially, by the first wave of skinheads from the 1960s.

According to Harry Hawke, the music of Toots and the Maytals typifies the tastes of the original skinheads of the mid- to late 1960s, with their song '54-46 Was My Number' representing one of the most popular 'skinhead hits' of the era (Knight 1982: 48). Meadows uses this track to score his credit sequence, which thrusts the spectator into the political and cultural milieu of the early 1980s through an eclectic montage of 1980s popular culture – including Roland Rat, Rubix Cubes, *Nightrider* and *Space Invader*, and news footage of Margaret Thatcher and Ronald Reagan, CND protests at Greenham Common, run-down council estates, the Falklands war (shots of Thatcher and dead soldiers are alternated to stress her personal culpability), the miners' strikes, racial attacks on British Asians' homes, Prince Charles and Princess Diana's wedding and National Front rallies. The juxtaposition of these archival images with the sound-track serves to build a complex and conflicted picture of British national identity. It celebrates the diasporic influence on post-war Britain while indicating the ongoing dismantling of working-class communities and backlashes against immigration therein – issues the film will go on to address within the microcosm of the gang.

Setting the agenda for *This is England*, Meadows contrasts a sanguine West Indian culture with the restrictions and hardships present in working-class British life in the 1980s. The selection of '54-46 Was My Number' – 54-46 being the prison number of singer Toots Hibbert following his arrest for marijuana possession – registers with the film's themes of imprison-ment and restriction; this includes Combo's incarceration that contributes, at least in part, to his radicalisation, but also the other characters' symbolic imprisonment within their social and economic circumstances. However, while the song serves as simultaneous escape from and evocation of the realities of Thatcher's Britain – including the swelling right-wing factions of skinhead culture – it instils what Svetlana Boym (2002) distinguishes as 'reflective' rather than 'restorative' nostalgia. Rather than wanting to restore a lost 'golden age', reflective nostalgia 'cultivates the bittersweet pangs of poignancy' and 'understands that deep loss is irrecoverable' (Reynolds 2011: xxviii). Meadows' use of music here serves to oppose the typically conservative impulses of restorative nostalgia, a particularly nefarious example of which is detailed in the neo-fascist rhetoric of Combo and the National Front meeting in the film. Ludovico Einaudi's melan-cholic piano compositions reinforce this sense of 'irrecoverable loss', mourning more the loss of individual innocence and belonging than a more innocent and communal past; these piano motifs are carried through into *This is England '86*, providing coherence across the two texts in light of the lessening of the gang's musical ties. *This is England '86* explicitly uses the diffusing of musical styles to signify the breakdown of the subcultural group, with a variety of popular artists such as Nena, the Housemartins and UB40 representing more of a musical backdrop than a communal aesthetic. The most consistent musical presence in the series – beyond Einaudi's score – is the Jam, who split up in 1982 and therefore help to reference back to the film's earlier subcultural moment.

Meadows' privileging of reflective over restorative nostalgia makes the scoring of Clayhill's cover version of the Smiths' track 'Please, Please, Please Let Me Get What I Want' (1984) over the film's final moments an interesting and ambivalent choice. Simon Reynolds highlights Morrissey's slippages between his reputation as the 'supreme poet of reflective nostalgia' and the 'restorative nostalgia danger zone'. Through his lyrics with the Smiths and in his solo career, 'Morrissey mourns a place and time (Manchester of the sixties and seventies) where he never stole a happy hour'. However, he has courted controversy through 'restorative', even blatantly racist, gestures such as playing his contentious song 'National Front Disco' draped in a Union Jack at a festival in 1992 and more recently, in a 2007 *NME* interview, attributing Britain's decline since his youth to, at least in part, Britain's immigration policies (Reynolds 2011: xxvii–xxviii). Meadows' choice of a contemporary cover version of the Smiths' song serves to distance the song from Morrissey's regressive politics while maintaining its reflective meaning.

As Shaun revisits scenes from his and the film's past, the song provides a fitting soundtrack for his reflection and rejection of the authoritative meta-narratives of heroism and nationalism that the St George's Cross flag (taken from the National Front meeting) has represented for him. Having thrown the flag into the sea, Shaun's final gaze directly into camera breaks the fourth wall, as 'Please, Please, Please Let Me Get What I Want' not only marks Shaun's shift from the conformity of the group to individual autonomy – the inevitable embrace of a Thatcherite ethos perhaps (the repetition of the singular: 'I' and 'me') – but also summons up a more fluid and positive sense of working-class male identity. With this act Shaun rejects Combo's gang and its racist values, but also indicates his loss of faith in the country which, as Combo reveals, sent his father off to die in a 'fucking phoney war'. Jon Savage (2007) draws intertextual links between the end of *This is England* and Jimmy's ultimate annihilation in the climax of The Who's *Quadrophenia* (Roddam 1979), both 'surrounded by the sea, confronted by physical limit and emotional space – if not actual ego dissolution'. However, Meadows reveals this symbolic gesture of discarding the flag into the sea as one of potential escape *not* annihilation for Shaun. Despite Meadows' nostalgia for the subcultural group, in *This is England*'s final ambiguous moments, Shaun casts off his subcultural identity, deciding to 'stand alone' rather than 'run with the crowd', as the poster's tagline reveals.

While the highly 'aestheticised' *This is England* might initially appear to be one of Frederic Jameson's nostalgia films, 'in which the history of aesthetic styles displaces "real" history' (1984: 67), it could be argued that Meadows' film 'rewrites' and 'reactivates' (Brooker and Brooker 1997: 7) – even resists – as much as it 'replicates and reproduces – reinforces – the logic of late capitalism' and its dominant representational modes (Jameson 1985: 125). Thatcher's Britain and 1980s subcultures are clearly simplified, stylised and filtered through an, at least initially, nostalgic gaze, but Meadows instils contradiction, complexity and comparisons with contemporary Britain's troubled political, economic and social landscape in his historically and geographically localised story. As with the best popular historical forms, *This is England* 'retain[s] memories of the past and contain[s] hopes for the future that rebuke the injustices and inequalities of the present' (Lipsitz 1999: 20). In parallel with developments in subcultural studies (Muggleton 2000; Bennett 2004), Meadows ultimately evinces a move away from the collectivity, commitment and ultimately conformity of the skinhead subcultures he represents, towards the individuality, fluid identity and mobility of the incoming era.

References

Aitch, I. (2007), 'Nazi salutes were part of the fun', *The Guardian*, 13 April, p. 3.
Bennett, A. and K. Kahn-Harris (2004) (eds), *After Subculture: Critical studies in Contemporary Youth Culture*, Basingstoke: Palgrave Macmillan.
Bochenski, M. (2007a), 'Original skin: Shane Meadows', *LittleWhiteLies*, *This is England* issue, April.
Bochenski, M. (2007b), 'The dance of the skin', *LittleWhiteLies*, *This is England* issue, April.
Boym, S. (2002), *The Future of Nostalgia*, New York: Basic Books.
Brown, W. (2009), 'Not flagwaving but flagdrowning, or postcards from post-Britain', in R. Murphy (ed.), *The British Cinema Book* (3rd edn), London: BFI-Palgrave Macmillan, pp. 408–16.
Brooker, P. and W. Brooker (1997), *Postmodern After-Images*, London: Edward Acton.

Chambers, I. (1985), *Urban Rhythms: Pop Music and Popular Culture*, London: Macmillan.

Clarke, J. (1973), 'The skinhead and the magical recovery of community', in S. Hall and T. Jefferson (2006) (eds), *Resistance Through Rituals: Youth Sub-cultures in Post-war Britain*, Oxon: Routledge.

Cohen, P. (1972), 'Subcultural conflict and working class community', in S. Hall (1980), *Culture, Media, Language: Working Papers in Cultural Studies, 1972–79*, London: Routledge.

Cohen, S. (2002), *Folk Devils and Moral Panics*, London: Routledge.

Donnelly, K. J. (2001), *Pop Music in British Cinema: A Chronicle*, London: BFI.

Driscoll, C. (2011), *Teen Film: A Critical Introduction*, New York: Berg.

Hebdige, D. (1979), *Subculture: The Meaning of Style*, London: Routledge.

Hebdige, D. (1988), *Hiding in the Light: On Images and Things*, London and New York: Routledge.

Hesmondhalgh, D. (2005), 'Subcultures, scenes or tribes? None of the above', *Journal of Youth Studies*, 8: 1, 21–40.

Hill, J. (1999), *British Cinema of the 1980s*, Oxford: Oxford University Press.

Hunt, L. (1998), *British Low Culture: From Safari Suits to Sexploitation*, London: Routledge.

Huq, R. (2006), *Beyond Subculture: Pop, Youth and Identity in a Postcolonial World*, London: Routledge.

Knight, N. (1982), *Skinhead*, London: Omnibus.

Lipsitz, G. (2001), *Time Passages: Collective Memory and American Popular Culture*, Minneapolis: University of Minnesota Press.

Lyotard, J. (1984), *The Postmodern Condition: A Report on Knowledge*, Manchester: Manchester University Press.

Malcolm, D. (2007), 'Brothers under the skin', *Evening Standard*, 26 April, p. 34.

Manzoor, S. (2007), 'Dedicated followers of Fascism', *The Guardian*, 13 April, p. 3.

Marchant, O. (2004), 'Bridging the micro-macro gap: Is there such a thing as post-subcultural politics?', in D. Muggleton and R. Weinzier (eds), *Post-subcultures Reader*, London: Berg, pp. 83–100.

McRobbie, A. and S. Thornton (1995), 'Rethinking "moral panic" for multi-mediated social worlds', *British Journal of Sociology*, 46: 4, 559–73.

McTear, C. (2007), 'Another country', *Telegraph*, 14 April.

Muggleton, D. (2000), *Inside Subculture: The Postmodern Meaning of Style*, London: Berg.

Muggleton, D. and R. Weinzier (2004), 'What is "post-subcultural studies" anyway?', in D. Muggleton and R. Weinzier (eds), *Post-subcultures Reader*, London: Berg, pp. 3–26.

Mungham, G. and G. Pearson (1976) (eds), *Working Class Youth Culture*, London: Routledge.

Murphy, R. (2009), 'Bright hopes, dark dreams', in R. Murphy (ed.), *The British Cinema Book*, Basingstoke: Palgrave Macmillan.

Redhead, S. (1990), *The End of the Century Party: Youth and Pop Towards 2000*, Manchester: University of Manchester Press.

Reynolds, S. (2011), *Retromania: Pop Culture's Addiction To Its Own Past*, London: Faber and Faber.

Romney, J. (2007), 'Natural shorn killer', *Independent*, 29 April, p. 6.

Savage, J. (2007), 'This is England', *Sight & Sound*, 17: 5.

Solomons, J. (2007), 'Shane Meadows', *The Guardian*, 25 April.

St John, G. (2004), 'Post-rave technotribalism and the carnival of protest', in D. Muggleton and R. Weinzier (eds), *Post-subcultures Reader*, London: Berg, pp. 65–82.

Stallybrass, P. and A. White (1986), *The Politics and Poetics of Transgression*, Ithaca: Cornell University Press.

Thornton, S. (1996), *Club Cultures: Music, Media and Subcultural Capital*, Cambridge: Polity.

Various authors (2009), 'Acceptable in the 80s', *The Guardian*, 11 April: www.guardian.co.uk/books/2009/apr/11/thatcher-and-the-arts (accessed 14 September 2009).

Vasagar, J. (2003), 'Misfit Morrissey finds new niche by signing with reggae label', *The Guardian*, 7 March: http://www.guardian.co.uk/uk/2003/jun/07/arts.artsnews (accessed 31 October 2010).

Warp Films (2006), 'This is England press notes'.

Watson, G. (1994), *Skins*, Church Stretton: Independent Music Press.

CHAPTER 9

Changing Spaces of 'Englishness': Psychogeography and Spatial Practices in *This is England* and *Somers Town*

Sarah N. Petrovic

Shane Meadows is a filmmaker whose use of space reflects the changing state of English society and culture. Following the British cinema tradition of social realism represented by Mike Leigh, Ken Loach and Alan Clarke, Meadows makes use of organic, improvisational filmmaking to explore the effects of multiculturalism in the working class, focusing predominantly on its youth. All of Meadows' films are driven by location and space, but in particular, two of Meadows' films, *This is England* (2006) and *Somers Town* (2008), contend with the issue of hybridity, or the melding of previously separated cultures, via the experiences of their young English protagonists, played in both cases by Thomas Turgoose. Though further work should certainly be done combining post-colonial and spatial theory and examining the relationship between space and character in all of Meadows' work, this essay is limited in scope to investigating this psychogeography in just two of Meadows' films and asserts that the contested ideological and spatial elements presented in *This is England* are transformed into a more fully and successfully realised hybridity in *Somers Town*.

In *The Practice of Everyday Life*, Michel De Certeau suggests that 'Every story is a travel story – a spatial practice' (1984: 115), and this is certainly true for Meadows' films, nearly all of which have spatial titles. In addition to *Somers Town* and *This is England*, Meadows' works include *Once Upon a Time in the Midlands* and *A Room for Romeo Brass*. Even the title *Dead Man's Shoes* suggests a personal perspective and space. In these films, characters are always overtly a product of their physical environments and therefore must be read in spatial terms. Space can reveal culture even in seemingly innocuous elements of daily life, and if individuals are substantially to determine and live out their own identities, they must acknowledge and exert agency within their own spatial practices against those practices and identities dictated to them.

Since the last quarter of the twentieth century, the social sciences and humanities have been critically preoccupied with the 'spatial turn', an investigation of space across the disciplines, and this theoretical concept can productively be applied to generate an increased understanding of Meadows' films. In his seminal text *The Production of Space*, Henri Lefebvre (1991) defines space as composed equally of three dimensions: the physical, the social and the mental. These three categories provide a framework by which to consider how Meadows' films recognise the multi-faceted nature of space and its effect on culture – space, which is portrayed as conflicted and fragmented in *This is England*, has the possibility for redemption in *Somers Town*.

Claire Monk describes the Sneinton setting of Meadows' early film *Small Time* (1996) as 'parochially marooned from the metropolitan centre' (1999: 185) of Nottingham. This isolation from the hegemonic majority is common in the director's work and breeds individuals fiercely dependent on their space, producing a unique psychogeography in Meadows' films. The physical space then, distinct from the country at large, is indicative of how characters in these two films define themselves as set apart from the larger society and seeking to find inclusive communities to which to belong.

The ways in which characters collectively engage with their space and the ways in which particular spaces influence community behaviour constitute the social space of a film. De Certeau suggests that spatial practices, our interactions with our surrounding physical environment, 'secretly structure the determining conditions of social life' (1984: 96) and defines space as 'a practiced place. Thus the street geometrically defined by urban planning is transformed into a space by walkers' (117). Thus, these spatial practices can and should be read in Meadows' films.

Finally, this essay considers mental space, or how characters conceptualise their space and themselves. When considering British texts like Meadows' films, it is important to remember how the British Empire established itself in its colonies through a manipulation of physical space that also dictated its cultural ideology to the inhabitants. This close relationship between the individual and place has been the purview of post-colonial theory (see Ashcroft, Griffiths and Tiffin 2002), and it is valuable to extend this reading of post-colonial space to Anglo-British sites, texts, authors and filmmakers to learn what the relationship between self and place is for those whose ideology has historically used spatial practices to gain and enforce power. For instance, just as post-colonial writers and critics seek to resolve a hybrid post-colonial identity (see Bhabha 1994 for the foundational post-colonial theory regarding hybridity and Kuortti and Nyman 2007 for more recent conceptualisations) with a spatially and mentally colonised one, so do Meadows' films.

This is England, set in 1983, is a post-imperial text contending with the white British experience of the effects of their colonialism; the result is an exploration of the white British struggle to reconcile psychological and social identity with spatial identity in a manner similar to what post-colonial texts portray. *Somers Town*, set in 2008, represents a more multicultural space and suggests how it might be representative of contemporary England, the realised hybrid space with which *This is England*'s characters contend. *This is England* is set in an unspecified part of England's Midlands, although significantly there is a coastline, and portrays twelve-year-old Shaun Fields and his encounter with skinhead culture and its appropriation by nationalist, neo-Nazi hatred. Despite not portraying the same characters, Meadows' next film, *Somers Town*, can be read as a coda to *This is England*. *Somers Town* follows Tomo, who ends up in the eponymous metropolitan neighbourhood after running away from Nottingham to London, as he meets Polish immigrant Marek, with whom he forms a friendship. Through these films, Meadows works through his contemporary culture's struggle to define 'English' and deal with hybridity, especially in response to the presence of immigrants both white and non-white, and he does so by exploring individuals' relationships to their space.

In one of the most powerful moments of *This is England*, Combo gives a speech on the state of England and begins to proclaim a nationalist, neo-Nazi ideology, discussing the wars of the twentieth century, saying, 'Men have laid down their lives for this. For this … and for what? So people can stick their fucking flag in the ground and say, "Yeah! This is England. And this is England, and this is England."' He points to the ground as if planting a flag for the first 'this is England', to his heart for the second, and his head for the third. He has defined the space of England: it is physical; it is emotional; it is ideological. These are the grounds on which Meadows builds his films and situates his characters, and they are the ones this essay explores.

This is England: physical space

The film *This is England* shows that it is not merely inner-city environments in which violence results from competing rather than co-operative ideologies and from a lack of acceptance of hybridity; similar issues occur in the small-town provincial East Midlands. It is significant to note that the location of *This is England* is not a specific, real place as in many of Meadows' other films. In one interview, Meadows notes it is 'the hardest [of his films] to place anywhere' because it is 'less specific and less identifiable', and he has also been quoted as describing the film as 'Nottingham-on-sea' (quoted in Harkness 2007). The film's setting seemingly portrays the East Midlands with a coast, which is an iconic geographical marker for this island nation. Indeed, even the accents of the various actors suggest a variety of origins, with no attempt to homogenise them. This blended location and range of dialects point to a more contemporary England that is more widely accepting of hybridity than the historical time of the film.

The physical space of *This is England* is covered with graffiti, a sign of people trying to project themselves onto the landscape and to define themselves by marking their territory. Initially, the graffiti in the film is that of band names (The Maytals, The Specials), slogans related to skinhead culture (Skins, Oi!) and personal messages (Lol 4 Woody, Kes 83). Near Shaun's house there is a small church with 'Maggie is a Twat' painted in large white letters; by itself, this slur on the British Prime Minister is humorous and indicative of the skinhead anger with the governing classes. Graffiti is used initially to represent the working-class skinhead credo, and it is not until Combo returns from jail that *This is England* shows graffiti being used in a more sinister way.

Once Shaun has joined Combo and that gang increasingly embraces a nationalist, neo-Nazi ideology, the graffiti in the film becomes a weapon for white English hegemony to reject any sense of blending or integration with what they do not consider English. One of the first actions the gang takes after attending a nationalist rally is to spray-paint racial slurs on the walls of the underpass where a number of workers of Pakistani origin walk to work. By doing so, Combo's gang is trying to suggest that the country itself, the physical walls of the town, is projecting their hate towards these immigrants. This graffiti incident occurs late at night without any interaction with those for whom the message is intended. Their vitriol is momentarily transferred to two white women who walk by; this group of white Anglo males call them 'whores' and throw paint cans at them, showing their animosity to any kind of diversity which might encroach on their white, homosocial community. Later on, the group grows bolder, and after threatening and intimidating a group of boys playing football and a Pakistani store owner, they spray-paint their slurs and 'Nashnil' (sic) ideology as a way of claiming a physical space. This tangible remnant of their racism remains, and at the height of Shaun's inculcation to Combo's gang, the film shows an image of him walking along a graffitied path super-imposed with another image, a close-up of the racist graffiti – he is surrounded and overwhelmed spatially on the screen by the graffiti and its emphatic rejection of hybridity.

The film uses its presentation of physical space to represent the internal experience of Shaun, and perhaps by extension English society, as it appears fragmented, then resistant to hybridity, and finally open to its possibility. Shaun's identity is initially unformed and uncertain. In an early scene, he goes outside by himself to wander and play. In a montage of shots, the film presents Shaun shooting at targets with a sling-shot in a vacant space; he then sits and eats sweets in a derelict rowing boat in the middle of a field; he rides his bike through a deserted car park; he walks along the beach. Each of these shots is unconnected to the others, tightly focusing on Shaun as he quietly passes time by himself; the audience does not see him travelling between these places, he is just there, and so these places do not exist in relation to each other. Each constitutes a tiny fragment of the physical space of Shaun's day, and Shaun's random wanderings mimic his non-unified identity. No other people exist in this world, highlighting Shaun's isolation. He is aimless but longing for direction, for somewhere to go, something to do, something to unify the fragments. His boat is grounded, his car park deserted, and his beach empty; he is alone and stuck. The film evokes this uncertainty and stagnation with an England in flux, grappling with rising unemployment; the Falklands war, where Shaun's father was killed; and increasing racial tensions. The future of the nation is unclear, especially to the youth. Just as Shaun is in search of a strong father figure, *This is England* portrays an English working-class youth population looking for direction. For Shaun and *This is England*'s English youth, this belonging and direction are temporarily found in the skinhead movement.

The skinhead subculture offers no long-lasting stability, but because of his encounter with it Shaun learns to look internally, not externally, for Truth. The final scene of the movie suggests the growth that Shaun has experienced through the same physical spaces that were used to portray his initial aimlessness. Now shown through continuity editing and contiguous space, Shaun walks towards the boat, stopping to take out the St George's Cross flag that Combo gave him, then continues through the field, which we now see overlooks the beach. The iconic significance of a flag is unavoidable in this sequence, as the political connotations of its cultural appropriation by racist groups are deployed to underscore the ideological consequences of Shaun's decision. But the scene is more than this: as Shaun throws the flag out to sea, he is, as Jon Savage describes it, 'confronted by both physical limit and emotional space'. However, the finality of the border between land and sea is not confining here but liberating in the distancing it represents (2007: 38).

Previously, Combo had drawn a line on the floor of his apartment and asked Shaun to cross it and join him; here, when Shaun throws the flag into the sea he rejects Combo's ideology by putting the most distinct physical separation – a shoreline – between himself and the flag. And while the boat Shaun passes is clearly not seaworthy, a visual connection between it and the sea, as the possibility for transportation, movement and growth, is now apparent. Just as the film's editing of the physical space has moved on from the earlier choppy fragmentation, the end suggests that there is hope for a more consistent future identity for Shaun and, by extension, England. However, this identity, as noted by William Brown, will not be 'an arbitrary notion of "nationality" defined by flags' (2008: 412) as evidenced by 'the desire to see the St George's Cross not waving but drowning' (415). The final shot of the film depicts Shaun staring unnervingly and directly at the camera, threatening the fourth wall boundary between himself and the audience. Recognisable as a recreation of the famous conclusion of François Truffaut's *Les quatre cents coups* (1959), this framing reinforces the location of Shaun as still isolated from society, but more steadfast in his reliance on himself to forge his own future apart from the ideology he has inherited and challenging the audience to consider examining their own beliefs.

This is England: social space

In the social space of the film, Shaun's spatial practices within the groups he joins, as seen in the rhetoric of his walking, reveal an ideological change from inclusion and hybridity to exclusion and singularity. When initially befriended by Woody's group and initiated into their midst, Shaun spends a day hanging out with the gang, which includes Milky (Meadows regular Andrew Shim), who is of Jamaican descent. They swim; they play football; they sit on park steps; they walk. Their walking is a joyous, bouncing affair, emphasised through the use of slow-motion. The boys and girls, sometimes separate, sometimes together, laughingly posture at being cool teenagers as they strut through their neighbourhood. Shaun, exuberant at his inclusion in the group, twirls and jumps in the centre and is playfully clocked on the head by Woody. For Woody and his gang, the skinhead movement is aesthetic, and having a gang is familial; while their music and fashion choices are chosen to place them in opposition to the general culture, they are not necessarily designed to intimidate but rather to align them with their own subculture, a sense of community that is then reflected in their spatial practices.

When Shaun leaves Woody's gang for Combo's, another pointedly parallel scene showcases the extreme difference in this group's purpose and ideology. No longer is there fluidity, fun, joy and unselfconscious hybridity; this group's walk is deadly serious and purposefully homogeneous. A straight line parallel to the screen comes towards the camera with Shaun standing tall, at the right hand of Combo, despite his comparative diminutive stature. This hyper-masculine group walks with militaristic precision, unsurprising as in the previous scene Combo reveals he considers them 'his troops'. The British-Jamaican Milky is not there; the girls Lol and Smell are not there, and because he questioned the dogma, Pukey is not there. Whereas the previous scene displayed a celebration of hybridity, the second walking sequence highlights white, male homogeneity. Combo is so aware of the power of their walk that he has Shaun and the others practise their walking back and forth across his apartment as they spew verbal abuse at imaginary immigrants.

Reinforcing a homogeneous society and rejecting a heterogeneous one, this intimidation is then put into action when Combo, Shaun and the rest return to an empty back alley where Shaun had previously played football with Woody's group on their day out. Now three Pakistani boys are likewise playing football, but they are quickly scared off. Combo threatens them and steals their football, saying, 'If I see you on my streets again … I'll slash ya. And it'll be a hundred fucking times worse. Now run home 'cause Mummy's cooking curry.' With this, Combo is claiming ownership of a public location and refusing entrance to the boys, not because of how they were using the space but because of his objections to their ethnicity. Instead of the alley being a hybrid location, where all could play together, physical violence is threatened, and verbal abuse is used to resist hybridity.

As Combo and Shaun become more committed to their nationalist ideology, their controlling violence moves from public to private spaces. They attack a convenience store where the owner had previously banned Shaun for reading comics without buying them. After misspelling their graffiti, the group enters the store and beats the owner while verbally assaulting him, pillaging the store and attempting to defecate on the floor. As Combo threatens the man with a machete, the owner repeatedly tells them to take whatever they want but to go. Combo does not allow him to dictate any of the group's spatial practices, however, and cannot leave without first emphasising that this is not a one-time violation of the man's private space. Combo tells him 'we'll be back here whenever we want because this is ours now', making clear that the man no longer has control over his space, that Combo has taken it from him. This colonising attitude allows them to feel entitled to space because of their race, differentiating this experience from a previous scene featuring the destruction of property by Woody's gang.

Earlier in the film, even before his head is shorn and he is officially initiated into Woody's group, Shaun is invited to accompany them when they go 'hunting'. This hunting consists of dressing up in an odd assortment of clothes (Woody in a kimono and umbrella hat, Gadget in a raccoon skin 'Davy Crockett' hat and goggles, and others with ammunition-laden military vests, a ladies' fur coat, a Japanese sword, a mask and snorkel, and a feathered cowboy hat), stomping through abandoned buildings, and smashing things up. While on the surface this is disconcertingly similar to Combo's outrageous assault on other people's space and spatial practices in its destruction, this hunting is actually more similar to what Guy DeBord (2010) and the Situationists termed a 'dérive' – a conscious psycho-geographic undercutting of the expectations of how one moves through space. Woody's group distinguish themselves from the general culture through their unusual garb and non-traditional use of space. While there is an undercurrent of anger in their destruction, Woody shows that this should clearly not be aimed at other people. When Gadget acts out against Shaun because Gadget feels that he's 'gone down in rank' with Shaun's arrival, Woody deftly manages the situation, making each boy explain his feelings, affirming each one's importance to the group, and ending with handshakes and hugs all around. In spite of their similarly destructive practices, ultimately, Woody's group affirms hybridity through inclusion and Combo's group affirms hate through exclusion.

This is England: mental space

Shaun's last name is Fields, and while this is certainly a nod to the auto-biographical nature of the film and Meadows' last name, this is also the location where we see him at his most vulnerable and introspective. The film begins with Shaun ideologically lost, unsure of how to act and who to be. As the film continues, it charts the battle for supremacy in Shaun's adolescent mental space as he questions what it means to be an Englishman and what would make his deceased father proud. The film includes radio reports and documentary footage from the Falklands war, but they are not directly addressed by the characters. Instead, the war hangs over the film like a silent cloud, reminding the audience of why Shaun is without a father, the terrible present absence that Shaun is continually feeling. Shaun is continually searching for his identity and attempting to fill the void left by his father. Though his mother, Cynthia, tries to be supportive and, in many ways, is a good parent, Shaun fails to connect with her, and their most significant interactions occur when talking about Shaun's father. Because Shaun is trying to discover his defining boundaries and edges, he seeks out associations with various groups and in particular tries looking to first Woody and then Combo as a father figure to help guide him in his mental displacement.

Woody, another terrain name, is the first man that Shaun attaches himself to in his search for a role model. While Woody offers an inclusive, hybrid society, he is ultimately unable to teach Shaun to replicate that ideology on his own, only to participate in it when with a group. The two first meet as Shaun walks home from the last day of school for the year, where Shaun had fought with another student for making fun of his trousers and his father. When teased by Gadget, before Shaun can even fight, Woody stops the other boy and has Shaun sit down with the group and tell him about why he looks so sad. The group is sitting in an underpass grafittied with skinhead band names consistent with their skinhead dress; they have their own space, and Woody invites Shaun, feeling isolated, into it. Shaun is then quickly embraced by the gang, an occurrence even sanctioned by his mother. During a group gathering, Shaun and Smell, one of the girls in the group, leave to have a sexual encounter of some kind (presumably Shaun's first), and, when he comes back, everything has changed; the world and the issues he encounters now are as an adult, however young he may be. Shaun's burgeoning sexual maturity foreshadows a rather more sinister rite of passage. Shortly after Shaun and Smell return to the group, Combo arrives, bringing with him a dangerous charisma which is fuelled by racist rhetoric. Combo's return precipitates the breakdown of the inclusive group and he directly challenges Woody's leadership.

Combo relates a racist story, complete with impressions, about a Jamaican man he met in prison. While a few people laugh, the majority, including Woody, Lol and Milky, are visibly uncomfortable, yet remain silent. Shaun's maturity is tested: he is not as independent as he tried to appear, and he is unsure of how to react without Woody offering a clear lead to follow.

Woody is not afraid to act out his own thoughts and ideology, though he is less willing to tell others outright what they should do. This is especially detrimental following Combo's 'This is England' speech about nationalist ideology when Combo singles out Shaun, who reacts angrily to mention of the Falklands. Combo virtually brainwashes Shaun, using Shaun's sensitivity regarding his father to convince Shaun that subscribing to Combo's nationalist rhetoric is honouring to his father's death and memory. At this point, Woody, Lol and Milky choose to leave as a sign of their rejection of this ideology. Though Lol urges Woody to bring Shaun with them, Woody says, 'There's nothing I can do if he wants to stay.' This perception is patently untrue and particularly dangerous after Combo's manipulation. This desertion is Woody's greatest sin. By leaving Shaun, sitting in Combo's apartment, Woody is abandoning him to Combo's racist – and extremely charismatic – influence. Shaun does not have the perspective to see the flaws in Combo's ideology and how it offers intolerance and exclusion, unlike Woody's.

Because Woody leaves Shaun to Combo, Shaun transfers his admiration and blind devotion to Combo, which Combo eagerly accepts, telling Shaun he reminds him of himself at that age. Combo's name may suggest hybridity but only ironically, as he is the film's most polarising figure. On the surface, Combo's nationalist ideology pits him against recent immigrants and those that do not fit his view of a white Anglo England; however, his racist vision and ideology of England have a complex background due to Combo's personal history. At one point in the film Combo, who is generally friendly with Milky, asks Milky if he considers himself to be English or Jamaican, and forces him to choose a side, specifically the English one, rather than allowing he might be both. The evening when Combo assaults Milky, though initiated by personal, non-racial motives, suggests to Shaun what the result of Combo's Nationalist neo-Nazi ideology truly is – hateful, senseless violence. Like Woody, Combo cannot fulfil the parental role that Shaun is craving, and Shaun is once again on his own.

By the end of the film, Shaun has been disillusioned by both Woody and Combo and claims neither as a father figure. Rather than seeking out either man after Milky's beating, Shaun stays at home with his mother and reminisces over photos of his dad, in particular one of the family at the beach. Shaun then returns to the field, the boat and the sea, those places the film demarcates as uniquely his. There he rejects Combo, and in so doing he is claiming for himself an identity that is still burgeoning but will be fashioned according to his own decisions and direction. Because he refuses the violence of Combo's xenophobic ideology and the passivity of Woody's inclusive one, Shaun has the potential to have a well-demarcated and hybrid identity.

New spatial practices in *Somers Town*

In many ways, *Somers Town* provides an interesting follow-up to *This is England* because it furthers the latter film's suggested hope for hybridity. Decisively positioned in a London neighbourhood depicted as multi-cultural, *Somers Town* shows contemporary English space mingling 'indigenous' and newly arrived cultures as its main characters make the transition from childhood to adulthood. Though the immigrants' role in England at the time of the film and how they are viewed by some English is not without problems and some defensiveness, Meadows' film largely focuses on the advantages of having a multicultural space. The physical space of *Somers Town* is hugely significant in setting the inclusive and progressive tone of the film. Tomo runs away from his home in Nottingham to London, just as Meadows himself filmically departs from his habitual use of Midlands settings. The area defined as Somers Town is heavily influenced by the railway system, and the film particularly features St Pancras Station. The sense of mobility suggested by the trains, connection to the rest of Britain, is augmented by the access to France and Belgium through the Channel Tunnel. While perhaps this inclusion of the station in the film is suspicious, given the feature's financing by Eurostar, which dictated the film's setting (Brouillette 2009: 835), Meadows was given the freedom as auteur to produce a film, not an advertisement, and the text can be read as a part of his artistic, not capitalistic, accomplishments. Unlike *This is England* with its grounded boat, the Somers Town boys have transportation that they can use to reconnect with Maria, the French waitress with whom they are both infatuated, at the end of the film – a movement that is significant enough to bring the film from black-and-white to colour.

Community is something that neither Tomo nor Marek truly has, but they find it with each other. Regardless of whether one believes the final moments to be actual or fanciful, earlier on in the film Tomo and Marek take Maria home and together create a unique social space that produces equality and harmony. Their walk together is their dérive, and, while far less destructive than the one in *This is England*, it is no less effective in providing an escape from monotonous spatial practices. Standing on their balcony, the boys see an abandoned wheelchair, which they deck out with streamers, flowers and a bell to create a 'special taxi' for Maria. As the two boys transport Maria home from her job at the café, the film lingers over their journey as they use this unusual travel method alternately to speed and meander through streets, parks and tunnels, passing by others who are sitting watching them. Initially, the trio interacts laughingly, but they soon lapse into silence, looking around and soaking in the surrounding space as they enjoy simply being with one another. When they reach Maria's home, she kisses both of the boys and tells them, 'Remember I love you both the same', and, even though they are seemingly in competition for her affections, the boys celebrate with each other. Maria's acceptance of them and this mutual joy stems from the spatial experience they have just shared, which was based on communal not individual achievement.

The characters' dérive is emblematic of the unspoken hybridity of the film, where nationality and ethnicity are not only unproblematic, but seemingly unimportant, although nevertheless recognised in the story. Tomo is English, Marek and his father Marius are Polish, Maria is French, and yet they each exist as characters, not stereotypes, and function harmoniously in the larger community. News articles from 2008 suggest that the place of Polish immigrants in English society was tenuous, as they were simultaneously admired for their hard work and feared because they held jobs (Kawczynski 2008; Moszczynski 2008), so Meadows' portrayal of them is significantly affirmative. Successful labourer Marek's strong accent and occasional struggles with English are never a point of contention or frustration between the boys, and Tomo never asserts a sense of superiority or natural right because of his English ancestry. Indeed, the film's only violent encounter occurs between English characters, when a gang of local boys beat up Tomo, fresh off the train from Nottingham, and take his things ostensibly because he is not from the area. This negative event is noteworthy in that the territorial violence is not shown in terms of nationalism, but more general thuggery, and the Somers Town community seems to embrace a variety of people without question. The film may seem unbelievably utopian, as critic Derek Malcolm suggests through his backhanded compliment, 'It is a genuinely pleasant watch. However, it is never quite tough enough to convince entirely', and to be sure the immigrants finding meaningful connections here are all white Europeans. But the film serves as a narrative to inspire rather than shock, to create hope, not to seedily titillate 'with drugs, for instance' as Malcolm advises for creating a story with 'more impact', and that is where its strength lies, in affirming the good that is and can be.

Tomo runs away from his home because he feels as though he has no space to belong, but he finds belonging and acceptance in Somers Town. When asked about his friends at home, Tomo's reply is that they are 'just people you know – useless waste of space. Like me.' He is mentally disconnected from his home space, where he found no value in the people around him or himself, and yet Tomo is presented as desperate to connect at the beginning of the film. His initial depiction shows the bloody Tomo posing as a tough guy, but the billboard behind him reveals his inner desires. The sign proclaims 'meet me' and shows a couple embracing and smiling at one another; Tomo, with arms crossed, looking tough with marks from his beating, is positioned directly under the 'me'. Tomo longs to connect with people, to establish meaningful relationships, and to be worthy of taking up space, all of which he finds in Somers Town. In addition to Marek, Tomo becomes acquainted with Graham, who lives in the same high-rise as Marek and employs the boys at odd jobs. Graham invites Tomo to move in with him at the film's end, and the work Tomo must do in exchange for board gives Tomo that sense of value and connection to the space that he had been searching for throughout the film.

Like Tomo, Marek is a lonely soul, looking for a space to belong. His father, Marius, works during the day and at night drinks with friends. When Marius and Marek have an argument, Marek asks him, 'What am I supposed to do here all day?' The 'here' implies not just the apartment, but also England. Revealed through a painful conversation with Marius, Marek views their lonely situation as temporary, expecting his mother to either join them in England or for them to return to Poland. Marius shares Marek's pain at the separation, but affirms that there is unlikely to be a reunion. Once Marek realises that his situation is more stable than he realised, and as his friendship with Tomo and Graham continues, he grows more comfortable and secure in his mental space, becoming more fully integrated into the community. The friendship of the two boys is a symbiotic bond. Both begin the film alienated, but, by the end, because of their acceptance of one another and their growing sense of inclusion in the larger community of Somers Town, they find significant connections.

Conclusion

Because *Somers Town* depicts a culture that is hybridised across all three of Lefebvre's categories of space, it is able to present a fully functioning and integrated community, rich because of its variety and fulfilling Bhabha's utopic view of hybridity 'without an assumed or imposed hierarchy' (5). This film can then be read as a coda to *This is England* of two years prior, overwriting the violence and hate fuelled by nationalism and celebrating hybridity, diversity and inclusion. In both *This is England* and *Somers Town*, characters' understandings of and interactions with space signify their ideologies and shape their identities. Just as the lead actor of both films has grown and matured, so too do these films portray a changing England between 1983 and 2008 as a nation increasingly hybridised in its acceptance of different cultures. The violence that comes with an inflexible national ideology, represented by the damaged Combo, has been replaced by a vision of a broader definition of self and country that can allow for meaningful, sustainable community; *Somers Town* suggests the type of inclusion that the area and country can aspire to by showing a vision of the possibilities available for a hybridised multicultural space.

References

Ashcroft, B., G. Griffiths and H. Tiffin (2002), *The Empire Writes Back*, London: Routledge.

Bhabha, H. K. (1994), *The Location of Culture*, London: Routledge.

Brouillette, S. (2009), 'Creative labour and auteur authorship: reading *Somers Town*', *Textual Practice*, 25: 3, 829–47.

Brown, W. (2008), 'Not flagwaving but flagdrowning, or postcards from post-Britain', in R. Murphy (ed.), *The British Cinema Book* (3rd edn), New York: Palgrave Macmillan, pp. 408–16.

Certeau, M. de (1984), *The Practice of Everyday Life*, trans. S. F. Rendall, Berkeley: University of California Press.

Debord, G. (2010), 'Theory of the dérive', 22 March: http://www.bopsecrets.org/SI/2.derive.htm.

Harkness, A. (2007), 'A history of violence', *The Scotsman*, 20 April: http://thescotsman.scotsman.com/features/A-history-of-violence.3278101.jp (accessed 5 January 2011).

Kawczynski, D. (2008), 'Poles in the UK are under attack. It's got to stop', *The Independent*, 25 April: http://www.independent.co.uk/opinion/commentators/daniel-kawczynski-poles-in-the-uk-are-under-attack-its-got-to-stop-815370.html (accessed 5 January 2011).

Kuortti, J. and J. Nyman (2007) (eds), *Reconstructing Hybridity: Post-Colonial Studies in Transition*, New York: Rodopi.

Lefebvre, H. (1991), *The Production of Space*, trans. D. Nicholson-Smith, Oxford and Cambridge, MA: Blackwell.

Malcolm, D. (2008), 'Runaway with a rose-tinted life', *London Evening Standard*, 8 August: http://www.thisislondon.co.uk/film/review-23542252-runaway-with-a-rose-tinted-life.do (accessed 26 November 2010).

Meadows, S. (2007), 'This is England: filmmaker Shane Meadows interview',

Future Movies: http://www.futuremovies.co.uk/filmmaking.asp?ID=203 (accessed 5 January 2011).

Monk, C. (1999), 'From underworld to underclass: crime and British cinema in the 1990s', in S. Chibnall and R. Murphy (eds), *British Crime Cinema*, London and New York: Routledge, pp. 172–88.

Moszczynski, W. (2008), 'Why Britain needs Polish migrants', *The Telegraph*, 3 April: http://www.telegraph.co.uk/comment/3556852/Why-Britain-needs-Polish-migrants.html (accessed 5 January 2011).

Savage, J. (2007), 'New boots and rants', *Sight & Sound*, 17: 5, 38.

CHAPTER 10

'Shane, don't film this bit': Comedy and Performance in *Le Donk and Scor-zay-zee*

Brett Mills

Le Donk and Scor-zay-zee is a significant film within Meadows' work because it is, as its DVD blurb attests, a 'comedy'. This places it at odds with the dominant assumptions related to Meadows, which, while acknowledging comic moments are common in his films, categorise him primarily not as a comedic director. This means that reviews and previews for *Le Donk* often note that while the film has clear similarities to others directed by Meadows, it is of a different sort from what is normally expected of him. For example, in *The Observer* Sean O'Hagan notes how Paddy Considine's performance, in other films thought of as having a 'dark intensity', 'is here reined in' (2009: 4); the implication is that not all of Considine's acting muscles are stretched in *Le Donk*, even though many reviews acknowledge the extent that the film draws on his improvisational skills for much of its content. Marc Lee, in *The Telegraph*, questions the cinematic nature of *Le Donk*, suggesting that it is more akin to television, because 'it isn't begging for the big-screen treatment' (2009: 11); it therefore fails to adhere to the notions of 'art cinema' (2009) that David Forrest sees as emblematic of the majority of Meadows' work. And Ben Hopkins, in the online magazine *ClashMusic*, enjoys the film, but calls it 'rather lightweight' and a 'stopgap' (2009), arguing in a manner similar to many other reviewers that *Le Donk* is an interesting experiment on the part of Meadows and Considine, but that we need to look elsewhere if we want to encounter their more substantial work. In all, then, *Le Donk and Scor-zay-zee* is commonly positioned as of minor significance in Meadows' output, and it is no coincidence that such responses should be engendered by a film which foregrounds its comic intent. That is, while the film succeeds in its aim to be funny, this appears to be perceived as having lesser artistic value, or social weight, than Meadows' other films, which are understood to be more 'serious'.

What this demonstrates is that it is commonly assumed that there is some kind of distinction between comic and serious culture, and that distinction not only resides in the 'meaning' of the text, but also suggests something about the social value of such culture. Yet examining the comedy in *Le Donk* is useful precisely because such humorous material is just as capable of pointing towards significant social truths as material in other films which appear more obviously didactic. It has been noted that 'the nature – and failure – of masculinity' (Hoggard 2007) is a recurring theme in Meadows' films. Indeed, Donk is a comedy character precisely because his attempts at carrying out certain kinds of masculinity repeatedly fail, and, as an audience, we are invited to find this funny because humour often alights on such social inadequacies. Many of the male characters in Meadows' films grapple with the ambiguities and challenges of contemporary masculinity. Yet the characters in most of these films are avowedly serious, and carry the serious intent of the film with them. The question that arises here, then, is why should a similarly flawed character such as Le Donk, who is engaged in an examination of his own masculinity just as many characters in other Meadows films are, be *funny*? The fact that we might laugh at Le Donk – when we would no doubt find some other Meadows men threatening or frightening – suggests that masculinity can be explored through both comedy *and* seriousness, even if certain kinds of representations encourage a comic reading rather than a serious one.

Key to the film's comedic mode is the mock-documentary format it adopts; the DVD blurb calls the film 'Meadows' hilarious rockumentary'. Early in the film we see Meadows, playing himself, turning up at Donk's house with his camera crew and explaining that he is making a film in which he will simply follow him. Donk seems pleased by this, partly because of the exposure it will give his protégé Scor-zay-zee (the real-life British rap artist Dean Palinczuk, playing himself), but clearly also because of his own ego. The mock-documentary format sets up a particular relationship between audience and character, precisely because it means that we are watching a character who knows he is being watched. For the majority of fiction film characters are unaware that their actions are being observed, and audiences are commonly offered a god-like position from which to peer on the action. In a mock-documentary, on the other hand, characters are aware that they are being observed, and so can, for example, break the fourth wall and speak to the audience they imagine is watching them. The mock-documentary format has been very important for television comedy in the last decade or so, in series such as *The Office* (BBC2/1, 2001–3), *Marion & Geoff* (BBC2, 2000–3) and *People Like Us* (BBC2, 1999–2001).

The comedy in such series works because many of the characters behave in inadequate ways – Roy Mallard in *People Like Us*, for example, is an extremely incompetent documentary filmmaker – but is given an extra inflection because the characters are happy for their inadequacies to be captured on camera or, worse, are utterly unaware of how they might be perceived by others. Both David Brent in *The Office* and Keith Barret in *Marion & Geoff* seem oblivious to the perceptions others will have of their behaviour, and the reason why such comedy is often referred to as 'a theatre of embarrassment' (Lewisohn 2003: 588) is because we are discomfited by characters who seem utterly lacking in self-awareness.

A significant amount of literature exploring the nature and consequences of mock-documentary now exists, with recurring themes being the representational strategies of such texts, their exploration of the relationships between filmmakers and their subjects, and the roles factual forms play in contemporary culture. As Jane Roscoe and Craig Hight note, 'Documentary holds a privileged position within society, a position maintained by documentary's claim that it can present the most accurate and truthful portrayal of the socio-historical world' (2001: 6). Such a position is often predicated on the production processes behind documentary, in which it engages with recording or capturing a previously existing world, and therefore functions as some kind of historical 'document'. Mock-documentary aims to critique and question the privileged position of documentary by actively foregrounding the processes and relationships which 'traditional' documentary merely assumes and relies on for its status. It does so partly by showing how easy it is to recreate the 'docu-real look' (Caldwell 2002: 268) in fictional forms (which is why, sometimes, audiences are 'fooled' into thinking mock-documentaries are 'real'), but also by commonly taking the relationship between filmmaker and subject as its main theme. In doing so, mock-documentaries often aim to recreate the 'documentary experience' (Juhasz and Lerner 2006: 7) of presenting a text that engages with the real world, but only via the practice of critiquing the very processes by which such documents come into being. That is, both documentaries and mock-documentaries aim to say something 'truthful' about the real world, but mock-documentary does so by engaging with, and critiquing, the normalised processes by which documentary carries out this act. Catherine L. Benamou therefore sees the mock-documentary as 'a carnivalesque exercise in poking fun at publicly revered sources of institutional authority' (2006: 151), where one of these authorities is documentary itself. And it is worth noting that in defining the form as 'carnivalesque' Benamou acknowledges that mock-documentary is often playful, funny, humorous and ridiculous: this is in opposition to the 'traditional' documentary, which commonly adopts a 'discourse of sobriety' (Nichols 1991: 3). The reviews of, and responses to, *Le Donk* summarised above suggest that Meadows' films are commonly assumed to be similarly sober; indeed, the 'real' documentaries that Meadows has made – such as *The Gypsy's Tale* (Channel Four, 1995) and *The Living Room* (2009) – adopt a more serious tone than *Le Donk*, and this distinction parallels the serious/comic distinction related to documentary and mock-documentary. In that sense, there is a formal relationship between *Le Donk*'s mock-documentary format and its comic content.

Indeed, Roscoe and Hight suggest that while the mock-documentary encompasses a wide range of texts, recurring tropes can be discerned within the genre, suggesting that the possibilities for the mock-documentary are as defined as those for the documentary 'proper'. They delineate three kinds of mock-documentary: the parody, which is a 'benevolent' form where 'documentary aesthetics are appropriated largely for stylistic reasons' and 'humour is emphasised' (2001: 68); the critique, which adopts a 'social-political stance' (70) towards a topic in a manner similar to most documentary, but whose material does not come from the same journalistic processes as the documentary; and the 'deconstruction', whose 'intention is to engage in a sustained critique of the set of assumptions and expectations which support the classic modes of documentary' (72). The latter's aim is quite different to that of the first two forms, for it sees the very legitimacy of documentary as something to be interrogated, while the 'parody' and the 'critique' necessarily rely on cultural understandings of the documentary for some of their pleasures. While the existence of Meadows playing himself in *Le Donk* might suggest that there are elements of the 'deconstruction' mode here, it is hard to make an argument that the key aim of the film is one that sees the documentary as a troubling social phenomenon. Instead, the film is more easily categorised as a 'parody', as it adopts the conventions of the documentary form primarily in order to offer spaces within which humour can be found in the film characters. In that sense, it follows in the tradition of other mock-documentaries about the absurdities of the music business – such as *The Rutles: All You Need is Cash* (BBC2, 1978), *The Comic Strip Presents ... Bad News Tour* (Channel Four, 1983) and *This is Spinal Tap* (Rob Reiner, 1984) – whose primary intent is not a sustained critique of the documentary form.

However, it is worth noting that *Le Donk* does not neatly adhere to these categorisations. For example, there is confusion in the film over the extent to which actors are playing themselves or characters. So, while there is, in

a manner common to fiction cinema, a distinction to be made between
Paddy Considine (the actor) and Donk (the character), this division is not
so neat for Shane Meadows, who is playing himself (or, at least, he is
playing a character that has the same name as himself). Furthermore, while
Scor-zay-zee plays himself, that persona is itself a fictional creation, the
rapping moniker for the 'real' person, Dean Palinczuk. That these three
different relationships between the on-screen and off-screen persona can
coexist in the same text makes neatly categorising the film's content and
aims difficult. Yet the mock–documentary format allows for such playful
transgression of the 'fact/fiction divide' (Beattie 2004: 146–60) in a manner
unavailable to the majority of fiction or the 'traditional' documentary.

Indeed, it is significant that *Le Donk* adopts the mock-documentary
format, when this is not an approach common in Meadows' films; why
mock-documentary for *this* narrative and *these* characters if Meadows has
not felt the need to adopt this style for his other fictional films? David
Forrest places Meadows' films within an 'art cinema' tradition, arguing
that the 'documentary authenticity' (2009: 192) of British social realism
has become a limiting yardstick by which such film has come to be
measured. In arguing for an acceptance of, and engagement with, the
'poetic dimension' (193) of such films, Forrest suggests art cinema encourages audiences to engage with texts 'in an increasingly profound manner'
(194), a text–audience relationship lacking in the limiting and pragmatic
format of something such as documentary. In that sense, adopting a mock–
documentary format for *Le Donk* means that a set of techniques become
unavailable to Meadows in making the film. Indeed, it is hard to find
evidence in *Le Donk* that a 'poetic dimension' is on offer, and the film could
be argued to be more visually 'flat' than the majority of Meadows' work.
Yet, as noted above, the mock-documentary format opens up a series of
spaces between filmmaker and subject which are perhaps unavailable with
the 'art cinema' tradition. Indeed, the auteurist connotations of art cinema
necessarily posit the filmmaker as the central guiding force within the text;
Forrest argues that the 'excessive aesthetic foregrounding' of art cinema
points towards 'positive affirmations of authorship' (194) that help uphold
the legitimacy of auteurism. The mock-documentary format, on the other
hand, repeatedly belies the processes by which cinema comes to be made,
and posits the director as merely another player within filmmaking practice.
Seeing 'Shane Meadows' in *Le Donk* failing to communicate adequately
with his subjects, and running around after them not knowing what they're
going to do, highlights the extent to which filmmaking is, quite often, done
on the fly, and is therefore a far more hit-and-miss procedure than the

notion of the 'auteur' seems willing to allow. Stella Bruzzi outlines how the pleasure of texts associated with documentary-makers such as Nick Broomfield is seeing 'the hassling director enacting the process of making a documentary', but, in doing so, such films make problematic our under-standing of the 'persona he performs on camera' (171). This 'performative mode' (Nichols 1994: 95) of documentary results in films that question their own status even as they come into being, while simultaneously offering representations of a documentary-maker that may be as performed as anything within fiction. By this account, *Le Donk* encourages us to question the auteur construct labelled 'Shane Meadows'.

This disparity between self-perception and actual perception is apparent at a key moment in *Le Donk and Scor-zay-zee*, where the eponymous leads practise their performance in a hotel bedroom in front of the camera crew and other assorted hangers-on. Le Donk's contribution consists solely of telling a list of random names to 'calm down', and the camera crew and Meadows laugh in hysterics not only at the absurdity of the list, but also at the disparity between this performance and the norms associated with certain forms of rap. Le Donk gets angry at the reception of his performance and leaves the room, insulting many of the people in it as he goes. When he has gone, Meadows and the others are quite shocked, and Meadows says, 'I thought he knew it was funny'. At this moment there is a disparity between self-perception and actual perception, and the moment is comedic because of this incongruity. It is noticeable here, though, that both sides misunderstood what was going on: Le Donk thought it was 'obvious' he was serious, whereas the film crew thought it was 'obvious' that he was not. In that sense, the film crew are as lacking in awareness as Le Donk is, and this interplay between performance and perception is a key one when thinking about the comedic nature of the film.

This idea of social 'performance' draws on the sociological work of Erving Goffman. In *The Presentation of Self in Everyday Life* (1969 [1959]) Goffman argues that social behaviour is *always* a performance because it responds to, and recreates, social conventions and norms for any kind of interaction. The term 'performance' is not intended to suggest that people *lie* in social interactions, and, by performing, are failing to reveal their true selves. Instead it suggests, in Goffman's words, that there is 'a crucial discrepancy between our all-too-human selves and our socialized selves' (56), and that learning to be a part of a society is about learning the parameters within which social interaction takes place. Quite often these parameters might clash with our individual desires or needs, or what might be thought of as instinctive, gut reactions. This idea of performance is useful for thinking about mock-documentary and comedy because it is often the disparity that Goffman refers to which such texts offer up as funny. The jokes only make sense if we know what the appropriate behaviour for a socialised self is, against which we can then measure the actual behaviour of individuals. It is the fact that comedy often works by offering up characters that fail to conform to social norms that has led to long-standing debates about whether most humour is conservative or radical: authors such as Aristotle (1980 [c. 350 BCE]) and Michael Billig (2005) argue that, as we laugh at inappropriate behaviour, we reassert social norms and mock those who fail to conform; conversely, writers such as Patricia Mellencamp (1992) and Kathleen Rowe (1995) argue that, in acting in unsocialised ways, comedy characters embody a rejection of such norms and therefore function as powerful critiques of social conventions. Whatever the consequences of such comedy are, it is clear that this humour *highlights* social norms and, by presenting characters who fail to conform to them, demonstrates such norms are nothing other than social constructions which are capable of being transgressed.

Le Donk fails to engage in socially appropriate behaviour in a number of places in the film. This is perhaps most evident in the scenes either involving his ex-girlfriend, Olivia, or in which he reflects on their failed relationship, often talking to the camera crew. For example, Le Donk's masculinity is threatened by Sonic, the man who is now dating Olivia and will be present at the birth of the child Le Donk and Olivia are having. Confronting him on the stairs in Olivia and Sonic's home, Le Donk makes a number of threats to him, eventually resulting in challenging him to take his trousers down so they can compare penis size. Tellingly, the film crew intervene at this point, informing Le Donk this is something they don't really want to see, which makes clear that such behaviour is deemed socially inappropriate and, perhaps more pertinently, something which they don't want to be part of the film; that is, not part of a text which will exist within a public arena. In a number of such scenes it appears vital to Le Donk that he is in control not only of the filming, but also of the performance he makes of himself. For example, he seems quite happy, early on in the film, to recount to the camera crew trying to get Olivia to have an abortion, even though this is a story which, he clearly knows, is not something likely to endear him to anyone viewing. This shows how Le Donk is capable of revealing socially damaging pieces of information, but appears comfortable doing so only when he is in charge of what is and isn't revealed. He makes this apparent early in the film when he negotiates the parameters of the filming with Meadows and his crew, stating that 'The thing that fears me about it, Shane, is if I'm too exposed. I don't like to be too exposed. [...] I just don't want to be exposed as a meany [...] It happened to the fucking Osbournes, they just showed all the tantrums.'

This is shown by what occurs when others control the information, and reveal facts which Le Donk has not sanctioned. This is perhaps best exemplified in the film when we first see Le Donk with Olivia, and their conversation turns to a negotiation of what will happen when their baby is born. Olivia reveals that she plans for her new partner, Sonic, to be at the birth rather than Le Donk, and so Sonic, sensing that his presence is not helping the debate continue, decides to leave Le Donk and Olivia alone. Olivia states that it is fair for Sonic to be at the birth as he has been her partner at the antenatal classes she has attended, and Le Donk asks, 'Why didn't you tell me about the classes? I would've come with you'. Olivia responds: 'I did, and you said "what a load of shit"'. There follows a pause, and Le Donk turns to the camera and says, 'Shane, don't film this bit, mate'. We then hear Shane, off-screen, ask, 'What?', and Le Donk replies, 'It's weird having you film this bit, because I'm trying to talk privately'. This is followed by Olivia asking, 'Why did you come here with cameras?', and Le Donk reasons, 'Because I thought it was going to be pleasant, but it's turning a little bit fucking disruptive now'. After some disagreement between the two, Le Donk again appeals to Shane: 'This situation's a bit sore to me, so I'd rather you switched it [the camera] off'.

We could see this moment as emblematic of the recurring theme of masculinity in Meadows' films, for Le Donk's discomfort is predicated on his realisation that his masculinity is under threat, especially as he is being told that he is not required to fulfil the 'New Man' (Schneider 2007) roles associated with contemporary fatherhood. Yet what is more telling for this moment is that Le Donk is less concerned about the conversation between himself and Olivia, and more that that conversation is being *seen*. More than that, it is being *recorded*. His exhortation to Shane that he 'not film this bit' is evidence of the fear of what the conversation being seen by others might mean for the version of masculinity he is trying to carry off. There is nothing in this conversation that suggests it is not of a kind that has occurred between Le Donk and Olivia many times before; indeed, it appears to be the kind of interaction which dominates their communication (and which, perhaps we can assume, is one of the reasons why their relationship foundered). While feigning nonchalance, it is clear that Le Donk never forgets that the camera crew is there and, consequently, is therefore always actively aware of the performance of himself he is attempting to portray. Le Donk's concern over the camera crew, then, is emblematic of a fear of a lack of control concerning how he might be perceived by others, and this fear of failing to convince others of the intended performance can be understood within the context of the surveillance society.

Much contemporary sociological research argues that we now live in a surveillance society, in which the possibility of being seen, usually by unidentified others, is part of everyday life. In a society with widespread CCTV we are observed and recorded multiple times each day, and the knowledge that this may, or may not, be taking place at every moment, contributes to the ways we modify our behaviour for fear of being spotted engaging in any kind of misdemeanour. This means that TV, film, CCTV and other media forms can be seen, in Gareth Palmer's words, to be the 'technology of social control' (2003: 35). It is through the fear of being seen that society regulates behaviour, and therefore controlling *how* you are seen becomes vital to how you are understood by others. Michel Foucault argues that such regimes mean we live in 'a disciplinary society' (1977 [1975]: 216), wherein disciplining others for inappropriate behaviour becomes a justified and vital role played out by governments, families and individuals. Notably, Foucault goes on to argue that the fear of such discipline becomes embodied by the individual, who regulates their behaviour in order to pre-empt any punishment that may be meted out on them. Foucault argues that it is these regimes of self-discipline that are the most powerful, because once they exist they do not necessarily require social structures to support them. That is, if we are all making sure we don't behave badly, we don't need the state to monitor our behaviour. In Le Donk's fear over how he will be understood via the film he is taking part in we can see the disciplinary society in action. The fear of social censure in response to his behaviour is enough to force him to modify that behaviour – or, more accurately, to force him to attempt to *hide* that behaviour from others. If he can convince Shane to 'not film this bit' then he can maintain mastery not only over his performance, but also over whether or not he will be censured by others. It is therefore being seen that remains the biggest threat to his idea of his own identity, and it remains the case throughout the film that Le Donk tries to control the version of himself witnessed by others.

Of course, the fact that this character calls himself 'Le Donk' at all demonstrates his desire to construct an image for himself and to control the access others have to his life. Indeed, in the scene between Olivia and Le Donk explored above, the one point at which Le Donk seems truly perplexed is when Olivia calls him by his real name – Nicholas – and he repeatedly asks her to call him Le Donk instead, stating, 'My name's not

Nicholas'. When Olivia replies that it is, he relents, but asks her not to call him it in front of the camera crew, showing how there is a version of himself which he is happy to have filmed: a version of the self which is distinct from his given name and the access to the private self that that implies. This desire to withhold the private is also seen later in the film when Le Donk, Scor-zay-zee and the camera crew arrive at the hotel in Manchester and make their way to their rooms. Le Donk enters his and immediately stands in the doorway, barring everyone else from entering, saying, 'This is where Le Donk says "au revoir"'. When Shane asks if he can come in and film him in his room, Le Donk replies, 'No, I don't want the crew following me around all day, you've got to give me some time on my own', and eventually reveals that he 'wants to have a shit in peace' because he 'can't have a shit if there's someone in my room'. Here Le Donk happily acknowledges his bodily need, but refuses to let others witness it. This shows how, within contemporary society, it is being seen that is the context which most defines social behaviour, and this film as a whole finds humour in the problems individuals encounter when attempting to maintain the social self once they agree to let others witness them.

The notion of the witness in comedy is important because it raises questions concerning how the audience, the collective group that engages in witnessing, is positioned relative to the humorous material. Steve Neale and Frank Krutnik argue that all comedy offers viewers a 'privileged' (1990: 185) audience position where we have 'spectatorial superiority' (73). That is, it situates us as omniscient viewers of events actively engaging in our spectatorhood – it is for this reason that television sitcoms have commonly had laugh tracks, which foreground the 'privileged' position we, and those others we can hear laughing, are offered. The mock-documentary functions as a development of the sitcom laugh track, in which the viewer of the event – in this case, the film crew – is made explicit, and the audience is consistently offered a viewing space aligned with those filming the action. It may be for this reason that *Le Donk* adopts a mock-documentary format for a film intended to be comic; in its foregrounding of the relationship between audience and text the mock-documentary is a mode well suited to comedy. As Paul Ward notes, 'Although not all mock-documentaries are necessarily comedies … the comedic mock-documentary certainly predominates' (2005: 72). In putting on display the processes by which texts come into being, the mock-documentary cannot help but disassociate itself from the 'reality effect' of dominant forms of social realism which attempt to deny their 'constructedness' (Lacey 1995: 69). But it is telling here that while mock-documentary's purpose has commonly been to critique the assumed norms of the 'traditional' documentary, *Le Donk* seems uninterested in such concerns. That is, there is little critique of the filmmaking process within the text, and nothing to suggest that 'Shane Meadows' and his filmmaking technique deserve analysis. As noted earlier, the television series *People Like Us* shows the incompetency of the documentary filmmaker; *Le Donk*, on the other hand, presents the character of Le Donk as worthy of ridicule, and the majority of the film's comic moments invite us to find him as the butt of the joke. In that sense, *Le Donk* reconfirms the validity of the documentary project, and offers little analysis of the relationship between documentary-maker and subject in a manner that finds the filmmaker to be the one required to think about what he is doing.

This means it is also worth thinking about who is standing in for the audience here; who is the on-screen presence representative of our spectatorial superiority? It is, of course, Shane Meadows and his film crew. That is, it is the filmmaker who we are invited to align ourselves with, and who adopts the position from which Le Donk's behaviour is rendered comic. The autobiographical nature of many of Meadows' films has been noted many times, with characters – especially those played by Thomas Turgoose – standing in for Meadows. In *Le Donk and Scor-zay-zee* we have no such surrogate character; Meadows plays himself, and the film reveals very little about what we are meant to make of him as a filmmaker. The comic butt of this film is very definitely *not* Meadows, for Meadows is one of the personas finding Le Donk funny; this is in sharp contrast to much of Meadows' other work, where laughable characters can be equated with some sense of the filmmaker's self. In this way, in *Le Donk* Meadows adopts an on-screen persona which occupies the superior spectatorial position which renders Le Donk a comic figure and which aligns Meadows' laughter at him with that of the audience. The exhortation from Le Donk for Shane to 'not film this bit' might therefore serve as a warning to all who agree to display their lives in front of the camera. But perhaps we need to think about the existence of moments such as these in a mock-documentary which features a filmmaker playing himself. What are we to make of a resolutely non-autobiographical film from a filmmaker who often uses the medium to explore his own history, and is there anything to be made of the fact that this film adopts a format and (comic) tone not foregrounded in his other work? As noted at the outset, critics have seen *Le Donk* as a minor film, and not worthy of as much analysis as others made by Meadows. That Meadows doesn't explore his own sense of self in *Le Donk*, and instead we get a film in which the filmmaker is aligned with the audience, laughing at a character with a flawed sense of self, seems to say that once humour becomes the key thing in a film, Meadows is far more comfortable hiding behind the camera. Le Donk spends the film negotiating the access to his life he wants to give the filmmakers; Meadows has done this in his other, more autobiographical, films, but resolutely avoids it here. In that sense, perhaps it is Meadows in *Le Donk*, referring to his own life (but not those of others), who most extols the dictum 'don't film this bit'.

References

Aristotle (1980 [c. 350 BCE]), *The Nicomachean Ethics*, trans. D. Ross, Oxford and New York: Oxford University Press.

Beattie, K. (2004), *Documentary Screens: Non-Fiction Film and Television*, Basingstoke: Palgrave Macmillan.

Benamou, C. L. (2006), 'The artifice of realism and the lure of the "Real" in Orson Welles's *F for Fake* and other t(r)eas(u)er(e)s', in A. Juhasz and J. Lerner (eds), *F is for Phony: Fake Documentary and Truth's Undoing*, Minneapolis and London: University of Minnesota Press, pp. 143–70.

Billig, M. (2005), *Laughter and Ridicule: Towards a Social Critique of Humour*, London: Sage.

Bruzzi, S. (2000), *New Documentary: A Critical Introduction*, London and New York: Routledge.

Caldwell, J. (2002), 'Prime-time fiction theorizes the docu-real', in J. Friedman (ed.), *Reality Squared: Televisual Discourse on the Real*, New Brunswick, NJ and London: Rutgers University Press, pp. 259–92.

Forrest, D. (2009), 'Shane Meadows and the British New Wave: Britain's hidden art cinema', *Studies in European Cinema*, 6: 2–3, 191–201.

Foucault, M. (1977 [1975]), *Discipline and Punish: The Birth of the Prison*, London: Penguin.

Goffman, E. (1969 [1959]), *The Presentation of Self in Everyday Life*, Harmondsworth: Penguin.

Hoggard, L. (2007), 'I was a skinhead myself in 1983', *The Observer*, 1 April: http://www.guardian.co.uk/film/2007/apr/01/2.

Hopkins, B. (2009), 'Film Review', *ClashMusic*, 25 October: http://www.clash-music.com/reviews/le-donk-and-scor-zay-zee.

Juhasz, A. and J. Lerner (2006), 'Introduction: phony definitions and troubling taxonomies of the fake documentary', in A. Juhasz and J. Lerner (eds), *F is for Phony: Fake Documentary and Truth's Undoing*, Minneapolis and London: University of Minnesota Press, pp. 1–35.

Lacey, S. (1995), *British Realist Theatre: The New Wave in its Context, 1956–1965*, London and New York: Routledge.

Lee, M. (2009), 'DVD of the week', *The Telegraph*, 31 October, Art section, p. 11.

Lewisohn, M. (2003), *The Radio Times Guide to TV Comedy* (2nd edn), London: BBC Worldwide.

Mellencamp, P. (1992), *High Anxiety: Catastrophe, Scandal, Age, and Comedy*, Bloomington and Indianapolis: Indiana University Press.

Neale, S. and F. Krutnik (1990), *Popular Film and Television Comedy*, London and New York: Routledge.

Nichols, B. (1991), *Representing Reality: Issues and Concepts of Documentary*, Bloomington and Indianapolis: Indiana University Press.

Nichols, B. (1994), *Blurred Boundaries: Questions of Meaning in Contemporary Culture*, Bloomington and Indianapolis: Indiana University Press.

O'Hagan, S. (2009), 'It's a rap: This is England, economy rate', *The Observer*, 27 September, Review section, p. 4.

Palmer, G. (2003), *Discipline and Liberty: Television and Governance*, Manchester: Manchester University Press.

Roscoe, J. and C. Hight (2001), *Faking It: Mock-Documentary and the Subversion of Factuality*, Manchester: Manchester University Press.

Rowe, K. (1995), *The Unruly Woman: Gender and the Genres of Laughter*, Austin: University of Texas Press.

Schneider, A. (2007), *The New Man: Masculinity after Traditionalism and Feminist Reaction*, Texas: SocioThought.

Ward, P. (2005), *Documentary: The Margins of Reality*, London and New York: Wallflower.

CHAPTER 11

'Them over there': Motherhood and Marginality in Shane Meadows' Films

Louise FitzGerald and Sarah Godfrey

As has been highlighted in this collection, Shane Meadows' persona as a white, working-class man from a deprived community in post-industrial Britain is inexorably connected to his status as a contemporary British auteur. Recurrent links between his proletarian Midlands background and the thematic and aesthetic concerns of his films made by both critics and the filmmaker himself reinforce the narrative construction of Meadows as a filmmaker with a particularly authentic worldview (Romney 2004). Meadows' cinematic vision is informed by and indebted to his own position at the 'social and geographical margins' (Fradley 2010: 290); the worlds he presents are the down-trodden and deprived communities which had been ravaged by the inexorable march of post-industrialisation. Indeed, it seems that it is precisely Meadows' own marginality – his distance from the London-centric media world – that distinguished him from many of his contemporaries and helped to garner critical acclaim for his films.

Meadows began making films in 1994; this was a moment in time where the confluence of 'Cool Britannia' commingled with discourses of 'new' lad culture, neoliberal meritocracy and 'girl power' to produce a particularly contested cultural terrain of gender and class politics. Imelda Whelehan notes that the aspirational discourses of 'new laddism' were often far removed from the 'lad on the street ... disenfranchised by his own lad heroes whose massively inflated salaries serve to underline the growing chasm between the rich and poor' (Whelehan 2000: 74). It was in this complex and often contradictory historical moment that Shane Meadows made the featurette *Small Time* (1996). In this low-budget semi-amateur film, Meadows invites the viewer into a parochial world of small-time criminals living in a deprived provincial town that 'ain't fucking London, this isn't even Nottingham, man, this is Sneinton'. Meadows introduces a cacophonous cluster of characters seldom represented by 1990s mainstream popular culture other than as a social problem in talk shows; the beginning of the social stereotyping that would later harden into the figure of the 'chav'. Meadows' 'affectionate' testimony in *Small Time* to the endurance and inventiveness of communities of men bonded through their experiences of disempowerment and social marginalisation marks a thematic concern that underpins much of the director's subsequent work.

In this chapter, we suggest that the framing concept of community as a way of understanding Meadows' work is something of a misnomer, because invariably his films refer specifically to a community of men. Women, while present, are only of peripheral significance within this male milieu, and their predominant narrative function is, we suggest, to serve in the recuperation of disenfranchised masculinity. Our aim in this chapter is to bring the marginal woman to the centre of our analysis to explore what we claim are derogated representations of working-class women and working-class femininity within an authorial world frequently acclaimed for its authenticity. In so doing, we will suggest the disjuncture between Meadows' position as a director whose work is understood as being decidedly invested in questions of British identity, British masculinity and the British class system is at odds with his articulation of a homogenised, transnational discourse of femininity which frequently elides important national and regional specificities.

While the focus on male identity is taken as a given of Meadows' films and is invariably the aspect of his work that is most explicitly commented on, Meadows' films do not present us with an entirely homosocial environment in the same way that films by his contemporaries such as Guy Ritchie or Nick Love do. There are numerous female characters throughout Meadows' oeuvre, such as Carol (Ladene Hall) and Sandra (Julia Ford) in *A Room for Romeo Brass*, Auntie Iris (Pamela Cundell), Pat (Annette Badland) and Jo (Jo Bell) in *TwentyFourSeven* and Lol (Vicky McClure), Trev (Danielle Watson) and Smell (Ros Hansen) in *This is England*. These women are at times highly visible members of the communities that constitute Meadows' cinematic vision, and so it is not the case that Meadows' preoccupation with masculinity is symptomatic of an inherently masculinist gender politics (Monk 2000: 157) or, as Steve Chibnall claims of Guy Ritchie's films, that 'the general absence of female characters is less an expression of hatred of women than the irrelevance of women to the stories Ritchie wants to tell, and the concerns he wants to address.' (2009: 378). Rather, with the exception of Lol in the *This is England* saga, the various female characters in Meadows' work are often endowed with what we see as a somewhat limited narratological function; it is this that we wish to explore in more detail in this chapter.

It is also worth noting how the representation of women within Meadows' television work has taken an interesting and potentially more progressive direction than seen in his cinematic output. Vicky McClure – who plays Lol in the *This is England* television series – draws attention to this apparent shift in a recent interview: 'Finally, it's so good seeing Shane Meadows using a female lead and to see a really strong female character' (Pook 2012).This comment is significant for two reasons. Firstly it highlights *This is England '88* as a programme which places at its centre a female character. But secondly, it also acknowledges that this shift in Meadows' treatment of women may be long overdue. Indeed, the opening frames of *This is England '88*, which begin with Lol waking up, suggest that her character is becoming increasingly central to the narrative; throughout the first episode of *'88* Meadows offers a sensitive portrayal of maternal alienation and dislocation; the cinematography emphasises Lol's loneliness, her isolation and her fatigue as she struggles to cope with the often exasperating and exhausting task of bringing up a child alone. Lol's dislocation is further articulated in the confrontation with the community nurse – a woman who appears to signify all that Lol lacks; the friendship that forms between these two women later in the series is, for us, possibly Meadows' most sympathetic and compelling rendering of female experience and community to date. The religious subtext that accompanies Lol's overdose is not without problem in its recourse to conservative discourses of gender and family, but it is clear from the series that Meadows' work does not simply marginalise or ignore female characters.

Despite Meadows' apparent new direction in the television *This is England* series, there remains an overall lack of attention paid to the ways in which women's lives are presented within his work. This is in spite of Meadows' own comments on how his memories of oppressive attitudes towards working-class women are central to the cultural landscape his films draw from. With specific reference to his film *Dead Man's Shoes*, Meadows explains 'that's the sadness with them people, there was never any respect for women ... there was no fuckin respect there' (Field 2004). The issue of respect towards women is centralised in the 2010 television and online short film Meadows directed as part of a government campaign to raise awareness of the seldom-discussed problem of sexual violence in adolescent heterosexual relationships (see http://thisisabuse.direct.gov.uk; film available to view on YouTube: http://www.youtube.com/watch?v= RzDr18U YO18). Associating himself with a project on domestic violence reinforces a sense of Meadows as actively engaged with gender politics, consolidated by the director's insistence in an interview for BBC News that the advert portrays 'a message I fundamentally believe in ... about finding another way of leading your life' (http://news.bbc.co.uk/1/hi/uk/8515601.stm). The film, which was commissioned with a teenage audience in mind, brings a very difficult social issue to the fore and powerfully urges teenage boys, in particular, not to use violence against women. However, the means by which the film achieves its message is potentially problematic in limiting the female position (perhaps inevitably?) to that of victim and refusing her any capacity for agency. The film is set in a girl's bedroom and features a teenage boy abusing his girlfriend verbally, emotionally and physically for refusing to 'have some fun' (sex) with him. The scenario escalates to the point where he throws her mobile phone across the room and grabs her by the hair while admonishing her for 'making him do this'. As the violence continues the frame is split by a two-way mirror where the boy's 'rational' alter ego looks on and remonstrates with his violent self, telling his 'bad self' to leave the girl alone. The advert is clearly aimed at changing male behaviour and getting boys to recognise any bullying as abhorrent, and it responds to its brief with verve and eloquence. But, acknowledging that they may not have been the director's editorial choice, the commercial's narrative and the *mise-en-scène* inadvertently have the effect of making the girl featured in it more of a passive victim; in failing to accord her the same process of self-remonstration as the boy, it effectively denies her an opportunity to take control over her own life. There is no attempt in this particular instance to suggest that the girl can leave her violent boyfriend; rather it proposes that this is a male problem. Thus questions of female experience and subjectivity are foreclosed and, arguably, become subsumed within wider discourses of male crisis and violence.

The young girl in Meadows' advert clearly plays an important narrato-logical role but is accorded scant subjectivity, and we suggest that the sidelining of the female perspective witnessed in this advert is, in fact, a defining feature of the gender politics of Meadows' cinematic work to date. While, as noted earlier, his films might contain a number of female characters, it is very rare that their lives drive the narrative. For instance, in *TwentyFourSeven*, the experiences of female characters are appropriated in order to frame narratives of flawed masculinity. The abuse that Pat (Annette Badland) suffers at the hands of Geoff (Bruce Jones) and that provokes the anger of Darcy (Bob Hoskins) is used less in its own right and more as a pretext for presenting male victimisation and disenfranchise-ment. Pat, like the girl in the advert, has no agency within her personal relationships; rather it would seem that the emphasis is less on female challenge than on male redemption and recuperation. In both examples, the subtext is that Pat and the nameless girl in the advert have no recourse to action, that in their enforced passivity they can only wait and hope that the male partner will change his behaviour. The issue of male violence towards women is a recurrent thematic concern running through Meadows' work: *Dead Man's Shoes*, *A Room for Romeo Brass* and *Small Time* all feature instances of male physical abuse, while Lol in the television series *This is England '86* is another woman victimised and abused by a man, in her case her own father. These narratives all serve to highlight the oppression of working-class women and the fundamental lack of respect that Meadows himself sees as characteristic of their experience within a male-dominated environment, but there is little evidence in his *films* – at least to date – of an explicit critique of those power dynamics and their impact on women's lived experience.

A family business: *Small Time*

Small Time (1996), a film read by Claire Monk as 'a social comedy of gender' (1999: 186), is, for us, an example of how Meadows' challenge to female oppression may be limited in political and critical purchase. The film invites us to accompany life-long friends Jumbo (Shane Meadows) and Malcolm (Mat Hand) and their gang of rag-tag small-time thieves as they go about their daily lives, offering a low-key celebration of their benign ineptitude. Jumbo, described in one review as 'a loveable rogue' (Dyja 2010), is, in fact, violent and abusive towards his partner Ruby (Gena Kawecka). Monk's claim that 'Ruby may be a battered woman but her confident, self-contained sexuality and indifference to Jumbo make it clear that his violence towards her is an expression of impotence rather than power' (1999: 187) is, for us, deeply problematic. While Jumbo is clearly codified as a risible character, his violence towards Ruby should not be so easily dismissed; the violently sexualised threat to 'shove a screwdriver up yer arse' is nasty and deeply unpleasant behaviour from a character who is supposedly a 'loveable' rogue. The cinematography appears to emphasise rather than dismiss Jumbo's threat in this scene as he leans over Ruby, who remains trapped on the sofa. Indeed, throughout the film Jumbo's ineptitude is juxtaposed with his abusive tendencies, and his behaviour towards Ruby should not be mitigated on the basis of her apparent resilience. It is the character of Kate (Dena Smiles) who offers the film's most explicit critique of Jumbo's violence when she accuses her partner,

Malc, of colluding in Ruby's abuse by failing to challenge his friend's behaviour. This gestures to a desire to raise consciousness and critique domestic violence within the film, but this narrative thread remains peripheral and is not picked up to any great extent; as a result Ruby and Jumbo are too easily read as a combative but essentially benign partnership of equals.

Small Time is particularly interesting among Meadows' earlier work because it does feature two prominent female characters whose stories run parallel with the male narratives concerned with homosocial camaraderie, socioeconomic marginality and criminality. Kate and Ruby are neighbours and the mothers to Malcolm's and Jumbo's respective children. One of the very first pieces of dialogue in the film emphasises the centrality of family to the narrative; as Jumbo narrates, 'we all just started out as mates and now we're a family, a family business. That's what I believe in, see. There's my missus and Malc's missus … we've got kids and we ain't fuckin' going anywhere.' What becomes apparent, however, as the narrative progresses is that this is a family dominated by men, while women present a threat to male relationships and male communities: when Kate and Malcolm are talking about their relationship Jumbo interrupts and challenges Kate's 'claim' to his friend (made viable because she is his long-term partner and the mother of his child), exclaiming 'How long 'ave you been around for … three years? Four years? Five years? Whatever … I've known him me whole life, I've been there 'is 'ole life.' Thus the maternal figure (and the women's role as mothers) is acknowledged but subsequently relegated to the margins in relation to male camaraderie. The maternal role is further derogated when Jumbo proclaims that his and Malc's 'missus' 'sit around watching telly all day … as long as my tea's on the table that's fine with me'. This could all be read in comic or satirical terms as evidence of Jumbo's idiocy, but in subtle ways the film also gives credence, perhaps unintentionally, to certain views expressed by him (and he is, after all, also played – and improvised – by the director himself). Crucially, Kate and Ruby are seldom seen actively mothering their children, the last scene of the film standing out as the only one where Kate and her children are engaging with each other. However, this refusal to show Kate and Ruby 'mothering' their children does not preclude the film from differentiating between good and bad motherhood through other means. Ruby's maternalism is implicitly derogated: she sleeps off the effects of an afternoon drinking session; she demands to be allowed to join in with Jumbo's all-male group, who are drinking and taking drugs; and her apparently insatiable (yet crucially secretive) sexual desire immediately places her at odds with the appropriate sexuality of 'good' mums. Ruby's 'self-contained sexuality' (Monk 1999: 187) represented by her secret use of a vibrator might be read as positive, but one might equally argue that her enjoyment of masturbation is presented as both monstrous and comedic. Moreover, Ruby's sexuality is, rather curiously, equated with motherhood in a scene where she is pictured hidden under the bed clothes, legs akimbo, panting, groaning and gurning in a pose which explicitly evokes giving birth – an analogy which is emphasised by the positioning of the camera at the foot of the bed.

Ruby's position as the derogated mother of the narrative is seemingly confirmed when she and Kate are in the pub celebrating Malcolm's birthday. While Kate explains that she has to be home by 7.30 for the babysitter, Ruby casually comments that she has left her children with 'them down the road, with the lady with the Dalmatians'. Kate's credentials as the 'better' mother are demonstrated throughout the film despite her lack of explicitly maternal activity. Her middle-class aspirations are valorised as a reflection of her 'good' or appropriate maternalism. Kate takes courses to improve her education, her children's handprints adorn the kitchen wall and she is presented as mindful of the household chores. Moreover, her threat to take the children and leave Malcolm because he is failing to provide the life she wants for her family and because he is a bad influence on the children is juxtaposed with Ruby's more ambivalent attitude to the effects of Jumbo's violence on her and her children's emotional world. In this way, Meadows appears to offer a straightforward replication, rather than critique, of the means by which it is always middle-class values which can equate to good maternalism (Douglas and Michaels 2004: 200–2).

The consistency with which these tropes occur in Meadows' work seems to add another perspective to the ways in which Meadows is understood and celebrated as offering an authentic working-class sensibility within a national cinema that is predominantly middle-class and Southern-centric. Whether unwittingly or not, Meadows reproduces this conservative and oppressive discourse about working-class women and working-class motherhood, perpetuating the ideological binary of good and bad motherhood. The cultural negotiation of femininity via the prism of motherhood, as used by Meadows, is a persistent narrative concern within both British and American contemporary cinema. As Louise FitzGerald argues, images of the working-class mother 'dependent on the state, living in social housing and raising delinquent children have been systematically employed within a vast spectrum of political, cultural, social and economic discursive practices, promulgated by the media throughout the last twenty years'

(FitzGerald 2009: 36). Such media representations have contributed to a cultural hierarchy of motherhoods, establishing a discourse of 'good' and 'bad' mothering, determined by class and race, referred to by Susan Douglas and Meredith Michaels as 'The Mommy Myth' (2004), which then impinges on all understandings of femininity, whether maternal or not. This transnational female hierarchy has, within a British context, invariably been predicated on class (see Tyler 2008 on discourses of the 'chav mum' and 'pramface'); indeed, the earlier example of Kate's aspirational maternalism appears to correspond directly with such discourses.

Meadows' claim to an authentic and specifically regional purview is problematised, we would argue, by his representation of the mother figure. Similar criticisms have been levelled at the work of US director John Singleton, whose films, invariably couched in similar discourses of authenticity and lived experiences, have been critiqued for precisely the ways in which they subsume the figure of the mother in order to elevate the role and status of the father in ways that are problematically masculinist and oftentimes misogynist (hooks 1994: 131). Although we would be cautious about suggesting that Meadows' approach to gender politics is as problematic as his American counterpart, it is the case that the authenticity of both Singleton and Meadows is invariably attributed to their upbringing within socially and economically deprived environments and that these environments are invariably characterised by an emphasis on tough and physical masculinity. Just as in the social and political world, where the role of the father is deemed paramount, at the heart of Meadows' films is a concern with the need for acceptance and a longing for role models who are *always* and only ever masculine – thus the typical narratives of 'father hunger' (Modleski 1991: 88–9), as seen in *TwentyFourSeven*, *A Room for Romeo Brass*, *Once Upon a Time in the Midlands*, *Dead Man's Shoes* and *This is England*. Despite the tendency to banish the mother figure to the margins of the narratives – for example in *TwentyFourSeven* and *Dead Man's Shoes* neither Pat (Annette Badland) nor Richard and Anthony's (nameless) mother is accorded anything more than minimal screen time – the mother is nonetheless consistently alluded to in the articulation of the troubled masculinity of both fathers and sons (see Andrew and Johnson forthcoming).

A notable exception to this is, of course, *Once Upon a Time in the Midlands*, a film which focuses much more on the narrative of the mother and daughter characters. Shirley (Shirley Henderson) is the central focal point of the film but is characterised as a rather pallid and passive character; her counterpart, Carol (Kathy Burke), is a significantly more vibrant character but is contained rather than actively used in the narrative. The fact that this is a film from which Meadows has actively sought to distance himself and which is often cited as anomalous within his oeuvre is significant for the fact that his status as an auteur has remained rooted to a contemplation of masculinity. Maternalism is returned to once more in *Le Donk and Scor-zay-zee*, and here, as in *Small Time*, maternal sexuality is deployed for comic effect when Le Donk (Paddy Considine) is repelled by the thought that his heavily pregnant ex-fiancée is having sex with her new partner. The dynamics of this particular narrative appear once more to use the question of female subjectivity and, in this instance, sexuality as a way of critiquing male possessiveness and ridiculing Le Donk's over-wrought squeamishness. As noted earlier, this greater engagement with questions about maternalism and femininity more broadly appears to be a developing aspect of Meadows' work. It is within this context that we want to examine three particular texts in detail for their representation of various modes of maternalism. We begin with *Somers Town*, a film that posits the mother as a spectral threat, and then consider the role of the lone mother Cynth (Jo Hartley) in the first instalment of *This is England*. Finally, we turn our attention to *A Room for Romeo Brass* in order to explore the ways in which race complicates Meadows' depiction of women and mothers.

Ghostly motherhood in *Somers Town*

While the literal threat of the mother is pivotal to the narrative of *Small Time*, in *Somers Town* the mother's destructive presence hangs over the narrative, providing, albeit spectrally, a culturally recognisable and common-sensical figure to explain Marek's (Piotr Jagiello) and Tomo's (Thomas Turgoose) social dislocation and their emotional investment in the extremely romanticised surrogate mother figure, Maria (Elisa Lazowski). While it might be argued that Maria is the object of their pubescent desires, her insistence that she loves them both the same is the very same rhetoric used by mothers to pacify sibling jealousy. The problematic mother figure is alluded to in a key conversation between Marek and his father, Mariusz (Ireneusz Czop). The father and son share a moment of emotional intimacy after Maria has left the country; Marek, who reacted to this departure by getting drunk, is pining for his lost love. The father acknowledges his son's anguish and admits that he too 'would turn to drink if I lost a woman like that'. This conversation initiates the first and, more notably, the only recognition within the film of Marek's absent mother, who remains behind in Poland. Indeed, the loss of Maria acts as the narrative device to enable Marek to speak of his grief about the absence of his mother, and for his father to speak of his loss. The film's surrogate mother figure is conflated with his actual mother in this scene, and it is hardly coincidental, then, that Mariusz *has* himself turned to drink because he *has* lost a woman like that. *Somers Town* reinforces the oedipal narrative which insists on the separation of the mother from the son. Marek's mother remains distanced from him in another country, and so too must the surrogate mother figure of Maria in order for Marek to progress to mature hetero-normative masculinity.

Maria's French nationality complicates the national and cultural specificity of gender politics in Meadows' films. But by making her French the narrative is not only able to fulfil the cosmopolitanism of its remit (as a commercial for Eurostar), but is also conveniently able to break the bonds of surrogate motherhood that Maria represents to Marek and Tomo; as she is sent back to her country of origin to deal with a family issue, she is the dutiful daughter, *not* the abandoning mother figure, and thus is able to remain romanticised. Maria's national identity – her association with Paris in particular – appears to facilitate her position as a romantic figure for the two boys, but she remains an otherwise essentialised, undifferentiated form of female identity narrativised through her position as a surrogate mother figure and object of desire. The film's nuanced rendering of the oedipal narrative, through Maria, Marek's absent mother and Mariusz's paternalism, reflects the persistent positioning of neoliberal discourses of fatherhood as the essential factor in the successful development of mature masculinity. Once Maria has departed, Marek and his father reconfigure their relationship in a moment of male bonding that simultaneously liberates the son and redeems the father. Marek and Tomo can visit Maria in France because she is repositioned within a liminal space and thus her threat to paternal authority is negated and contained. The threat of Marek's mother is also contained by her immateriality. Not only does her physical absence ensure that the threat to the father/son bond is contained at the margins but, more significantly, her chimerical presence is the very thing that consolidates the father/son relationship.

Spectral father and lone mother: *This is England*

In *This is England*, it is precisely the longing for a father and Shaun's subsequent search for this symbolic male figure that locates his mother, Cynthia (and in this instance she is a lone, widowed mother), as a problematic figure. What is significant in this film is the way in which Shaun's masculinity is coded as incomplete and is even maligned by his peers precisely because of his fatherless status. By highlighting the inadequacies of the lone mother through her failure to provide the 'right' sort of clothes and, more significantly, emotional sustenance and guidance for her son as he traverses the perilous journey from child to man, Cynthia's inadequacy as a suitable channel for the learning of the culturally sanctioned performance of masculinity is indicated. The fact that Shaun turns (albeit briefly) to the extreme politics of Combo not only signifies a rejection of perceived feminisation as a result of his fatherlessness, but also signifies a symbolic desire to return to the patriarchal certainties of family and national life as dictated by right-wing political ideologues. In so doing there is a suggestion that the male child of a single mother is vulnerable to the patriarchal certainties of this community because of the ways in which it feeds his father hunger. As such, then, the single mother is implicated for not being able to provide a suitable father figure to guide her son through the maturation process.

This trope of inadequate lone mothers of troubled sons recurs within contemporary mainstream British and American cinema, in *About a Boy* (2002), *The Full Monty* (1997), *Bullet Boy* (2004) and *Pay it Forward* (2002), to name a few examples. Despite the cultural currency of these narratives, the trope of the damaging mother is not a new phenomenon. Since at least the 1950s, narratives of damaging motherhood have been a cornerstone of US popular cinema in films such as *Rebel Without a Cause* (1955) and *Psycho* (1960). More recent deployments of this narrative device consistently position the lone mother/son dyad as the most potentially damaging form of motherhood in films including *Fight Club* (1999), *The Sixth Sense* (1999), *Baby Boy* (2001) and *Jerry Maguire* (1996). In many instances, fatherhood is elevated in the re-enactment and reconfiguration of more conservative forms of masculine identity, and specifically fatherhood, which are posited as intrinsic to a cohesive and stable national identity.

Similarly, in *This is England*, Shaun can only learn how to be a 'proper' man under the tutelage of a father figure which, in this film, comes in the guise of various surrogates, including Woody and Combo. The loss of Shaun's father in *This is England* is rendered particularly poignant precisely because he is constructed as an epitome of British male citizenship as a result of his military career, and Shaun's bereft status is returned to throughout the film – he frequently looks at the photograph of his dead father which adorns his bedside table. Despite the shift in Cynthia's portrayal over the course of the following television instalments, within the film her maternalism is, much like that of Shirley in *Once Upon a Time in the Midlands* (2002), passive and inept. While this functions as a structuring device for

Shaun's story, the questions about maternal experience that her character raises become subsumed within a narrative which appears to be mainly concerned with questions of male experience and development.

Maternal hierarchies in *A Room for Romeo Brass*

The figure of the lone mother features again in *A Room for Romeo Brass*, where she, alongside other female characters, is used once more to frame and facilitate the redemption of damaged and dysfunctional masculinity. The film, which is based, albeit loosely, on Meadows' and co-writer Paul Fraser's adolescence, once more deliberately evokes the notion of Meadows' work as being 'authentic'. The story centres on the friendship between the eponymous Romeo Brass (Andrew Shim) and his next-door neighbour, Gavin 'Knocks' Woolley (Ben Marshall), but, as Mark Kermode suggests, it is also the story of what he terms 'a succession of odd couples: two young boys, an estranged husband and wife, a misfit and his unattainable siren'(Kermode 2000). *A Room for Romeo Brass* offers a rather different rendering of motherhood than the earlier *Small Time*, but one that is no less problematic and typifies some of the central questions around female characters and the discursive construction of motherhood within Meadows' work.

In the broader culture, the lone mother is, as we have already discussed, invariably constructed as a marginal and dangerous figure. In his position as Chair of the think-tank the Centre for Social Justice, Conservative MP Iain Duncan Smith (just one voice among many across the political spectrum) has repeatedly emphasised the connection between lone mothers and 'Broken' Britain. In 2009 he delivered a speech to charity directors in which he outlined key findings from five years of research at the Centre for Social Justice; after noting problems of unemployment, addiction and entrapment in social immobility, he argued that 'most significantly, however, a catalyst and a consequence of these pathways to poverty is the breakdown of the family … without strong families violent and lawless street gangs, whose leaders are often school age, offer a deadly alternative' (Smith 2009). In addition, a range of social commentators, including unorthodox female voices such as Erin Pizzey and Fay Weldon, have weighed in on the debate, which insistently positions the lone female parent as harmful to society. The marginalisation of working-class lone mothers by a neoliberal cultural hegemony which privileges conspicuous consumption serves to position working-class and poor single mothers as particularly resonant scapegoats for a range of societal problems. Moreover, there is a further troubling conflation of gender, race, class and lone motherhood in *A Room for Romeo Brass*. For all the claims to authenticity and regional/ national specificity that are made about Meadows' work, this film offers a problematic representation of black lone motherhood which relies on a transatlantic and homogenised discourse of race and maternalism. In stark contrast to the nuanced narratives of male characters, the character of Carol appears to reflect a much more generalised and over-determined understanding of black lone motherhood that has informed the politics of American society since the days of slavery but which has also been refracted within British culture and history. According to William Du Bois, in his 1970s tract on African American families, the black lone mother is emotionally distant from her male child, decidedly violent towards him and crucially unable either to teach him appropriate forms of male identity or to protect him from developing culturally derogated (and criminalised) forms of black masculinity (Du Bois 1979). It is this resigned acknowledge-ment that leads Reva Devereaux (Angela Bassett) in John Singleton's *Boyz n the Hood* (1991) to hand over Tre (Cuba Gooding Jr) to his estranged father in order that he learns how to become a 'proper' black man. Similar concerns lead Beverly (Claire Perkins) to seek help and guidance from the Pastor (Curtis Fraser) in Saul Dibb's British film *Bullet Boy* in order to protect her younger son (Luke Fraser) when she is forced to acknowledge her own ineptitude in raising her wayward ex-con eldest son (Ashley Walters). This form of maternal resignation is an integral part of a trans-national and homogenised paradigm of black motherhood. Within Meadows' work this paradigm is in evidence in *A Room for Romeo Brass*, where Carol's inability as lone mother to foster a protective and supportive relationship with her male child is central to the narrative. Carol does not intervene in the deeply troubling relationship between Romeo and Morell until Romeo has been on the receiving end of Morell's psychotic behaviour. Carol's ambiguity towards her son is juxtaposed with the emotional support given to Romeo's friend Gavin by his white married mother, who is maternalised according to a very different set of discursive norms.

Significantly, the film shows Gavin and his mother sharing intimate space in the son's bedroom. Gavin is lying in his bed recovering from back surgery and his mother is comforting him; the depth of their bond is demonstrated through their physical proximity and the closeness between them. This scene sharply contrasts with the spatial organisation of a similar scenario between Carol and Romeo, in which the physical distance between mother and son (who are both sitting on Romeo's bed) suggests a concomi-tant emotional distance between the two. This distancing serves to highlight not just maternal hierarchy but a racial hierarchy, which is maintained through the persistent configuration of lone black motherhood as ambivalent and the black lone mother/son dyad as psychically damaging. Furthermore, in the climactic sequence in which Morell seeks out Romeo, it is Gavin's mother who actively supports her husband and is shown protecting and comforting the boys. Pointedly, Carol's reluctance to intervene distances her from the role of mother and protector. Indeed, she is rendered the voyeur, contained within the safety of her home, watching the events unfold from the vantage point of her window. In this way the black lone mother is distanced from the preferred image of maternalism that Gavin's mother embodies as a white, married mother.

Equally pernicious is Meadows' depiction of Carol as a violent mother; but it is also important to note that this violence is only ever targeted towards her son, reinforcing historical narratives of black lone motherhood as abusive. Du Bois makes the point that black lone mothers use violence against their sons as a way of punishing them for the sins of their fathers in a way that seldom extends to their daughters. *Monster's Ball* (2001) rehearses the same scenario of black maternal violence towards the male child, wherein the black lone mother, Letitia (Halle Berry) attacks her fatherless son (Coronji Calhoun) for being overweight and failing to meet the dictates of black American masculinity. In *A Room for Romeo Brass*, Carol is only able to access an acceptable configuration of motherhood once the nuclear family is re-established through her reconciliation with Romeo's white father, who had been expelled from the family home as a result of his violence. Interestingly, it is this exact characteristic – his violence, which the film positions as inappropriate – that is also the key to his redemption and reconfiguration as a protective father and the reunification of Romeo's nuclear family. When the father's violence is enacted under the guise of paternal protection, with his physical attack on Morell, his role within the family is restored and the patriarchal family structure is regenerated. While the final scene of the film appears to celebrate the nuclear family, the whimsical, soft-focus fantasy sequence challenges the plausibility of this fairy-tale ending (Godfrey 2010: 290). Nonetheless, it sees patriarchal gender roles and family structures restored and the 'problem' of the black lone mother contained and resolved at the hands of white working-class masculinity (as in *Monster's Ball*).

Conclusion

As this chapter suggests, the absence from Shane Meadows' film work of a detailed and deliberate consideration of female experience sits in sharp contrast to his dominant thematic concern: what it means to be a man. This chapter should not be read as critiquing Meadows for not focusing on women per se, nor are we suggesting that Meadows *should* switch his focus or that he should prioritise women-centric narratives in his work. Rather, in analysing and critiquing Meadows' female characters we are suggesting that the representational palette he employs for female characters is limiting and oftentimes problematic. His television work co-written with Jack Thorne, and the central positioning of Lol in the *This is England* series, suggests the possibility of a new direction. But within his film work to date, there exists a marked dichotomy in Meadows' treatment of gender that elaborates on questions of British working-class masculinity at extensive length and in great depth while simultaneously containing and limiting female narrative agency, thus truncating the representational spectrum of British working-class femininity. In this way there are parallels with social discourse too and the ways in which specific forms of female agency have been increasingly undermined through the persistent referencing of chav culture and the concomitant deployment of the single mother as a derogatory catch-all for all working- and underclass women. We have suggested that the female characterisations in Meadows' films appear to be much less developed than those of Darcy, Morell, Richard, Woody, Combo and the other male protagonists. Where Meadows' men are nuanced and complex, his female characters often draw on unexamined or commonsense assumptions about working-class femininity. This invariably functions, as in the case of Singleton's work, to frame these women within a transnational discourse that simultaneously denies them agency while implicating them in the dislocation of masculinity. That Meadows' cinematic work to date has consistently overlooked the gendered and racial aspects of the social economic structures which he seeks to critique means that, for us, he, albeit perhaps inadvertently, perpetuates the very forms of social exclusion that he seeks to comment on.

References

Andrew, J. and B. Johnson (forthcoming), 'Dead Man's Shoes: revealing the subtext of the lost maternal', *Journal of British Cinema and Television*.

Centre for Social Justice (2009), *Every Family Matters: An in-depth review of family law in Britain*: http://www.centreforsocialjustice.org.uk/UserStorage/pdf/Pdf%20reports/CSJEveryFamilyMattersWEB.pdf.

Chibnall, S. (2009), 'Travels in Ladland: the British gangster film cycle, 1998–2001', in R. Murphy (ed.), *The British Cinema Book* (3rd edn), London: BFI.

Douglas, S. and M. Michaels (2004), *The Mommy Myth: The Idealization of Motherhood and How It Has Undermined All Women*, London: Free Press.

Du Bois, W. (1979), *The Negro American Family*, Chicago: University of Illinois Press.

Dyja, E. (2010), 'Shane Meadows' *Small Time* and *Where's the Money Ronnie!* on DVD', *Suite101*, 27 September: http://suite101.com/article/shane-meadows-small-time-and-wheres-the-money-ronnie-on-dvd-a290483#ixzz27m3VbLxs.

Field, J. (2004), 'Shane Meadows', *Lazarus Corporation*, 15 September: http://www.lazaruscorporation.co.uk/articles/shane-meadows.

FitzGerald, L. (2009), 'Negotiating Lone Motherhood: Gender, Politics and Family Values in Contemporary Popular Cinema' (PhD thesis, available at https://ueaeprints.uea.ac.uk/10577/).

Fradley, M. (2010), 'Shane Meadows', in Y. Tasker (ed.), *Fifty Contemporary Film Directors*, London: Routledge, pp. 280–8.

Godfrey, S. (2010), 'Nowhere Men: The Representation of Masculinity in Nineties British Cinema' (PhD thesis, available at https://ueaeprints.uea.ac.uk/20540/).

hooks, b. (1994), *Outlaw Culture: Resisting Representations*, New York and London: Routledge.

Kermode, M. (2000), 'Review: *A Room for Romeo Brass*', *Sight & Sound*, February, p. 51.

Modleski, T. (1991), *Feminism Without Women: Culture and Criticism in a Post-feminist Age*, London: Routledge.

Monk, C. (1999), 'From underworld to underclass: crime and British cinema in the 90s', in S. Chibnall and R. Murphy (eds), *British Crime Cinema*, London: Routledge.

Pook, L. (2012), 'Interview: Vicky McClure', *Stylist*, 6 June: http://www.stylist.co.uk/people/interviews-and-profiles/interview-vicky-mcclure.

Romney, J. (2004), 'Shane Meadows: Shane's world', *Independent*, 3 October: http://www.independent.co.uk/arts-entertainment/films/features/shane-meadows-shanes-world-6160552.html.

Smith, I. D. (2009), 'Government, Poverty and Voluntary Organisations', in *Charity Times*: www.charitytimes.com/pages/ct_features/april-09-iain-duncan-smith.html

Tyler, I. (2008), '"ChavMum, ChavScum": class disgust in contemporary Britain', *Feminist Media Studies*, 8: 2.

Whelehan, I. (2000), *Overloaded: Popular Culture and the Future of Feminism*, London: The Women's Press.

CHAPTER 12

'What do you think makes a bad dad?' Shane Meadows and Fatherhood

Martin Fradley and Seán Kingston

The term 'father' can signify many things.
Stella Bruzzi (2006: vii)

Like its predecessors in Meadows' hugely popular film and television cycle, *This is England '88* (2011) begins with a poignantly hauntological montage of archival news footage from the 1980s. Evocatively fuzzy, the sweepingly impressionistic series of analogue video images reaffirms Meadows' insistence on understanding the 1980s as a kind of national primal scene: a traumatic era in which social and political upheaval becomes irrevocably entangled with popular and personal memory. This expressionist strategy is exemplified by what are perhaps the most disturbing moments in Meadows' career to date. The protracted sequence featuring Lol's hospitalisation following a suicide attempt powerfully conflates personal biography, subjective trauma and prosthetic memory. Overlaid with an undulating sound mix of prayer, Catholic incantation and the voice of her dead father, Meadows splices together a highly condensed affective *bricolage*: religious iconography is interspersed with joyless sexual coupling; Lol's aborted marriage to Woody appears next to horrific footage of children cowering behind gravestones during the Loyalist massacre at Milltown Cemetery; grotesque close-ups of a leering Combo sit uneasily alongside blurry shots of emaciated African children. The emergency purging of Lol's stomach is conflated with the violently incoherent regurgitation of her fractured selfhood, the sacred and profane overlapping in an emotionally affective and necessarily over-determined melange of love, rape, guilt, spirituality, post-colonial fallout, murder, procreation and humanitarian catastrophe. Tellingly, however, the traumatic epicentre of these unnerving non-linear flashbacks is the recurrent appearance of a haunting, heavy-breathing spectre: Lol's sexually abusive father, Mick.

Anyone familiar with Meadows' films will know that fathers – both real and symbolic – abound in the director's body of work. From mournful patriarch Bartley Gorman in *The Gypsy's Tale* (1995) through to the lacerating portrayal of incestuous abuse and its legacy in Channel Four's *This is England* TV series, Meadows has been compulsively drawn towards paternal figures and the contested institution of fatherhood. For all its brash wit and roughshod charm, *Small Time* (1996) is emblematic of Meadows' sustained critique of immature masculinity and neglectful fathers. *Small Time*'s distinction between the arrested development of Malc and Jumbo is ultimately mapped across their paternal trajectories: Jumbo's 'bad' dad ends the film in prison, while Malc is redeemed through his rejection of the suburban trap of Sneinton in favour of familial bliss in Skegness. Indeed, Meadows' films have remained unambiguously father-fixated from his earliest films through to *Le Donk and Scor-zay-zee* (2009). As Martin Fradley (2012) has suggested elsewhere, 'whether absent, inept or brutal, the problematic nature of fatherhood remains arguably *the* dominant ideological trope in Meadows' *oeuvre*'. In her own work on cinematic fatherhoods, Stella Bruzzi argues that a clear distinction should always be made between 'films that offer active discourses of fatherhood and those that merely happen to have fathers in them' (2006: ix). Needless to say, Meadows' work is firmly entrenched in the former category.

As Graham Fuller comments, it is 'the perpetual crisis of blighted masculinity – and the struggle to overcome it – that endows Meadows' work with its power and fascination' (1997: 45). From the doomed provincial youths of *TwentyFourSeven* (1997) and the lost adolescent waifs of *A Room for Romeo Brass* (1999) and *Somers Town* (2008), to the violent psychotics of *Dead Man's Shoes* (2004) and *This is England* (2006), Meadows' male melodramas invariably portray working-class male identity as fragile and unstable. Yet while androcentric interrogations of 'masculinity in crisis' are perhaps the defining hallmark of Meadows' career, we contend that they are far from masculinist in their political outlook. With his unsteady fluctuations between violent rage, dope-fuelled camaraderie, authoritarian polemic and childish tears, Combo's behaviour in *This is England* typifies the deeply troubled and psychologically divided terrain of masculinity in Meadows' work. Consistently emphasising the fragmentations of a post-industrial neoliberal Britain, Meadows' tales of beset menfolk register the psychosocial continuum between social depriva-tion, poverty and mental instability. Moreover, Meadows' investigation of the failings of his male characters dependably highlights paternal failure as its most persistent motif.

If Meadows' films are unarguably preoccupied with the often fraught relationships between fathers and sons, his work certainly does not exist in a vacuum. While numerous critics have pointed to the thematically gendered terrain of Meadows' work (Fuller 2007; Savage 2007; Monk 1999; Fradley 2010, 2012; Godfrey forthcoming 2013), many key British films of the last twenty years have also knowingly engaged in various ways with social, cultural and ideological 'daddy issues'. Popular movies such as *The Full Monty* (1997), *About a Boy* (2002), *Billy Elliot* (2000), *Brassed Off* (1996), *Nil by Mouth* (1997) and *Fever Pitch* (2005) are exemplary in this respect. This phenomenon is directly associated with the interminable 'crisis' of masculinity in the wake of a supposed shift towards a post-patriarchal era, a period characterised by a heightened state of social and political castration anxiety grounded in a familiar roll-call of social and economic transitions. These include de-industrialisation and the move to post-industrial service economy; the pre-eminence of a consumer culture grounded in the logics of neoliberal capitalism; the shockwaves of a post-feminist culture; and the decline of the traditional father-headed nuclear family unit and the associated male breadwinner role (Monk 2000b; Robinson 2000; Godfrey forthcoming 2013).

This preponderance of anxious cultural narratives about contemporary British masculinity and fatherhood is exemplified by the 'lad lit' of best-selling writers such as Tony Parsons and Nick Hornby and the political posturing of activist groups such as Fathers4Justice. In his book *Cultures of Masculinity* (2006), Tim Edwards points to three broad sociological factors which – rightly or wrongly – have continued to inform narratives of beset fatherhood. Firstly, a greater cultural awareness of male-perpetrated domestic violence, child abuse and absentee fatherhood (all of which, notably, are issues which Meadows has engaged with repeatedly). Secondly, the decline of the male 'provider' role and scientific advances such as IVF which have rendered biological fatherhood all but redundant. Finally, Edwards points to the high-profile antics of Fathers4Justice, noting that 'it is now well known that the judicial process tends to favour women or mothers as primary carers of children', according to notions dependent on perhaps anachronistic modes of parenting. 'Taken together,' he suggests, 'these factors would seem to present a somewhat pessimistic future for the position of men within the family' (12).

Conversely, however, feminist commentators have interpreted this high-profile fascination with embattled fathers and struggling sons as an insidiously recuperative strategy which allows straight white men to claim entitlement and victimisation simultaneously (Robinson 2000; Rehling 2009). In an influential study, Tania Modleski (1991) argues that the valorisation of paternal figures in popular culture serves to reinstate male power by systematically marginalising women even further as men aggressively appropriate traditionally 'feminine' roles. For Nicola Rehling (2009), the ongoing fixation on fatherhood is suggestive of a political need 'to reiterate and shore up the paternal function at a time of heightened anxiety over absent or neglectful fathers and eroded paternal authority':

> In the last few decades, fears about how absent fathers damage their children have been endlessly articulated in the U.S. and British media, as well as neo-conservative and neo-liberal political rhetoric, with the supposition that only a restoration of paternal authority will heal male pain and, by extension, the ailing social body. (65)

Elsewhere, Imelda Whelehan (2000) concurs with Modleski and Rehling's sceptical analyses of 'male crisis', arguing that in the wake of moral panics about the growing number of mother-headed single-parent families, cultural narratives such as popular film and 'lad lit' emphasise the primacy of 'male bonding of the father–son variety'. 'This most particular concern about fathers', Whelehan argues, 'reflects underlying anxieties among middle-aged men about how to find a model of masculinity which incorporates the duties of fatherhood' (132).

Given their father-fixated outlook, it would be easy to bracket Meadows' work within the kind of dubiously recuperative trends outlined by Modleski, Whelehan and Rehling. What we argue here, however, is that Meadows' work is much more nuanced and progressive than such readings would allow. We are not, of course, the first to adopt this critical perspective in relation to Meadows. For example, Claire Monk (1999) marks out *Small Time* for its progressive gender politics in contradistinction to the fashionably regressive 'lad culture' which characterised the majority of British 'underclass' crime films in the mid- to late 1990s, and Sarah Godfrey mounts a similar argument in relation to *TwentyFourSeven*'s rejection of laddism (forthcoming 2013). While Meadows' films are unquestionably male-centred, then, we nevertheless contend that they are far from masculinist in their cultural politics. In other words, while Meadows' patented brand of post-patriarchal angst is in many ways emblematic of representations of masculinity in British films of the past few decades, in the remainder of this essay we argue that these themes are markedly more complex and ambivalent in Meadows' work than in most other associated cultural representations.

Serving as something of a thematic template, it is entirely symptomatic that Meadows' debut feature, *TwentyFourSeven*, begins with a patriarchal figure in his death throes. Acting as an ersatz 'father' to a disenfranchised, combative and perpetually unemployed group of male youths in the

Midlands' provincial hinterlands, *TwentyFourSeven* documents the philanthropic travails of Alan Darcy as he undertakes the role of nurturing paternal figure. Set in a bleak social universe populated by fathers whose behaviour ranges from selfish and neglectful through to violent domestic tyranny, the flawed and unsympathetic patriarchs in *TwentyFourSeven* – typified by local businessman-cum-gangster Ronnie and the violent and abusive Geoff – offer feeble role models for their directionless and warring sons. By contrast, Darcy's gentle *paterfamilias* founds an amateur boxing club which serves to communicate traditional working-class virtues of self-discipline, mutual respect and collective agency. Ultimately, like so many of Meadows' adult males, Darcy is unable to sublimate his own frustrations and crippling lack of self-worth. The boxing club eventually descends into chaos and disarray, and Darcy's depression manifests itself in a shocking bout of violent brutality. Consumed with guilt and regret, Darcy's subsequent psychological breakdown and descent into alcoholism typifies the way Meadows insistently maps social trauma across damaged male subjectivity.

As the first of Meadows' many neo-patriarchs, Darcy provides the local disenchanted 'lads' with a place to vent their energies. Acting as an introjective ego-ideal, Darcy carefully fosters a spirit of collectivity and class-based commonality for the demoralised sons of a dying Midlands town. With its emphasis on embattled working-class masculinity, widespread unemployment and the lifetime of social marginality faced by the film's young men, *TwentyFourSeven* typifies the thematic emphasis on socioeconomic castration in many British films of the post-Thatcher era. For James Leggott (2004), the trope of father–son relationships in such films is often mobilised as a way to explore 'the anxieties that accompany the diminishment of homosocial authority, tradition and territory' (163) in a post-patriarchal era. In Leggott's view, the altruism of Darcy's self-appointed role as homosocial mentor – a performative conflation, *pace* Modleski, of maternalism and paternalism – is politically undermined by his endorsement of a physically honed and virile male body, the sanctioned violence of boxing and his insistence on restoring an exclusively homosocial territory for his young charges. Although he compares *TwentyFour-Seven*'s 'ambivalent' worldview favourably against the more ideologically transparent *Billy Elliot* and *The Full Monty*, Leggott nevertheless argues that Darcy's 'reclamatory project is revealed to be regressively masculinist, nostalgic and untenable' (166).

This reductively orthodox reading of *TwentyFourSeven* structurally requires the critical erasure of several prominent thematic elements in the film. There is little acknowledgement in Leggott's reading that *Twenty-*

FourSeven very clearly marks out Darcy's nostalgic idealism as ideologically untenable in neoliberal Britain. Furthermore, Leggott confidently posits that it is a combination of Geoff's mockery and 'the contamination of his hallowed homosocial realm by Ronnie's sponsorship' (166) that triggers Darcy's violent rage. However, this reading casually elides Darcy's exasperation over Geoff's persistent physical abuse of his wife and son and refuses to acknowledge how the film clearly grounds Darcy's frustration in decades of unemployment, social neglect and civic decay. As Paul Dave (2006) points out in his overview of the film, 'Darcy's "failure" with the boxing club is perhaps more a reflection on his own struggle to come to terms with an era in which, as he puts it in his diary, working-class men such as himself feel that they are "casualties" who are "not really living"' (85). As Jill Steans astutely points out elsewhere in this book, Darcy's nurturing relationship with the broader community clearly functions as an allegorical rebuttal of – and ideological counterpoint to – the debilitating conditions of post-industrial Britain in the wake of Thatcherism.

Leggott's overarching view that *TwentyFourSeven* regressively endorses the restoration of a physically potent male subject barely tallies with the film's thematic trajectory. Darcy's close-bonded but hopelessly unfit lads – exemplified by Tonka's corpulent bulk and Fag Ash's perpetually stoned bonhomie – are easily quashed by an aggressively honed rival boxing club. Indeed, in a provincial world marked out by a wholesale lack of social welfare, Darcy's quasi-paternal role is best understood as a form of *de facto* social work which nurtures and fosters an inclusive range of male identities. Given the film's mournful post-Thatcherite locale, Darcy's pro-social idealist functions less as a reclamatory paternal substitute and more as a necessary stand-in for an all-but-absent welfare state. Rather than simply acting as an oedipal role model, then, Darcy's interventionism ultimately confirms the latent sociality within the local community, something gently underscored by the understated invocation of social renewal at Darcy's funeral in the film's closing moments.

A Room for Romeo Brass and *This is England* develop the director's preoccupation with the paternal. Both films feature mother-headed households and absent fathers, and both pivot on the emergence of insidious paternal substitutes. Just as significant, however, is the way both films register the ghostly absent-presence of dead fathers. The lingering paternal shadows of various male figures is a key trope in several of Meadows' films, and it is this absence which emotionally structures the relationships between Romeo and Morell in *A Room for Romeo Brass* and Shaun and Combo in *This is England*. Psychologically and emotionally, Shaun, Romeo,

Morell and Combo all respond in different ways to the debilitating legacies of missing fathers, and all four manifest symptoms which register the enduring influence of these absent patriarchs.

Although *A Room for Romeo Brass* is ostensibly about the friendship between adolescent neighbours Romeo and Gavin, the film ultimately tells an archetypically Meadowsian tale of fractious father–son relationships. Biological fathers in Meadows' films typically fall into one of several categories: absent, hopelessly inept or brutal, and the fathers in *A Room for Romeo Brass* serve as illustrative examples of these Meadowsian archetypes. Gavin's father, Bill, is selfish, immature and seemingly indifferent to the welfare and emotional needs of his frail son. Bill's arrested development is underscored by his covert stash of pornographic magazines – happily appropriated by Romeo – while his paternal limitations are comically illustrated when he visits his son in hospital after an operation for a spinal condition. 'How long do people normally visit you for?' he enquires of Gavin, visibly exasperated that he has served a mere thirteen minutes of his torpid hour-long paternal obligation. Joe Brass, meanwhile, has abandoned his wife and two children following an affair. Living in a matriarchal household with his mother Carol and older sister Ladine, the film soon establishes Romeo's domestic life as tense and fractious. In *A Room for Romeo Brass*'s opening tableau, Romeo returns from the local chip shop having devoured most of the family meal en route. Furious with her son, Romeo's teenage appetite serves as a trigger for Carol's broader frustrations with her feckless husband. 'Pack yer bags, find yer dad, go and fuckin' live wi' 'im,' she rasps, 'cos you and him are both greedy, selfish bastards! Goarn, piss off!' Romeo is subsequently drawn towards Morell, a twenty-something stranger who intervenes when Gavin and Romeo are bullied by older boys. Owning his own car and offering idiosyncratic life lessons to the two young men, Morell's entertaining man–child subsequently emerges as a quasi-paternal figure to the impressionable Romeo.

Joe's unexpected – and unwanted – return to the family he abandoned exacerbates Romeo's growing bond with Morell, and it is Joe's re-emergence into his son's life which ultimately bookends the paternal narrative of *A Room for Romeo Brass*. Downtrodden, unemployed and begging forgiveness from his disinterested family, Joe cuts a singularly pathetic figure. By contrast, Morell's posturing machismo and bizarre 'warrior' persona offer an empowering magnetism that neither Joe nor the sickly Gavin can match. When a beleaguered and frustrated Joe physically threatens Morell, Romeo's worst fears about his untrustworthy father are confirmed. By contrast, the accommodating Morell takes Romeo back to his flat, assuring him that '[my] door is open twenty-four hours a day and you're welcome in it, anytime'. Alongside his inclusive homosociality, Morell's individualist credo appeals directly to his impressionable young soldier-in-training. 'Trust no fucker,' Morell sagely advises an attentive Romeo. 'Look after number one.' Despite the schizophrenic contradictions of Morell's personal philosophy, their bond is confirmed when Morell draws an empathetic parallel between Joe and his own late father:

> I know what it's like, man, when you don't get on with yer dad. I had a fuckin' life of it, man. I had things what was done to me that I wouldn't even tell you about. I had my head smacked off every fuckin' wall in this house, man, till me ears bled. I never stopped loving my dad … but he never gave anything back.

Beyond this mournful confession, Morell's father is a spectral presence registered only in inherited bric-a-brac and his son's many neurotic quirks. When Romeo is first invited to Morell's house, the young boy is swiftly ushered out of a bedroom. 'Don't go looking around, it's me dad's old flat', Morell snaps. 'You've depressed me now.' Material possessions – such as an oxygen tank standing beside the unused bed – function as fetishised substitutes for the paternal lost object. Socially isolated and living in what has become a low-rent mausoleum, Morell lingers mournfully in the otherwise unused room surrounded by the grim detritus left behind by a father simultaneously mourned and loathed by his son.

In keeping with the film's dystopic paternal themes, *A Room for Romeo Brass* implies that Morell's impeded socialisation and increasingly unhinged behaviour stem from a cloistered life spent with his abusive father. Morell's child-like naivety is initially underscored by the wayward 'poetry' he employs to woo Ladine, but the flipside to Morell's emotional immaturity is manifested in his disturbing attempts at sexual coercion. Indeed, Morell's crude sexual overtures and wholesale incomprehension of contemporary romantic mores ('go on, suck it!') culminate in an attempt to date rape Ladine. Given British cinema's fascination with 'damaged' masculinity in the 1990s (Monk 1999), we would argue that Morell's wayward emotional and psychological state should be interpreted as – to borrow Sally Robinson's (2000) useful phrase – socio-somatic. As Fradley notes, mental illness and male sociopathology are recurrent tropes in the work of a director who 'clearly understands low self-esteem and dysfunctional behaviour to be symptoms of social fragmentation' (2010: 285). To this end, Morell's disturbed personality and contra-social outlook ('trust no fucker', 'look after number one') should be understood as a cruel parody of the norma-lised pathologies of neoliberal individualism. Morell's avowal of aggressive individualism as a self-empowering response to social abjection is symptomatic of the remasculinisation of the state under neoliberalism in which a virile, market-led 'daddy state' replaces the post-war welfare 'nanny state' (Wacquant 2009; Dave 2011). With no apparent state support despite his obvious mental ill health, and oscillating between vulnerable sociability and self-aggrandising individualism, Morell is ultimately both a victim of, and atomised cipher for, the logics of contemporary neoliberal culture.

Morell's neurotic machismo reaches its zenith when he arrives at Gavin's house threatening to murder Bill and his family. Psychotic and incoherent, Morell's behaviour ultimately serves as a performative staging of social impotence. Deliberately humiliating Gavin's meek father in front of the women and children of both Brass and Woolley clans, Morell's violent performance of masculinity is subsequently mirrored by that of Joe. Arriving just in time to intervene, Joe beats and throttles Morell in full view of his estranged family. Joe's performativity at this juncture underscores the gendered theatricality of his violent protectionism. 'Now you listen to me,' Joe bellows at an infantilised Morell. 'If you ever come near my family again I'll put a knife straight through your heart and fuckin' kill you!' Tellingly, Meadows inserts a cutaway to Ladine's distressed and appalled reaction to her father's physical intimidation. Rather than a recuperative remasculinisation of Joe's estranged *paterfamilias*, then, his cruelty is – like Morell's – ugly, regressive and predicated on the staged abasement of an obviously weaker scapegoat.

A Room for Romeo Brass thus climaxes with a bout of regenerative violence which provides a wholly unconvincing solution to the narrative problems the film raises. As such, the film's fantastical conclusion offers a tentative rejection of this bleakly masculinist impasse. The closing moments of *A Room for Romeo Brass* seem to underscore a reading of the film as ideologically recuperative: both families are reunited and Joe is happily reintegrated into the Brass household. However, the highly condensed and self-consciously phantasmatic scene covertly instils Meadows' patented critique of normative masculinity. Their friendship rekindled, Romeo and Gavin perform a magic show for the assembled families. In a shrewd parody of the doubling of Morell and Joe, the camp theatricality of Gavin's foppish magician's outfit is echoed by Romeo's slow-motion appearance in full drag as 'Magical Maggie'. Like their magic show, then, the surreal cross-dressed conclusion to *A Room for Romeo Brass* communicates a craving for alternatives to the pitiful models of masculinity Gavin and Romeo are offered by Joe, Bill and Morell. Distancing itself from social realist convention, *A Room for Romeo Brass* knowingly offers the 'happy ending' itself as a magical illusion, simultaneously providing a fleeting glimpse of a more egalitarian post-patriarchal future.

The sense of irresolution at the end of *A Room for Romeo Brass* is repeated in *This is England*. With his father a casualty of the Falklands war, Shaun Fields is – like so many of Meadows' male characters – a lost man-child in search of paternal guidance. Bullied at school, Shaun is initially drawn towards the gregarious and companionable skinhead Woody, the first of two adoptive father figures he encounters. Set in 1983, the film is haunted by what Louise Hadley and Elizabeth Ho (2010) dub the social 'trauma' of Thatcherism. In an important critical analysis of Meadows' work, Paul Dave (2010) argues that the director's films 'make the remnants and resources of working-class sociality central, exploring them from the perspective of the domestic, personal, familial and semi-autobiographical, while maintaining a sense of the immediate context of political crisis':

> The film's central character is the young boy Shaun whose grief and isolation after the loss of his father in that war intensifies the sensitivity to others he possesses as a child. His need for others and his impressionability highlight issues of 'tending' and 'growth'. It is the child's experience that becomes the criteria by which to judge the quality of the community offered him by the gang of skinheads associated with Woody. (33)

Dave's argument that Meadows' work should be understood as simultaneously intensely personal and sociopolitically allegorical is astute. By contrast to Woody's benign inclusivity, the older Combo offers a more muscular sense of authority combined with a righteous ideological militarism. Combo's impassioned neo-fascist oratory on unemployment, national identity and the political obscenity of the Falklands conflict proves all too seductive to Shaun's grieving *naïf*. Combining nationalist pride with aggressive anti-Thatcherite rhetoric, Combo comes to embody a series of potent paternal metaphors – nation, flag, warrior, father – which imbues his ersatz fatherhood with a seductively metonymic resonance.

Paralleling the oedipal bond between Morell and Romeo, Combo attempts to make good his own fractious relationship with an abusive father by symbolically restaging the father–son dyad with Shaun. In this fraught oedipal psychodrama, Shaun finds his yearned-for role model in Combo's would-be righteous English 'soldier', while Combo, in turn, becomes the fabled 'good dad' *he* never had. It is barely insignificant that after Combo's violent implosion the film cuts to the same image of paternal stoicism that opens the film: Shaun's bedside photograph of his father in full uniform. Inevitably, Combo's authoritarianism and blood-and-soil rhetoric serve as a poor substitute for the nurturing sociality he obviously craves. When Milky warmly describes the mutuality and communal ethos of his extended family, Combo interrogates Milky with the question that haunts Meadows' entire body of work. 'What do you think makes a bad dad? I know you had a good dad, what do you really think makes a *bad* dad though?' Unable to assuage the skinhead's self-hatred, Milky becomes the victim of Combo's self-defeating rage. Having lost all faith in paternal authority, Shaun's doleful gaze into the camera at the end of *This is England* serves as mute testimony to masculinity's uncertain future in Meadows' films. Rather than simply mourning the passing of old certainties, Meadows' post-patriarchal films repeatedly ask the unanswered question: what comes next?

Although not obviously a film about fatherhood, similar troubling questions lie at the heart of *Dead Man's Shoes*. On a literal level the film deals with the story of two brothers, Richard and Anthony, and their conflict with a quasi-familial collective of low-level drug dealers. As Clair Schwarz points out in her essay in this book, however, through the doubling of Richard and gang-leader Sonny the trope of father figure as leader and flawed role model remains central. In many ways a gothic sequel to *Small Time*, *Dead Man's Shoes* replaces the earlier film's raucous comedy with a disturbing vision of homosocial dystopia. Despite the film's almost exclusively male universe, *Dead Man's Shoes* is neither Boy's Own adventure nor reclamatory patriarchal fantasy. As Joe Andrew and Beth Johnson (forthcoming 2013) point out, it is precisely the absence of women within the bleak provincial universe of *Dead Man's Shoes* that the film critiques. Moreover, *Dead Man's Shoes* depicts paternal authority as socially and ethically bankrupt, the oedipal paradigm itself a form of cruelly systemic abuse.

While the brutal Sonny is symbolic patriarch to the dishevelled rabble of overgrown toddlers who make up his gang, Richard adopts the role of surrogate father to his mentally disadvantaged younger brother. Much like the relationship between Shaun and Combo in *This is England*, this quasi-paternal relationship pivots on Anthony's idealisation of his older brother. Yet in the film's harrowing final scenes, Richard belatedly confesses his true feelings about Anthony: 'He was a fuckin' embarrassment to me.' Consumed with guilt, Richard nihilistically undertakes the role of avenging patriarch by slaughtering the gang. In a final twist, *Dead Man's Shoes'* subdued emphasis on the paternal metaphor is underscored. Mark, the final man on Richard's hit-list, is now married and a father to two young sons, and certainly not the 'monster' Richard expected to find. Allowing Mark to live, Richard passes on the burden of guilt by forcing Mark to become complicit with Richard's death. With blood on his hands once more, Mark flees the gothic ruins which house both Richard's corpse and Anthony's ghost. Heading back towards his family, Mark returns to take his own deeply uncertain place among the bruised and damaged patriarchs of Meadows' world.

The bleak patricidal conclusion of *This is England '86* could easily be interpreted as the logical end-point of Meadows' dystopian paternal imaginary. As sexually malevolent *deus ex machina*, Mick is the ultimate 'bad dad' in Meadows' canon. Like Jimmy in *Once Upon a Time in the Midlands* (2002) and Joe in *A Room for Romeo Brass*, Mick is an absentee father whose unexpected return to the domestic fold triggers cataclysmic emotional and psychological fallout. Prompting Lol's psychological fragmentation and a profound schism in the formerly close-knit group of friends, Mick's homecoming culminates in the horrific rape of Trev. While Lol's sexually predatory father was at the dramatic epicentre of *This is England '86*, the paternal motif is arguably more pronounced than ever. Shaun continues to grieve over his father's death while struggling to cope with his mother's new relationship with Mr Sandhu; Meggy's illegitimate fathering of a son with Trudy remains unresolved; Woody struggles with adult responsibilities while agonising over 'turning into me dad'; and Harvey is violently beaten by his abusive father. Meanwhile, *This is England '88* continues the theme in its depiction of Milky's absentee father and his ambivalent relationship with Lol and their baby daughter.

Yet Meadows' two most recent features suggest a potentially more progressive direction in his representation of fatherhood. Polish migrant Mariusz in *Somers Town* and Paddy Considine's 'Donk' in *Le Donk and Scor-zay-zee* are fathers who, though flawed, represent optimism for the future. Both films are also more wistful and lighter in tone than the majority of Meadows' features; perhaps not coincidentally, both were released after Meadows had himself become a father for the first time. In *Somers Town*, Mariusz arrives home from work to find his son drunk, his flat in chaos and a giggling Nottingham runaway half-naked on the couch, and there is a palpable expectation of violence. It is the same latent threat of physical thuggery the viewer senses when Milky, stoned and soporific, grins at a simmering Combo, or when Joe Brass's animosity towards Morell verges on unhinged brutality. But in this film both Marek and Tomo – and viewers accustomed to the familiar trajectory of Meadows' work – are spared. The scene in question ultimately acts as the catalyst for a tender exchange between Mariusz and his son. The following morning, Marek explains the root cause of his recent behaviour to his father, confessing his struggles with feelings of loss over both his absent mother and his burgeoning romantic interest in the kindly, maternal Maria.

Like earlier scenes featuring Mariusz patiently teaching Marek to speak

English, these moments of reciprocal bonding between father and son represent something of a shift in Meadows' representation of fatherhood. *Somers Town* thus tallies with the cultural re-evaluation of fathering and masculinity in a 'post-patriarchal' era. As Whelehan points out, '[n]o-one seems to want to repeat the tendency to emotional distance of our forefathers' (132). Indeed, it is productive to understand *Somers Town* as an optimistically sentimental riposte to some of the troubling questions posed about masculinity, fatherhood and national identity in *This is England*. Joanna Rydzewska (forthcoming 2013) shrewdly points to the potential ideological limitations of *Somers Town*'s idealisation of hard-working Polish migrants, yet this is to elide the obvious fact that Mariusz's heavy drinking, 'laddish' homosociality and valorisation of manual labour and masculine strength are clearly encoded as a sublimation of his depression vis-à-vis his estranged wife. Like Darcy, Morell, Richard and Combo, Mariusz's masculine performativity is grounded in the repression of vulnerability and sadness; unlike his predecessors, however, he breaks the chain of negligence and neglect begun by the myriad fathers of *TwentyFourSeven*.

Like Jumbo in *Small Time* or Jimmy and Dek in *Once Upon a Time in the Midlands*, Paddy Considine's delusional ex-roadie Le Donk in *Le Donk and Scor-zay-zee* is immature, chauvinistic and barely equipped for the responsibilities of imminent fatherhood. Though in his own absurd way he is as confused as any of Meadows' male characters, what ultimately makes Donk interesting is his eventual acceptance of both surrogate and biological paternity. Despite his comically strained relationship with ex-girlfriend Olivia and her new partner, he also makes a conscious – if characteristically belated – decision to participate in the life of his newborn son. This new-found maturity seems a deliberate echo of his acceptance of a permanent role in his infant son's life despite no longer being in a relationship with the child's mother. 'I can watch him growing up via the web,' he suggests enthusiastically, 'like a cyber pet!' His idiosyncratic approach to twenty-first-century fatherhood aside, Donk ultimately makes a positive addition to the catalogue of fathers in Meadows' films. Though clearly irresponsible and unsuitable as a day-to-day fixture in his son's life, Donk resolves to make good his commitment to this resolutely post-nuclear family unit. If the triumphant happy ending of *Le Donk and Scor-zay-zee* seems – like the conclusion of many of Meadows' films – curiously unreal, it remains Donk's enthusiastic embrace of fatherhood that lingers.

Shane Meadows' films are unquestionably preoccupied with the so-called 'crisis' of masculinity. Yet it is the role of the father – absent or present; real or symbolic; positive or detrimental – which remains the thematic cornerstone in Meadows' Midlands tales. It may well be true, as Stella Bruzzi's (2006) work on fatherhood in popular cinema argues at length, that the longing for an idealised paternal figure as evidenced in much popular cinema belies a fundamentally conservative outlook. However, we have argued that mapping this ideological trajectory onto Meadows' body of work seems incongruous given the clear-eyed critique of masculinity, homosociality and fatherhood his films so often provide. Rather than following a reclamatory or recuperative political trajectory, the persistent recourse to the paternal in Meadows' work offers a sustained critique of traditional definitions of masculinity, gender imbalance and familial relations. In what is perhaps the most iconic image in Meadows' work to date, Shaun bitterly tosses away the English flag he has so closely associated with Combo's homosocial mentoring. In this gesture and elsewhere, we argue, Meadows consistently foregrounds the rejection of patriarchal authority as an unambiguously progressive social move.

References

Brown, W. (2009), 'Not flagwaving but flagdrowning, or postcards from post-Britain', in R. Murphy (ed.), *The British Cinema Book* (3rd edn), pp. 408–16.

Bruzzi, S. (2006), *Bringing Up Daddy: Fatherhood and Masculinity in Post-War Hollywood*, London: British Film Institute.

Dave, P. (2006), *Visions of England: Class and Culture in Contemporary Cinema*, Oxford and New York: Berg.

Dave, P. (2011), 'Tragedy, ethics and history in contemporary British social realist film', in D. Tucker (ed.), *British Social Realist Art since the 1940s*, London: Palgrave Macmillan, pp. 17–56.

Edwards, T. (2006), *Cultures of Masculinity*, London and New York: Routledge.

Fradley, M. (2010), 'Shane Meadows', in Y. Tasker (ed.), *Fifty Contemporary Film Directors*, London: Routledge, pp. 280–8.

Fradley, M. (2012), 'Shane Meadows', in E. Bell and N. Mitchell (eds), *Directory of World Cinema: Britain*, Bristol: Intellect.

Fuller, G. (2007), 'Boys to men', *Film Comment*, 43: 4 (July–August), pp. 44–7.

Godfrey, S. (forthcoming), '"I'm a casualty, but that's OK": *TwentyFourSeven* and British masculinity in the nineties', *Journal of British Cinema and Television*.

Hadley, L. and E. Ho (2010), 'The Lady's not for turning: new cultural perspectives on Thatcher and Thatcherism', in L. Hadley and E. Ho (eds), *Thatcher and After: Margaret Thatcher and Her Afterlife in Contemporary Culture*, London: Palgrave Macmillan, pp. 1–26.

Leggott, J. (2004), 'Like father? Failing parents and angelic children in contemporary British social realist cinema', in P. Powrie, A. Davies and B. Babington (eds), *The Trouble with Men: Masculinities in European and Hollywood Cinema*, London: Wallflower Press, pp. 163–73.

Modleski, T. (1991), *Feminism Without Women: Culture and Criticism in a 'Post-feminist' Age*, New York: Routledge.

Monk, C. (1999), 'From underworld to underclass: crime and British cinema in the 1990s', in S. Chibnall and R. Murphy (eds), *British Crime Cinema*, London: Routledge, pp. 172–88.

Monk, C. (2000a), 'Underbelly UK: the 1990s underclass film, masculinity and the ideologies of "New" Britain', in J. Ashby and A. Higson (eds), *British Cinema: Past and Present*, London: Routledge, pp. 274–87.

Monk, C. (2000b), 'Men in the 90s', in R. Murphy (ed.), *British Cinema in the 90s*, London: British Film Institute, pp. 156–66.

Rehling, N. (2009), *Extra-Ordinary Men: White Heterosexual Masculinity in Contemporary Popular Cinema*, Lanham, MA: Lexington Books.

Robinson, S. (2000), *Marked Men: White Masculinity in Crisis*, New York: Columbia University Press.

Rydzewska, J. (forthcoming), 'Masculinity, nostalgia and Polishness in *Somers Town*', *Journal of British Cinema and Television*.

Savage, J. (2007), 'New boots and rants', *Sight & Sound*, 17: 5, 38–40.

Wacquant, L. (2009), *Punishing the Poor: The Neoliberal Government of Social Insecurity*, Durham, NC: Duke University Press.

Whelehan, I. (2000), *Overloaded: Popular Culture and the Future of Feminism*, London: The Women's Press.

CHAPTER 13

Is This England '86 and '88? Memory, Haunting and Return through Television Seriality

David Rolinson and Faye Woods

This chapter will discuss the Channel Four serials *This is England '86* and *This is England '88* in their specific television contexts. Although these serials form a transmedia narrative as sequels to the film *This is England*, we seek to engage with their televisuality, both textually (their style, their reference to antecedents and their use of archive television footage) and extra-textually (their promotional strategies and place within institutional discourses). Our analysis is framed by the serials' key themes – the weight of the past as revealed in returns, hauntings and traumatic memory – which are facilitated by the larger space of serial television and the multi-year timespan. Although the titles underline their period settings, the representation of Britain's collective past is not the serials' primary focus. Historical markers such as archive footage serve less as nostalgic cultural artefacts, sociopolitical interrogation or subcultural exploration and more as manifestations of memory in service of theme and characterisation. In particular, Lol's status as tragic centrepiece reveals a concern with subjectivity facilitated by the texts' interplay of different types of memory.

This chapter will begin by exploring how Channel Four sought to position *This is England '86* as both 'event serial' and youth drama in its bid to assimilate the filmic into the televisual. The traces of television drama found across Meadows' work are made more explicit, leading us to explore the echoes of television past. This will take us into a discussion of the serials' use of archive television footage in montages and diegetic footage, the use of television past to explicate narrative. Finally, we consider the serials' core concern with the memories and hauntings experienced by Lol. For this is a haunted text – by television itself as much as by the characters' own pasts. As we shall see, these narrative, stylistic and institutional features interrelate in distinctive ways.

Assimilations and echoes: *This is England* becomes televisual

We begin with the contemporary contexts in which these serials were commissioned, mindful that, as Philip Drake summarised in his study of Hollywood films set in recent decades, 'what we call the past is accessible only through private and publicly articulated memories, narrated through the perspective of the present' (Drake 2003: 184). The 'remembered, memorialised past' in these films was dependent on 'audiovisual representations' according to Drake, following David Lowenthal's labelling of *'memorial knowledge'*: our sense of the past is 'based upon selective and strategic remembering in the present' and 'made up of a mixture of personal memory and public memories' that 'become fused and indistinguishable' (Drake 2003: 183–4). This chapter will place Lol's struggles, and the serials' use of archive footage, in the context of these debates on mediated memory, but first the serials' textual and extra-textual concern with invoking the past should be placed in 'the perspective of the present'.

Drawing on the 'quality' status legitimised by its filmic roots and British 'auteur', *This is England '86* played a key role in Channel Four's 'creative overhaul' following the cancellation of *Big Brother* in 2010 (Sweney and Holmwood 2009). As part of this the channel pledged £20 million for original drama in the mould of previous critical successes *The Devil's Whore* (2008) and the *Red Riding* trilogy (2009). Like these and subsequent serials such as an adaptation of William Boyd's *Any Human Heart* (2010) and Peter Kosminsky's Palestine piece *The Promise* (2011), *'86* was an 'event serial' offering period drama with a twist, positioned within a discourse of quality drama. We use 'event serial' here to refer to those high-profile, high-budget (often co-productions) 'authored' serial texts that are often BAFTA-nominated and serve as flagships for Channel Four's value as creative space and public service broadcaster. Single dramas such as *Boy A* (2007), *Mark of Cain* (2007) and *The Unloved* (2009) are also highly valued, but such one-offs tend to be more issue-led and contemporary, whereas the 'event serial' typically offers a historical narrative, though one with a more politicised or quirky twist than the mainstream BBC1 'classical serial' (Caughie 2000). *The Devil's Whore* presented the Civil War as a proto-feminist swashbuckling melodrama, while Yorkshire crime trilogy *Red Riding* revisited the late 1970s and 1980s with a dense, bleak approach far removed from nostalgia.

However, *'86* is simultaneously positioned as special 'event serial' (with a complicated relationship with the past) and within the channel's distinctive brand of contemporary drama series such as *Shameless* (Channel Four,

2004–13), *Skins* (E4, 2007–13) and *Misfits* (E4, 2009–). While the surrounding discourse foregrounded Meadows' authorship (Raphael 2010; Lobb 2010), he worked with creatives experienced in Channel Four drama: Jack Thorne (*Shameless*, *Skins*) co-wrote '86 and '88 while Tom Harper (*Misfits*) directed two episodes of '86; '86 shares *Shameless*'s domestic focus, its shaggy ensemble of low-income outsiders, comic impulses and point of view from *within* a working-class community, and its 'anti-social realism' (Creeber 2009: 436). Yet '86 and '88 move away from *Shameless*'s fondness for comic surrealism and farce, slipping into a darker worldview with Lol's emotional unravelling.

Channel Four's initial promotion positioned '86 within its reputation for documenting the British youth experience. The teaser trailer features the cast crammed together and joyously pogo-ing in slow motion, sound-tracked by Wayne Smith's '80s dancehall classic *Under Me Sleng Teng* as Woody's voiceover fondly (re)introduces the characters to the audience. The actors are lit brightly in shots that concentrate on faces and bodies in movement, and are abstracted in a darkened studio, removed from their period setting and landscapes that could signify a downbeat social realism. The trailer communicates youth, energy and pleasure: the cast smash together and embrace, while Woody proudly reiterates 'This is us'. The temporal dislocation paradoxically heightens the sense of the contemporary: the 1980s reference points provided by their costumes illustrate Drake's observation that films construct 'a memory of the past through the recycling of particular iconography that metonymically comes to represent it'. However, the serials emerged in a period of 1980s revivalism, embraced by *Skins*' tendency towards constructing its cast's identities from reassemblages of past youth cultures, their promotion illustrating Drake's point that 'the styles of the past' can help texts to 'be branded and marketed to audiences' (Drake 2003: 183), here both the nostalgic Generation X-ers and the Millennials targeted by British youth television. The trailer's aesthetic brings connotations of the distinctive early trailers for *Skins*, in which bright lights pick out youthful bodies in darkened rooms of destructive hedonistic partying, while Woody's introductions also echo the Frank Gallagher voiceovers which open each *Shameless* episode. Thus it positions '86 as youthful, fun and decisively 'Channel Four'. However, as the serial unfolds this pleasurable companionship is tested by the weight of the past, and pop cultural nostalgia is problematised by more complex and disturbing representations of the past shown in archive footage or embodied in references to challenging dramas from the period.

While the serials marked Meadows' television debut, he has long been connected with the medium. He has benefited from television's funding and production convergence with cinema: his backers have included BBC Films and Film4, the latter co-funding *This is England*. Meadows' citation of Alan Clarke as an influence on *Dead Man's Shoes* (Kermode 2004) and *This is England* (Raphael 2010) is just one example of his awareness of convergence; promoting *'86*, he wrote that 'As a kid, I got my cinema through my TV: Mike Leigh, Alan Clarke, Stephen Frears all seemed to be making films for Channel 4 [...] so you'd have *Made in Britain* or *Walter* or a Ken Loach film' (Meadows 2010: 33).[1] Meadows was 'inspired by their social realism', and the influence of filmed television plays contributes to the layering of traces of televisual past visible in the text. By briefly noting echoes of Clarke, Leigh and Loach, we are not tracing their 'social realist' lineage but considering the ways in which these memories of earlier dramas circulate in the text – in service of theme – and the contemporary television landscape. Meadows' movement into television places his acknowledged influences within a different cultural context, a memory of value. Clarke devoted most of his career to television, enjoying greater creative freedom than he was afforded in cinema, while Loach debuted the particularly topical pieces *The Navigators* (2001) and *It's a Free World...* (2007) on television, the site of his many earlier impactful filmed pieces, rather than cinema, despite having become internationally renowned in that arena. John Caughie saw across Loach's work a 'fundamental shift' in terms of social impact between television drama *Cathy Come Home* (1966), which 'circulated as a national event and functioned as documentary evidence within the political sphere', and cinema film *Ladybird, Ladybird* (1994), which 'circulates within an aesthetic and a cultural sphere which is given prestige (and economic viability) by international critics' awards' (Caughie 2000: 198). Meadows' serials return to the 1980s in their setting, characters and production design, but their very existence in the schedules also recalls the era where such filmmaking was more prominent on British television. Indeed, Channel Four's post-*Big Brother* refocusing stressed its 'increased commitment to drama', with a creative range evoking the values which underpinned the channel's launch in 1982 (Anonymous 2009). Similarly, Meadows mentions Frears' *Walter*, which featured in the channel's first-night line-up, which was designed by Chief Executive Jeremy Isaacs as characteristically diverse, challenging and stimulating programming with fiction a vital component (Isaacs 1989).[2]

There are, therefore, implications when echoes of television's past occur. The serials feature sequences of static, formal establishing shots – their regularity partly generated by the interruptions of commercial breaks –

which recall strategies in the 1970s filmed plays of Leigh, Clarke and others but also emphasise spatial and character dynamics in their variations between symmetrical and off-centre framing (segmented by sky or buildings), which emphasises emptiness.[3] Echoes of previous filmmakers are grounded in characterisation: for instance, Lol and Woody's separation in '88 is reflected formally to such an extent that they are virtually in different films. Lol could be the protagonist of a Clarke drama, closely pursued by Steadicam: her striding walks across the estate in coiled fury during '86 – a dynamic female character ultimately rendered static and mute by Meadows' characteristic climactic trauma – and her walk along an institution's corridors in '88 make striking connections to Trevor in *Made in Britain* and other mobile Clarke characters of the 1980s.[4] '88 finds her inexpressively walking between background and foreground within static frames, her psychological state submerged, as in the movingly restrained *Diane* (BBC, 1975), whose titular character is imprisoned for disposing of a baby conceived to her father. By contrast, Woody is nearer to Leigh, as the social comedy of his unwanted workplace climbing peels away to reveal the psychological wounds festering beneath his scabs. As we shall see, even Meadows' most overt reference to Clarke is couched within several layers of discourse.

Television's past therefore constitutes one of the layers of memory at work in the serials, but others are even more important in tracing the serials' televisuality. We shall take these in turn: links with the film, and the use of archive television footage.

Memory traces: pop culture past and skewed remembrances

'I wanted to broaden the story of the gang, tell multiple stories', observed Meadows (2010: 33), 'and television is more suited to that than a 90-minute feature film.' In this movement into television, we find a reorientation towards the domestic, a look inwards. While this was important to the film – despite Combo's racist rhetoric, his attack on Milky was triggered by jealousy of his happy family life – the movement to television firmly orientates the narrative away from skinhead tribalism and towards domestic concerns, family conflict and character interiority. Here personal histories and the repercussions and memories of past events weigh heavily, with Lol's abusive father replacing Combo as the 'bad father' villain. As we shall see, the domestic space serves as a site where memory (at times contested) refracts through characters' present circumstances.

The relationship that characters and audiences have with personal and narrative past in '*86* and '*88* resonates with Amy Holdsworth's work on television memory and nostalgia, in particular her engagement with memory in serial drama. Holdsworth discusses longer-running dramas; however, Meadows' revisiting of *This is England*'s characters at intervals throughout the 1980s constructs long-developing personal narratives which echo Holdsworth's description of the 'backwards and forwards movement, patterns of return and retreat, and the "ebb and flow" of television' (Holdsworth 2010: 3). Both '*86* and '*88* open with the gang fractured and incomplete, separated by barriers created by past events and seeking to escape, atone or return to the fold. '*86* finds the gang long absent from Shaun's life after the divisive and violent events of the film, while '*88* finds Woody estranged from the gang and Lol suffering depression following her affair with Milky and her murder of her father, Mick, in '*86*.

The opening moments of '*86* bring together character and audience memory of the film's events, serving to assimilate the separate film text (which had been rebroadcast the weekend before '*86* began) into the televisual text with a short sequence set in the aftermath of Combo's climactic assault on Milky in 1983. Static establishing shots fix us in an abandoned industrial space at daybreak. Dockside we find a car stained with Milky's blood, in which a shell-shocked Shaun sits with a remorseful, bloodied Combo. A soft, melancholic piano score begins as Shaun walks away from the car, then stands in his back garden – still in his skinhead uniform – with his hand outstretched to touch the soft rain, which brings connotations of cleansing and new beginnings. In close-up he turns his face into the rain and the camera follows his gaze down towards his hand, when a cut takes us to an older hand catching raindrops. We track up to reveal ungainly 1986 Shaun about to take his final exam, the slow motion of the 'contemporary' footage bringing a contemplative tone, which positions the film footage as a memory.

Set between Shaun helping Combo to carry Milky's body from the flat and the coda in which Shaun walks to the sea's edge, the sequence of the child Shaun works as an aide memoire, an update which constructs the film as one part of an ongoing serial narrative. It recalls the film, yet renders that recollection problematic: although shot for the film, the sequence did not appear in it, and so this is Shaun's memory, yet one which the audience does not share. The disjunction between Turgoose's youthful broken innocence and his lumpen teenage body is stark and simultaneously humorous and melancholic. The cut moves us forwards in time, yet signals that the imprint of the traumatic event remains (if never really discussed when the gang is reunited). The sequence also establishes Combo's presence, allowing the memory of him to haunt audience and characters alike before his return at the close of episode three. Much of *'86* and *'88* will occupy this territory of spoken and unspoken memory, and will be characterised by 'the hauntings of and by characters, the traces that return and retreat', to utilise Holdsworth's (2010: 38) description of the evoking and employment of memory in serial drama and the pleasures of repetition.

The film is also recalled by the recurrence of one of its devices in both *'86* and *'88*: montage sequences of archive (usually television news) footage. To consider the methods and implications of such sequences' audiovisual representations of the remembered past, we will discuss one such sequence, before demonstrating how other returning traces – from elsewhere in the serial and from antecedents discussed earlier in this chapter – complicate their function.

After episode one of *'88* reintroduces core characters only to surprise us with their changing circumstances (notably the separation of Lol and Woody), the title sequence begins: a montage soundtracked by the Smiths' 1984 single 'What Difference Does It Make?' The montage features major news events from the period, but their narrative organisation and juxta-position with the song's lyrics also produce narrative expectations – a function of opening sequences – that are unsettling. The sequence begins and ends with Prime Minister Margaret Thatcher. We first see her pro-nouncing the 'British cure' for the 'British disease', and while her meaning – privatisation and free-market economics – is not explicitly stated, the cut to a sign reading 'BUY NOW PAY LATER' implies a critical reading of those policies' impact on contemporary Britain. Subsequent images indicate conspicuous consumption – consumer goods, champagne and Harry Enfield's satirical character Loadsamoney waving wads of cash – although the starkness of the frame-filling sign hints at narrative relevance, accompanied as it is by the song's first line: 'All men have secrets and here is mine' (Lol and Combo have secrets – will they pay later?). The lyric 'I can surely rely on you' motivates a cut to Prince Charles and Princess Diana dancing, which leads to the Duke and Duchess of York with newborn daughter Beatrice in August 1988. The contemporary viewer's awareness of each couple's future may bring irony to the initial lyric, but the lyric accompanying a shot of the baby seems in retrospect more applicable to Lol's baby: 'heavy words are so lightly thrown'.

Literal readings of lyric–image relationships in pop music montages are often problematic, but particularly here, given that grasping those relationships depends on memory not just of the news events pictured but of narrative events.[5] The same applies to the *choice* of song, which Simon

Goddard suggests contains a 'sense of regret, hopelessness and betrayal' (2009: 473). The perspective of the present is in play in the sequence's selections: protests against tuition fees and public sector cuts and images of Colonel Gaddafi echo contemporary news stories. However, the cut from anti-Thatcher protests to Thatcher dancing sedately among signifiers of affluence with her husband Denis (their left-to-right movement rhyming with the protest footage) is accompanied by the lyric 'What difference does it make?', and this sense of hopelessness is emphasised later by footage of famine victims, accompanied by the lyric 'But now you make me feel so ashamed', as if the images of suffering overwhelm uninformed recipients. Images of famine will recur in episode three, representing Lol's subjectivity, divorced from news context. The line 'But no more apologies' accompanies images of acid house raves, a sign of subcultural unity that will be missing in '88,[6] where we can anticipate the metaphorical equivalent of the homes broken by storms and the Lockerbie bombing, images of which follow. The serial's title appears over footage of Thatcher in the remains of a home, which opens a political reading – the destruction of communities attributed to policies implied earlier in the sequence – but is moored in character by the shot that follows the titles: an establishing shot of Lol's home.

The montage's images therefore contribute to the serials' discourses on memory. Noting that viewers may find irony, rather than historical record, in images of Charles and Diana is consistent with Maurice Halbwachs' work on 'collective memory', notably his point that 'a remembrance' is largely 'a reconstruction of the past achieved with data borrowed from the present', as we bring the past into the present (Halbwachs 1980: 69). These serials' use of news footage such as Wimbledon's giant-killing FA Cup win over Liverpool provides an invitation to remember, but in ways that have troubling implications for our understanding of characters' memories in these serials. Tracing various concepts of mediated memory, Drake (2003: 185) observes that the repetition of images – such as films or news footage of events such as Thatcher's resignation – leads to them being 'continually re-remembered and remade', their emotional resonance increased by repetition but the memory 'often the memory of a mediated experience in the first place'. The repetition of mediated memory may make it 'impossible to discern primary from secondary memories' – in Lowenthal's phrase, we are 'remembering things from remembering remembering them' (Lowenthal 1985: 196, quoted in Drake: 184). Their impact demonstrates Alison Landsberg's description of 'prosthetic memories', mediatised events which we have not directly experienced but which affect us sufficiently to 'become part of one's own personal archive of experience, informing one's subjectivity' (Landsberg 2004: 26). Meadows' serials deal in often rich secondary memories through their use of news montages, but these function alongside the aesthetic echoes of previous dramas as elements of televisual memory. Therefore, we will examine the combination of archive images with other televisual forms, and then end the chapter by considering how these factors contribute to Lol's battle for primary memory as archive becomes part of her subjectivity.

Episode four of *'86* uses images surrounding England's World Cup quarter-final against Argentina in ways that relate their emotional resonance (heightened by their repetition in popular culture) to narrative developments – however, these are integrated with other forms of televisual memory. After Lol's killing of Mick (a troubling scene to which we return below), Combo volunteers to take the blame to protect Lol and atone for his behaviour in the film (signposted by his repetition of 'let me do a good thing'), although in the process he problematically robs our previously active heroine of her agency. The latter scene is followed by news footage previewing England's match, which mentions boiling 'passions' and Argentina's apolitical desire to get 'revenge' for defeat to England in the latter's World Cup-winning 1966 campaign. This inverts traditional narratives in keeping with Lol's predicament and Shaun's doubts regarding his father's death during military victory against Argentina. While friends gather in the pub and at home to watch the match on television, Combo arrives in prison. His calling of name and number (6787) recalls Carlin (4737) in Alan Clarke's *Scum*, and the framing reinforces this memory. Like Carlin in the television (1977) and cinema (1979) versions, he is seen from behind in a shot which makes confining use of symmetry: he is flanked by officers on either side, positioned centre of frame with his head facing an authority figure at the centre of a table at the back of the frame, in a rectangular room whose space seems distorted by a wide-angle lens. The similarity also heightens difference – Clarke's ideological form parallels institutional discourse, but Combo is boxed in not by institutions but by the domestic. Another trace of cultural memory appears later in the montage when the football-watching characters' angry and confused reactions to Diego Maradona's handball goal against England crossfades to reveal a photograph of the act. The lingering fade connotes memory, an image imprinted on the public consciousness, so widely repeated as to resonate with people who did not watch the match. The moral and emotionally multifarious moment, with unfair defeat and victory earned through foul means, forms a surprisingly ambiguous backdrop to Combo's incarceration.[7]

Again, archive images are not the only returning traces in play. Combo's arrival in prison features another returning trace, as our view of him through the office window chimes with numerous window shots in the serial. In different episodes Lol's father, Mick, looks out of a window, on which we see the reflection superimposed – the estate outside – as if he is trapped by the space to which he has returned. At another point, a cut takes us from a shot of Combo asleep left of frame (with space right of frame) to Mick, right of frame, distorted behind patterned glass (with undistorted space left of frame), aligning the two returned bad fathers, but contrasting the peaceful Combo with the nightmarish wheezing Mick. The shot of Mick anticipates his distorted appearances behind a screen during Lol's nightmare in '88, but windows connect Combo to Mick and to Lol, in his discovery of Lol's crime through the house window. This is returned to in episode three of '88 when Lol visits Combo in prison, a shot/reverse-shot pattern in which their faces combine in reflections on the screen between them.

Hauntings and trauma: Lol's battle

However, Lol's visit with Combo evokes another returning trace: television images of prison seeded throughout '88 which return Combo's incarceration to Lol's already haunted mind. Considering these earlier prison images helps us to consider the way that returning traces (images from archives and the serial's narrative past) contribute to an understanding of Lol's subjectivity and her capacity to negotiate forms of memory. In the first episode of '88, Lol watches Pauline Fowler visiting Den Watts in prison during an *EastEnders* Christmas special.[8] We have seen how archive montages evoke circulating memories, but archive footage works differently in the three scenes featuring *EastEnders*: it is used diegetically and subjectively, in that it raises the question of our access to Lol's thoughts and memories.

The first scene to feature *EastEnders* opens on a television set showing Pauline, whose surprising visit to her nemesis prompts Den to ask cynically, 'Got a fit of the community spirits, have you?' *EastEnders* then cuts to a reverse shot of Den, and the way that the soap cuts in response to dialogue will inform the serial's cutting to Lol in response to dialogue potentially applicable to her. Den's line 'Cos you always were such a *family* person, weren't you?' prompts a cut to Lol, watching from her sofa, wrapped in a blanket. The shot of Lol is held as Den baits Pauline: 'Feeling maternal? Well, I'm shocked.' Den's questions chime with Lol's self-doubt on the

sensitive subjects of family and her doubts as a mother, indeed her post-
natal depression. A further cut to a closer angle emphasises the sense that
this, while not an internal monologue, is vocalising her concerns. Similarly,
her concerns about Combo's imprisonment are mirrored by the soap's
handling of this awkward fictional visit, as if a subjective take on Lol
visiting Combo, darkening the soap's dialogue and emphasising Lol's guilt.
Pauline's description of Den's predicament as 'the best present I've ever
had' seems bleakly ironic when viewed in parallel with Combo's gift to Lol.
If we listen to *EastEnders* for clues as to Lol's state of mind, it is because
we are not privy to Lol's thoughts, except for understated performative
cues in response to the diegetic text: McClure's twitching of an eyebrow
during Den's line about Pauline being happy he is inside, and of a lip
during Pauline's acidic reply. Similarly, the angle of the medium close-up
– with Lol's right shoulder closer in the frame than her face, rising and
falling – makes her breathing seem relatively heavy, as if agitated.

Shots of Woody and Lol bookend this *EastEnders* sequence (the previous
scene cuts abruptly from Woody's warm but disconnected new family set-
up with his parents and straight-laced girlfriend), connecting them through
their unspoken feelings regarding their isolation. Editing forms their only
connection – they do not meet until the climax of episode three – and we
actively seek connections between them, to the extent that this scene's
opening shot of the television set does not confuse (whose television is
this?), as the abruptness of the cut between scenes implies a connection,
which we would expect to be between Woody and Lol.[9] Watching *EastEnders*
at Christmas serves as cultural shorthand for Lol's solitary state, but the
association of her thoughts with a soap, rather than the clothes, music and
friends with which we have previously associated her, emphasises the leads'
eroding sense of self and ability to communicate.

The second appearance of *EastEnders* begins not with the television set
but with Lol as viewer. Pauline's continued approval of Den's incarceration,
'banged up in here out of the way of decent people', reflects Combo's self-
imposed situation but also Lol's, until Trev arrives with drinks. Lol
describes *EastEnders* as 'fucking depressing', but does not elaborate: is this
a general observation or an indication that the prison storyline is troubling
her? The soundtrack hints at the latter, with Den's transferable point that
'You must have a lot on your mind this time of year'. Lol and Trev leave
their mutual traumas from '86 unsaid, but Den's continued opinions on
Pauline's family's recent misdemeanours hint at Lol's self-made exclusion
and the pressure of guilt: 'I think I prefer to be in my prison rather than
yours'. Lol's question to Trev about 'Woody's new bird' seems less abrupt

if we view the soap as part of the conversation. Lol feels that Woody 'deserves to be happy', and a cut to his caring parental home could suggest that he is, yet doubt has already been created.

When Woody escapes by riding round the streets, 'After Laughter (Comes Tears)' by Wendy Rene is held over a melancholic montage of the gang's karaoke session and Lol and Trev playing cards, unifying the gang across space yet signifying their enforced separateness. The card game opens the third scene to feature *EastEnders*: now it is in the background, and a prisoner's manhandling of Nick Cotton draws Trev's comment that it's 'so much shit'. Lol's reply – 'Yeah, but I'm gripped' – seems dismissive, as though Lol disavows the soap's earlier connection with her guilt over Combo. Lol's comments also disavow post-modern implications in the soap's use: *'88* will also be, in part, grim festive viewing, and both serials turn to melodrama (although that too is echoed in Shaun's college perform-ance in a Victorian melodrama: 'you're coming back from prison'). *'88* uses *EastEnders* to parallel narrative events, but avoids the playfully self-aware implications of *Twin Peaks*' paralleling of its narrative with scenes from fictional soap *Invitation to Love*, unless we read serial returner Nick Cotton as the panto Combo. Yet, *EastEnders*' paralleling of narrative events, and Lol's seemingly troubled reaction to them, reinforces our point that the use of archive in these serials goes beyond nostalgic marking. In this case, they indicate subjectivity, signposting unspoken memories of the previous serial and unseen events between the serials.

Given our observation of the forms of textual and extra-textual memory at play in these serials, it is striking that Lol should be haunted by the past's existence in the present, a memory transformed into seemingly 'living' experience. In *'86*, the viewer cannot access her memories, as in contrast to montages' audiovisual representations of our collective past there is at first no direct visual corroboration of her abuse accusations against Mick. Returning to discussions of memory earlier in the chapter, if the remembered past depends on audiovisual representations, Lol is vulnerable to Mick contesting her account as selective and strategic remembering in the present. If personal and public memories do not just combine (as in the serial's situating of the personal around a football tournament as site of collective memory) but become indistinguishable, Lol will struggle to reclaim the 'remembered past' from contingency, as 'the memories of others' are 'necessary in order to affirm the validity of our own' (Drake 2003: 184). Mick's rape of Trev in *'86* episode three is horrific both on its own terms and as visual confirmation of Lol's own earlier abuse, as if memory is, in Halbwachs' formulation, 'always an act of reconstruction and representation' (Storey 2003: 103). Forced to stare by a long-held wide shot, whose composition makes us aware of a door which will not open to provide discovery and rescue, a shocking scene becomes part of our archive of experience. Trev will not openly discuss the events – she is problematically marginalised for the rest of '86 and '88 – but the match which forms part of England's collective memory plays out during a private nightmare she strives to forget. It is difficult to watch archive montages in the serials after this acknowledgement that the repetition of media images as a form of collective memory constructs a vision of the past closed to the subjugated knowledge of Lol, Trev and others. Lol kills Mick after the contestation of memory becomes reconstruction and he starts to attack her. Our own memory of Trev's rape and Mick's killing creates further traces across the serials – the family living room becomes a haunted space. In '88 Lol's daughter playing on the floor and Trev sitting on the sofa raise troubling associations, which are brought home by a later scene where we track from a disturbed Lol to reveal the apparition of Mick, reclining ominously in the chair beside her in this space imprinted by memories of violence.

Holdsworth's comments on the pleasure of repetition, 'the hauntings of and by characters, the traces that return and retreat' (2010: 38), are particularly interesting in relation to Lol's interaction with Mick across '86 and '88. Mick's return sweeps the darkness of her past into her unravelling present, reflected in his ominous, dank physical presence, with his heavy beard, wheezing breath and staring eyes; his dark bulk and oppressive stillness are a stark counterpoint to bleached-blonde Lol. Mick's presence is not erased with his death, as '88 manifests Lol's mental deterioration through her father's apparition, her past folding in on and stifling her present. These appearances use his wheezing breathing and looming stillness to create feelings of intense dread, the inescapable weight of Lol's guilt. The haunting places the viewer within Lol's psyche and, combined with the use of expressive *mise-en-scène* – the cold blue tones of her flat and chiaroscuro light closing down the edges of the frame into darkness – externalises her emotional shutdown. The Christmas-set instalment associates Lol with spiritual themes – her nurse offers prayers for her, she seeks sanctuary from her oppressive thoughts at Midnight Mass, and editing connects her with images of the Virgin Mary. The repeated presence of a choral score signals both the seasonal setting and Lol's disintegration in its atonal blend of voices which rarely resolve themselves into soothing harmony, instead crowding into dense, unsettling notes which communicate her dread of what this haunting and guilt means for her sanity.

A montage in episode three of *'88* marks the culmination of the use of archive as one level of memory interspersed with narrative memory to convey Lol's subjectivity and the working through of trauma. The violent pumping of Lol's stomach after her overdose is framed as a cathartic purging of her pain, a conclusion to the arc started by the film. This is signalled by the nurse's prayer in voiceover, the dedicated repetition in monotone of a request to save Lol which retreats to a mumble below night-marish warped sounds, which together with Lol's writhing body recall the audience's memory of *'86*'s climactic attack by Mick even before we are shown visual representations of those memories. The stomach pumping becomes an abstract montage, which intercuts Lol's thrashing body with flashes of her father, her mother's muffled screams in the waiting room, news footage of starvation, flashes from *This is England*, including a looming Combo, and flashes from *'86*, including Trev's rape and Lol's adultery with Milky. Lol's nightmare visions combine primary and secondary memories: things that happened to her alongside news images of events she has not directly lived but which, in Landsberg's terms, have become part of her 'personal archive of experience', including images of death which engender despairing powerlessness, guilt over events beyond her control. If memories 'do not just consist of what is remembered but also of what has been forgotten' (Storey: 105), this guilt extends to Lol's inability to memorialise her abuse to prevent Trev's rape: during this montage, Mick says to camera (Lol), 'You're the only one who knows'. Given that some of the images from the film and *'86* featured in the montage were not seen by Lol, the sequence can be read as a traumatic memory montage for the omniscient viewer who has experienced these events across the film and television narratives. This lends a darker meaning to Mick's comment to camera (the viewer).

The sequence is positioned as a climactic conclusion to the three-part (to date) *This is England* narrative, as the darkness that has haunted the narrative is purged for the viewer as well as Lol. This is signalled by the montage building to a frenzy which ends abruptly with the removal of the stomach tube. The conclusion of the nurse's prayer plays over Lol's silent hunched body, the stark drained colour of the waiting room cutting to the warmth of the nurse kneeling in the candlelit chapel. Lol's emptying out frees her from the weight of her past and the guilt that has haunted her, yet her renewal is only finally signalled by her reconciliation with Woody in the serial's closing scene. Having fought to have her individual memories valued in *'86*, she seems to purge her primary memories – but then, if 'memory depends less on a conscious decision to record than an inability to forget', this purging of guilt means confronting 'the echo and pressure of the past as it is configured in present-based struggles over the meaning of lived experience' (Grainge 2003: 2–3). It therefore marks another stage in the 'negotiation of memory' by Lol and, in their various textual and extra-textual strategies, the television serials.

Notes

1. *Made in Britain* was broadcast on ITV in 1983, one of four education-themed films by David Leland under the banner *Tales Out of School*. The series was repeated on Channel Four in 1985. Clarke only directed *Made in Britain*. One of the other films, *RHINO*, has more parallels with Lol's experiences raising a child. See Rolinson (2011).
2. Meadows' observation is enriched by the fact that David Rose, first commissioning editor for Film on Four, had worked with Clarke and others in the 1970s as head of BBC English Regions Drama, resulting in continuities of personnel and style between 1970s television films – a neglected cinema movement – and Film on Four's cinema output. See Rolinson (2005, 2010).
3. These devices also mark the serials as contemporary and challenge critics' emphasis on Meadows as auteur: *Misfits*, on which Harper worked, also uses artfully composed, fragmented establishing shots and compositions which emphasise the contrasting lines of concrete housing against unexpected bursts of green and the sky, to locate its own dark comedy about a working-class ensemble in a vivid milieu.
4. Although this chapter's focus is textual, these earlier filmmakers' techniques are also echoed in other ways. Leigh's practice is recalled in the space for script-guided improvisation and actor collaboration, facilitated by the production environment; in Meadows' case, the cast largely lived together or, for '88, were tactically kept apart, with Lol and Woody separated until the end of both the story and filming. Loach's practice is recalled in Meadows' methods to generate the intensity of spontaneous response, as in Woody's surprise reunion with the gang near the 18-Hour Café or his belief that Lol had died in hospital, regarding which the actor was, respectively, unprepared and misled.
5. Admittedly the sequence also contains some bluntly literal juxtapositions of lyrics and images – 'now you have gone' accompanies Edwina Currie, who resigned as a health minister in December 1988 after the salmonella scare.
6. Though rave culture and the Hacienda nightclub would be the focus of a planned return visit to the group set in 1990 (Harvey 2011).
7. The soundtrack choice for the end titles, The Jam's 'The Bitterest Pill (I Ever Had To Swallow)', reinforces this. There is also, in Maradona's description of the incident as 'the Hand of God', a connection to the religious threads uniting Combo and Lol across the serials and a reply to The Smiths' contention at the start of the episode that 'the devil will find work for idle hands to do'.
8. BBC1, 22 December 1988.

References

Anonymous (2009), '"18 months to transform the schedules" as C4 calls time on Big Brother', *Channel4.com*, 26 August: www.channel4.com/info/press/news/18-months-to-transform-the-schedules-as-c4-calls-time-on-big-brother.

Caughie, J. (2000), *Television Drama: Realism, Modernism and British Culture*, Oxford: Oxford University Press.

Creeber, G. (2009), '"The truth is out there! Not!": Shameless and the moral structures of contemporary social realism', *New Review of Film and Television Studies*, 7: 4, 421–39.

Drake, P. (2003), '"Mortgaged to music": new retro movies in 1990s Hollywood cinema', in P. Grainge (ed.), *Memory and Popular Film*, Manchester: Manchester University Press, pp. 183–201.

Goddard, S. (2009), *Mozipedia: The Encyclopedia of Morrissey and The Smiths*, Ebury Press.

Grainge, P. (2003), 'Introduction: memory and popular film', in P. Grainge (ed.), *Memory and Popular Film*, Manchester: Manchester University Press, pp. 1–20.

Halbwachs, M. (1980), *The Collective Memory*, New York: Harper and Row.

Harvey, C. (2011), 'Shane Meadows and Vicky McClure on This Is England '88: interview', *The Telegraph*, 13 December: http://www.telegraph.co.uk/culture/tvandradio/8950839/Shane-Meadows-and-Vicky-McClure-on-This-Is-England-88-interview.html

Holdsworth, A. (2010), 'Televisual memory', *Screen*, 51: 2, 129–42.

Isaacs, J. (1989), *Storm Over 4: A Personal Account*, London: Weidenfeld and Nicolson.

Kermode, M. (2004), 'Bloody minded? Dead right', *Observer*, 15 August: http://www.guardian.co.uk/film/2004/aug/15/features.review1.

Landsberg, A. (2004), *Prosthetic Memory: The Transformation of American Remembrance in the Age of Mass Culture*, New York: Columbia University Press.

Lobb, A. (2010), 'Stephen Graham on This is England '86', *The Telegraph*, 1 September: http://www.telegraph.co.uk/culture/tvandradio/7975572/Stephen-Graham-on-This-Is-England-86.html

Lowenthal, D. (1985) (quoted in Drake), *The Past is a Foreign Country*, Cambridge: Cambridge University Press.

Meadows, S. (2010), 'Gangland graduates', *Radio Times*, 4: 10 (September), 33.

Raphael, A. (2010), 'Shane Meadows's This is England gang will give Channel 4 a kick up the 80s', *Guardian*, 4 September: www.guardian.co.uk/film/2010/sep/04/this-is-england-86-shane-meadows

Rolinson, D. (2005), *Alan Clarke*, Manchester: Manchester University Press.

Rolinson, D. (2010), 'The last studio system: a case for British television films', in P. Newland (ed.), *Don't Look Now: British Cinema in the 1970s*, Bristol: Intellect, pp. 163–76.

Rolinson, D. (2011), *Tales Out of School* programme notes, Network DVD.

Storey, J. (2003), 'The articulation of memory and desire: from Vietnam to the war in the Persian Gulf', in P. Grainge (ed.), *Memory and Popular Film*, Manchester: Manchester University Press, pp. 99–119.

Sweney, M. and L. Holmwood (2009), 'Channel 4 to launch "creative overhaul" as it axes Big Brother', *Guardian*, 26 August: http://www.guardian.co.uk/media/2009/aug/26/channel-4-big-brother.

CHAPTER 14

After Laughter Comes Tears: Passion and Redemption in *This is England '88*

Robert Murphy

I just remember Christmas being shit … I wanted to make a sort of broken Nativity play.

Shane Meadows, ''Tis the season to be brutal', *Independent on Sunday*, 27 November 2011

This is England '88, set over three days at Christmas, begins starkly with three awakenings. Lol (Vicky McClure), her chirpy platinum-blonde hair from *'86* now a fierce Chrissie Hynde black, looks haggard and unhappy at being woken by a toddler whose appearance indicates that Lol's affair with Milky in *'86* has had consequences beyond their mutual betrayal of Woody. An alarm clock wakes Woody (Joseph Gilgun). We last saw him at the end of *'86* arranging a surprise wedding for Lol while she was battering her father to death with a hammer. Now he leaps out of the bed he is sharing with a buxom gingery blonde. Like Lol, he looks ten rather than two years older. His Paul Weller Mod haircut of 1986 is changed to a severe middle-aged neatness reminiscent of Bryan Pringle's cuckolded husband in *Saturday Night and Sunday Morning* (1960). Finally, to Shaun (Thomas Turgoose), who is lying in a close embrace with Smell (Rosamund Hanson), her elaborate hair moulded into an elfin bowl cut. He is no longer a child, but he sulkily resists her playful sexual demands.

Woody, Shaun and Lol are souls in torment, and their suffering is dwelt on with an intensity which darkens further the melodramatic denouement of *This is England '86*.

'Make me a clean heart, O God: and renew a right spirit within me'

Woody shares breakfast with his suffocatingly nice parents and his gigglingly bashful girlfriend, Jennifer. Her mid-length skirt and nunty pink-and-white embroidered cardigan suggest that she is all too ready to slip into his mother's fluffy slippers. He escapes to his car, muttering 'Get me the fuck out of here.' Driving to work, he passes Lol as she pushes a buggy up a steep Sheffield street, and Milky as he dismounts from a bus carrying a big white teddy-bear. But Woody is too self-absorbed to notice either of them. At work he is still in purgatory. He jokes with the men as he hands them their Christmas wage packets, but his pretence of jollity tips into Tourette's-like over-boisterousness when his boss offers him the prospect of promotion. Promotion would seal his fate and condemn him irrevocably to dull conformity. After a pre-Christmas meal with the family, he ducks out of a game of charades and goes out on his scooter. Wendy Rene's poignant 'After Laughter Comes Tears' plays over a montage which links him with the pub where the gang are enjoying a karaoke evening, and with Lol and Trev playing cards and drinking beer in her dilapidated maisonette. Outside the pub, Woody stands on his scooter and watches Chrissie, Kelly, Cynthia and Smell's performance with fond pleasure until Milky waltzes into view. With a curse he drives off, revealing his unexpunged bitterness about what he sees as Lol and Milky's betrayal and his abandonment by the gang. On Christmas Eve, after a meal with his boss, he makes another attempt to re-engage with his past life, taking Jennifer to the seedy 18-Hour Café. The gang are just coming out and in a long impro-vised scene, as messily realistic as an episode of *Night Cops*, Woody confronts the reality of loss and betrayal which he has tried so hard to avoid.

Woody's anguish and frustration and his sardonic sense of humour make him an endearing figure; Shaun seems to have less reason for discontent. Failing his school exams has propelled him onto a performing arts course, and he has landed the lead part in the Christmas play, as uncouth Yorkshire lad Bob Brierly in the Victorian melodrama *The Ticket of Leave Man*.[1] Fay (Charlotte Tyree), a middle-class girl playing the long-suffering but stout-hearted heroine, seems to offer an entrée into a more genteel, sophisticated world.[2] Smell, now his live-in girlfriend, has grown out of her dopey New Romantic phase and has become sassy, sensual and stylish. But Shaun's need to spread his wings pushes her into the role of possessive femme fatale. When we first see them they look a happily loving couple, but when Shaun wakes from sleep he is drained and grumpy, as if he has been conjoined with a succubus. Smell wails insistently when Shaun refuses to heed her sexual desires. Later, when she helps him learn his lines for the play, she yells at him and hits him round the head. Her Cleopatra-like collar and headdress and her serpentine hand movements at the karaoke evening make her seem otherworldly and exotic in comparison with Fay's nice-girl modesty. On the evening of the play's performance, when Smell goes backstage and finds Shaun and Fay kissing, and later in the evening when she discovers them in flagrante delicto, she acts like a vengeful painted doll. In the final montage sequence, a medium shot of Shaun glumly sharing his Christmas dinner with his mother and her lover Mr Sandhu is followed by a choker close-up of Smell staring pensively. Her sleepy, unblinking eyes and air of languorous sensuality make her look like a genie out of *The Thief of Bagdad* (1940). But she is obviously not going to be at Shaun's beck and call.

'A broken and a contrite heart, O God, thou wilt not despise'

If Shaun and Woody are trapped in worlds they are desperate to escape from, Lol is consigned to Dante's fifth ring of Hell, cursed by her impotent anger to smoulder and fester. Her mother tells her she 'looks like shit'; worn down by lack of sleep, she is irritable and impatient with her little daughter; at the community health centre she erupts in hate and envy at the nurse who tries to sympathise with her. When she tries to relax by submerging herself in the bath she is visited by an apparition of Mick (Johnny Harris), her dead father. She is afforded some relief in the evening when her friend (and fellow rape victim) Trev comes round to drink beer and play cards with her. But after Lol kisses Trev goodnight and goes upstairs to the bathroom, the ghostly Mick is lurking there. She steels herself and, telling herself 'this isn't real … this isn't happening … I'll be okay', she begins her struggle for redemption.

The next morning she goes back to the health centre and apologises to Evelyn the nurse (Helen Behan) for her outburst; Lol can now recognise that she is someone she can safely confide in. She then visits Combo (Stephen Graham) in prison and acknowledges the enormous debt she owes him for taking responsibility for Mick's murder. After reuniting with the gang to watch Shaun's play, she goes to Midnight Mass. She seems wretchedly out of place among the earnestly ordinary churchgoers, but catches a glimpse of redemption as she smiles at a baby. Horror returns when she realises that Mick is sitting in the pew behind her. Like a brazen and insistent demon he has followed her to where she might have expected sanctuary. He remorselessly torments her, countering the good effects of the support she's had from Trev, Combo and Evelyn the nurse. Her subsequent suicide bid and the attempt to save her life by dredging up with a stomach pump the tablets she has swallowed comes across more as an exorcism than a medical procedure.

Reggae got soul

Meadows' soundtracks are always good, a rich mix of old and new (Ludovico Einaudi and Toots & the Maytals, Aphex Twin and J. J. Cale), but that of *'88* is extraordinary in its eclecticism. The period is evoked through the titles montage sequence set to The Smiths' 'What Difference Does It Make?' – Mrs Thatcher, various royals, mobile phones the size of bricks, Eddie the Eagle at the Winter Olympics, Ronald Reagan and Mikhail Gorbachev, Lockerbie – and two bad but unforgettable songs: Samantha Fox's 'Touch Me' and Rick Astley's 'Never Gonna Give You Up'. Ken Boothe's rocksteady 'Everything I Own', which gives an appropriately bittersweet tone to the end titles, dates from 1974, but was re-released in 1988 to cash in on the success of Boy George's cover version. Tracy Chapman's internationally popular 'Fast Car', which we hear in Fay's bedroom, clearly differentiates her from the ex-skinhead gang singing along to Wendy Rene's 1964 recording of 'After Laughter Comes Tears', a song only dedicated northern soul fans would be aware of. Fionn Regan's 'Dogwood Blossom', with its intimations of suicide and love gone wrong, is the only contemporary song used and fits the tone set by the delicate, meditative music of Ludovico Einaudi. 'Il Fuori Dalla Notte' accompanies Woody's journey to work, where he drives obliviously past Lol and Milky, the two people who mean the most to him. 'Solo' plays over the heart of the film, beginning just before Evelyn the nurse tells Lol, 'I will help you and you will find peace', intensifying the emotion as they embrace and continuing rhapsodically over her journey to the prison and her slow-motion walk against a seemingly limitless concrete wall. Einaudi's gently nostalgic 'Berlin Song' links together Woody's Christmas meal and the gang watching Shaun's play, confirming that despite the noise and laughter, both events are disappointments leaving those involved unhappy and deflated.

'Thou shalt purge me with hyssop, and I shall be clean: Thou shalt wash me, and I shall be whiter than snow'

Christmas songs burble away in the background, from Frank Sinatra's 'Santa Claus is Coming to Town' to Wizard's 'I Wish it Could be Christmas Every Day', but more portentous religious music is used for purposes beyond aural wallpaper. Religion rarely figures in British films. Christian motifs haunt the films of Terence Davies and Derek Jarman, but in mainstream cinema there is little beyond the blessings and penances of Powell and Pressburger's *A Canterbury Tale* (1944), the camp religiosity of

Roy Baker's *The Singer Not the Song* (1961) and the tortured Catholicism of Graham Greene and Jimmy McGovern. *This is England '88*, despite the proliferation of crucifixes in the final episode, has more in common with J. Arthur Rank's Methodist-inspired *Hard Steel* (1942), *The Great Mr Handel* (1942) and *They Knew Mr Knight* (1946). But there divine providence settles easily on the shoulders of repentant sinners; Lol has to undergo a more violent exorcism before she can be at peace. In the central sequence where she is comforted by Evelyn's embrace, her shadowed face and imploring eyes make her look like a Renaissance painting of Christ on the cross. In the church, close-ups of Lol's anguished face as Mick whispers his poison into her ear are intercut with a huge wooden crucifix, the high angle seeming to emphasise Christ's suffering. At the hospital, crucifixes hang prominently in the surgery and above Lol's hospital bed. In prison, a crucifix nestles among Combo's letters and photos on the pin-board in his cell.

Mick is explicitly configured as a demon, though he's modelled less on the elemental forces of nature that crowd into M. R. James stories than on the cheap villains who used to haunt East End pubs waiting to be bought drinks on the strength of their association with the Kray twins. He is never violent, but his heavy breathing and reek of bad sex make him immensely disturbing. His presence is always signalled by religious music. Knut Nystedt's intensely eerie 'O Crux' forewarns of his materialisation when Lol is submerged in the bath. Gregorio Allegri's more harmonious penitential psalm 'Miserere Mei Deus', which has played over Shaun's journey into the quiet night after leaving Fay's house, and Lol tidying up and giving Trev a sisterly goodnight kiss, suddenly bursts back as Mick reappears in the bathroom mirror to shatter the mood of domestic tranquillity. The dissonant tones of Alfred Schnittke's 'That is Why I Live in Poverty' drown out Lol and Milky's conversation as Mick's presence fills the room where we witnessed him raping Trev. In the church the melodious chords of Britten's 'Hymn to the Virgin' give way to the congregation singing 'Silent Night' and, as the camera tracks back to reveal Mick sitting in the pew behind Lol, Einaudi's plaintively elegiac 'Distacco', which acts like a lament for Lol's shock and despair. The priest reiterates St John's message of hope, 'The light shines in the darkness, and the darkness has not overcome it', but as Lol scurries from the church it seems that evil is triumphant.

If Lol is plagued by her demonic father, she also has a guardian angel in the shape of Evelyn, the community nurse. Initially she seems like an ideal big sister's sister, someone that a dominant female like Lol can feel safe with. But her actions take her beyond sisterly solidarity. With prescient concern, she goes to Lol's home after midnight on Christmas Eve to check on her welfare. But the religious dimension only becomes apparent with her prayer ('for a sick friend'), which begins while Kelly and Trev summon an ambulance for the comatose Lol and continues over the stomach pump montage. Lol has entered the long tunnel of death. She will be dragged from it alive, but this rebirth is not an easy one. The stomach pump operation becomes an allusive collage – the insertion of a hose down Lol's throat and her violent thrashing around on the operating table intercut with her monstrous father raping Trev, whispering threats, attacking Lol, his bloodied head as she hits him with the hammer, and scattered images of Woody, Combo and Milky, a young and innocent Trev at the swimming pool, the priest at the altar, the wooden crucifix – the invasive exigencies of a procedure which will save her life linked to both rape and exorcism.[3] Evelyn's prayer is drowned out by a jumbled cacophony but returns as the tube is removed from Lol's throat and calmness descends. She ends with the plea:

> Lord, I don't always understand your ways. I don't know why my friend has to suffer, but I trust you. I ask that you look with mercy and grace towards Lorraine. Nourish her spirit and her soul in this time of suffering and comfort her with your presence.

And finally we see her, no longer in her nurse's uniform, kneeling at the altar. Later she appears at the hospital, sitting by Lol's bed, a crucifix above her head, praying that, with the demon expelled, the Holy Spirit can enter her soul.[4]

When Woody, wearing a novelty Chrimbo cardigan, which for such a dandy would be the equivalent of sackcloth and ashes, finally finds Lol in her white gown having a fag in the smoking room to the accompaniment of the Westminster Cathedral Choir's ethereal rendering of 'The Holly and the Ivy', she might be a purified soul awaiting entrance into heaven. But the pathos and comedy of their reunion obscures the fact that this isn't a happy-ever-after ending. Lol's debt for her salvation is to Combo, Trev and Kelly, whose love has drawn her onto the right path, and – through his intermediary Evelyn – to God.

This is England '88 proves that the provincial, the powerless, the ordinary lead interesting enough lives to provide drama and tragedy, and shows Meadows to be an extraordinarily sophisticated and complex filmmaker. If he looked more like an intellectual and didn't come from Uttoxeter, we might be comparing him to Carl Dreyer and Ingmar Bergman.

Notes

1. *It's Never Too Late to Mend* was written by the prolific playwright and journalist Tom Taylor in 1863. In the 1937 film version Bob is very much overshadowed by Tod Slaughter's villain, 'The Tiger'. The play was revived at the National Theatre in 1981.
2. Fay's house looks as if it is in Highcliffe Road, which is in the Hallam constituency of Sheffield, the wealthiest part of the city. Since 2005 the MP has been Nick Clegg, the leader of the Liberal Democrats.
3. There is also a subliminal shot of a small gold crucifix. David Rolinson and Faye Woods provide a detailed analysis of this extraordinary sequence in their chapter in this volume.
4. Evelyn's second prayer, 'Father I bring Lorraine before you today. I break the power of Satan from his assignments and activities in her life in the name of Jesus. Now, while Satan is bound, I ask you to send the Holy Spirit to share the good news of the Gospel in such a way that she will listen and understand it. As the truth is ministered, I believe Lorraine will come to know and love you, and so out of the snare of the devil', etc., is based on a Pentecostal prayer for 'an unsaved loved one'. This, combined with the predominance of crucifixes, would mark Evelyn out as a member of the Catholic Charismatic Renewal movement which began in the late 1960s.

Index

213